CW01667267

DRAGON ASSASSIN

ARTHUR SLADE

DAVA ENTERPRISES

Cover by Zhivko Zhelev

Map by Garnet Whyte

Created with Vellum

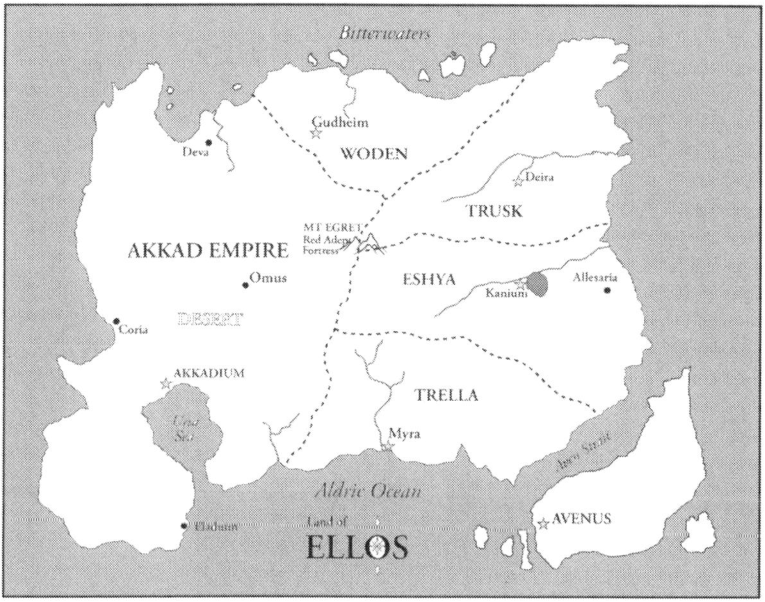
Bitterwaters
Gudheim
WODEN
Deva
Deira
TRUSK
MT EGRET
Red Adept
Fortress
AKKAD EMPIRE
Omus
ESHYA
Kanium
Allesaria
DESERT
Coria
AKKADIUM
TRELLA
Myra
Aldric Ocean
AVENUS
Land of
ELLOS

PART 1: TWIN FURY

1

AN EYE FOR AN EYE

I lost my left eye during blades training at assassin school. My twin brother did the deed using a clever feint and a quick crosswise cut that caught me by surprise.

"Well, Carmen, that'll leave a scar," Corwin had said. Then he'd laughed that snorty, snotty laugh that had grated on my nerves a thousand times since childhood.

My vision had been too blurry to aim a cutting blow at him, and I wasn't certain if I even wanted to. He was the only family I had. And despite his laughter, he may not have known how deep the wound was. He often made a silly joke when he'd done something stupid.

But when I stumbled and fell toward the floor, Corwin dropped his blade and caught me. "Aw, sorry, sis," he said, holding me against his chest. Then the healers rushed in with their bandages and salves and led me to the healing room. Maestru Alesius—my master—soon followed them, bringing the bad news:

"You will lose that eye, Carmen."

I was thirteen. I'd been ahead of my brother on the honor roll—the top of the class. I often wondered if a bout of jealousy inspired my blinding. The blades were sharp, but we students weren't supposed to cut each other—the idea was to keep the mind sharp as well. And I'd love to know where he'd learned the move. I'd never seen it before, and I was better with the sword than him. Did he have a secret teacher?

Everything was harder with only one eye—the sword fights, the dagger throws, learning to avoid traps; even the poisons and potions were more difficult to pour.

A half-blind assassin was a joke. I was pretty certain my fellow students had chuckled and celebrated as my position on the honor roll slipped. I had the knowledge and the skill. But the patch over my eye meant I had a weakness, and the school trained assassins to exploit weaknesses.

I'd have quit, perhaps to be a scullery maid or to work in the massive wheat fields of the Akkad Empire, if only to get away from the other apprentice assassins who had once been beneath me and who now scorned me. I especially wanted to flee from the kinder ones who looked at me with pity.

But Maestru Alesius had insisted I stay. "Adversity will toughen your mental bones," he'd promised. His support and my perseverance had kept me in school. Three years had passed since the incident. Three years of struggling to keep my spot. I was finally sixteen, in my final week of classes.

Corwin would graduate at the top of the honor roll. He was the best with bladed weapons, the best at hiding in shadows, the best assassin the school had seen in many years. He may even be better than the legendary Banderius. All the kings, queens, and archons would seek to hire Corwin. Maybe even Emperor Rima himself.

I'd be lucky to get hired at all.

2

THE FORTRESS

Red Adept Assassin School was a fortress built on the top of Mount Egret, and no one had ever conquered it. The small pocket of mountains was an area that no country was allowed to lay claim to—it belonged to the assassins. It was perfectly positioned on the border of the Akkad Empire and between the other five realms. The fortress had three hundred and eight secret gates locked by the strongest locks protected by ancient, powerful spells. Because no one could watch every door, the number of gates meant that there would always be a way out.

My brother and I were babies when we were left in a box in front of one of those gates. We never knew why we were abandoned, but we did know that a gate opened and an assassin took us inside. We were raised in that fortress—to work in the kitchen, to clean the floors, to wipe the latrines. But we watched the maestrus. We watched the students, and we practiced in the dark. And we were invited to attend the school when we turned twelve, which put us on the path to becoming assassins.

Anyone in the mortal lands who wanted to hire an

assassin could send a raven with payment, and soon after, one of the gates would open and an assassin would slip out. Or the assassin would saddle a giant black swan and take to the sky to land silently on a castle wall and complete his or her mission. Many nervous kings and noblemen, worried that their enemies had hired one of us, listened at night for those never-to-be-heard footfalls.

There was one group that should never fear us: upon our graduation, we swore an oath to never kill a child. We also only took the jobs that aligned with our moral beliefs. This system had worked for the last two thousand years, and there was no reason to believe it wouldn't work for two thousand more.

3

THE POINTS

My fourteen classmates surrounded me, all seated at a long table set with fifteen pestles, fifteen mortars, fifteen oil burners, and a selection of knives. Piles of dried leaves from several plants, including mint and basil to disguise the smell of any poison, sat in the center of the table. The final exam for Potions, Poisons, and Alchemy was about to begin.

We students were a variety of skin shades and body types and came from every realm and corner of the empire. The Red Assassin School wants its assassins to be able to fit in. The more shapes, sizes and colors the better. As much as the heroic stories have us dashing into houses and fighting, it's better to not stand out. We want to do our job then melt right back into the crowd.

My brother was at the far end of the table with his two cronies: square-jawed Gregum and willowy and cold-eyed Scyllia. I didn't like either of them because they brought out the worst in Corwin. Or he brought out the worst in them. I knew Gregum was from Trella because he bragged about how rich his family was and that he grew up in a walled mansion. The rest of us kept quiet about our countries because the less information you give an assassin, the better.

Megan of the red hair and perfect face was directly across the table. She'd given me the nickname Cyclops, so I'd decided to hate her forever. Next to her was Thord, whom I actually liked. He had blond hair and was larger than the other assassins, but despite his size, he'd always spoken kindly to me. To everyone, in fact. Though I could do without the pity I often saw in his eyes.

"Wort's poison," Maestru Nestor shouted. I shuddered at his barked command, then smiled. This was an easy one for me. I gathered the green leaves from a jar, crushed them, and mixed in the oil from black ivy seeds, knowing each portion perfectly. I was done before everyone else. Maestru Nestor came over to sniff my concoction. He nodded without smiling. I'd never seen him smile.

Despite my grinding, slicing, and pestling talents, I was at the bottom of the graduating class. For each assassin skill, a student would receive points, and I lacked points in the sword fighting, grappling, dagger work, garrotting, and other hand-to-hand combat techniques, all because my missing eye made it so hard to judge distance. But I excelled at alchemy, logic, and finding hidden messages in secret scrolls.

"You look puffed up and proud, Carmen," Maestru Nestor said. He had never liked me. Well, he didn't like any of his students. "Remember, we aren't training you to be an apothecary who cures boils on goats. I expect perfection."

I nodded, and he moved on.

My empty eye socket itched behind the black patch. I preferred people to see right away that I was blind in one eye, instead of having them goggle at a glass eye, wondering why it wasn't moving along with my good eye. Or worse, the junior students laughing when the glass eye stared off to one side.

After Maestru Nestor had inspected every other student's work, giving them all emotionless nods, he shouted, "Brillig's acid."

I had the list of ingredients memorized. I gathered them from the piles on the table, including vitriol of Damen, petra salt, and alum. Once they were mixed together, it would become an acid that had to be carried carefully in glass vials. It would eat through metal, wood, and flesh.

I used the pestle to grind the salt. Holding the bowl in one hand meant I always knew where it was. And, after a few more additions, I mixed all the ingredients together. I risked a quick glance at the surrounding students. I had to turn my head quite far to make up for my lack of peripheral vision.

Everyone else was still grinding. Even Corwin looked like he was struggling with getting the right consistency. Good! I grabbed one of the small glass balls in front of me and uncorked it. The ball was designed to be thrown at an enemy or at a wall, the glass smashing to release the acid. All I had to do was use the funnel to the pour the mixture into the container. I lined it up, confident I wouldn't miss.

The smell of acrid smoke alerted me to my mistake. Stupid, stupid eye! Several drops of the acid splashed onto the table, thankfully missing my fingers. But my good eye watered up, and I pushed back from the smoke, slid on my bench, and nearly fell over. I dropped the decanter and a huge hole began burning in the stone floor.

I looked up to see Maestru Nestor looking down. A smile crossed his face. "Not satisfactory, Carmen. Not satisfactory at all. You lose five points. Now clean all this up."

I did clean it, using soda powder to neutralize the acid.

The whole time, I avoided looking at the other graduates. What a stupid way to end the class.

An hour later, the freshly inked grades were hung up, and I discovered my mistake meant I wouldn't have enough points to graduate. The other students backed away, happy with their own marks, but I was still staring at the numbers.

"Can I help?" Corwin asked. He gently lowered his hand onto my shoulder. He was in one of his brotherly moods. "I'd feel horrible if you didn't get your Red Assassin cloak."

"I don't know what to do," I said. "I can't get those marks back. And we graduate in three days."

"You could find a swan egg." He said it so quickly I wondered if he'd been thinking about it for some time. "Ask your maestru—he'll be able to figure out how many points to assign you. I looked into it when I thought Scyllia might graduate above me...but I don't need the points now. You could do it."

"It's dangerous. Wild black swans could easily kill me."

He waved his hand, dismissing my fears. "You eat danger for breakfast. Remember when we practiced our flying skills?" We had jumped from cliffs into deep water and had to learn to maneuver ourselves through the air on the way down. It was supposed to make us better at landing on parapets. We got points for each jump. "You nearly beat me!"

I had felt fear during those tests, but I had felt exhilaration too. It turned out I loved flying, if only for a few seconds.

"It might be possible," I said.

"Good! I see the competitive fire in your eyes." He slapped my back. "Get a swan's egg and you'll graduate. I'm sure. And if you fail, you could still be an apothecary. One of the best."

"I don't want to be an apothecary!"

"You don't give up, do you? I love that about you. Just ask Maestru Alesius for the extra points. He dotes on you."

"He doesn't dote." I pointed at Corwin. "At least my maestru likes me." Maestru Nestor was his.

"I don't need you to be liked." He chuckled. "But I'm sure you can get an egg, sis."

I stared at my marks. All that work almost lost. "Yes. I might be able to do it. Thank you," I said.

"We're in this together." He often ignored me, so this sudden softness from him surprised me. "You're the only family I have."

And that was the truth. Despite everything aggravating about him, he was my brother. And the slash that took my eye was most likely an accident.

Or, if it was intentional, perhaps he regretted it.

He walked away. I'd never seen anyone with such a confident stride. It was as if he'd been born knowing exactly where every step he took in life would land.

"You'll need feathers if you're going egg hunting," a voice said beside me. I shuddered and pivoted.

It was Thord. His smile showed his perfect white teeth.

"Were you eavesdropping?"

"No!" He blushed. Assassins were trained not to blush unless it was part of a deception. I was pretty certain this was a real blush. "Your brother talks loud. I heard him say something about a swan egg, and I put the rest together."

"Then you snuck up on me?"

"I'm sorry that I surprised you." I couldn't get a good read on him. He was talented with weapons and above average with all the other skills, but he just seemed too nice. There was no such thing as a nice assassin! Or was it all a show to keep us off our guard?

He had curly blond hair. And blue eyes. And was always friendly to me. That kept me on guard too.

"Why would you give me feathers?" I asked.

"Because I collected them from the swannery. For an art project."

"An art project? Assassins don't do art."

He crossed his muscled arms. "What I do in my spare time is my business."

Who has spare time? I nearly asked. I did remember that he was particularly adept at constructing devices and had once made a clockwork owl that impressed the maestrus. And the rest of the students. Even me. So maybe he did artwork for fun.

"And," he continued. "The reason I am offering the feathers is because we will be part of a guild once we graduate, and guild members help each other. So, don't look for some deep motive."

"I would have to owe you for this," I said.

"No strings attached. Only feathers." He said the last line with a smile.

Why was he being so kind to me? I couldn't come up with a reason to say no. "I will take your feathers," I said. "And I will owe you nothing."

"That's the deal. No. Wait, I want a story—I want to hear how you got the egg. Because I know you'll be able to do it."

"Fine. I'll take the feathers, and I will owe you a story. It's a deal."

We shook hands. His was pleasantly warm.

4

THE EGG

The nesting ground of the massive black swans was a four-hour hardscrabble journey from the fortress. The way was rocky, and the climb to the flat peak nearly impossible. But Red Adept Assassins needed wings. The giant black swans were a great asset to every assassin. They would silently carry their masters to the tops of castles or hover near bedroom windows, so the assassins could jump in, do their work, and jump out.

And that was why I had undertaken the journey. Night had fallen by the time I reached the top of the rocky precipice. Exhausted and sweating, I crept through the nesting grounds of the black basilisk swans.

This place was even more dangerous than the journey. The swans themselves were not like the little swans in lakes. These were at least six to eight feet tall with a wide wing-span, razor-sharp beaks, a sleek muscular back, and long talons on their webbed feet.

I had ridden on the backs of several swans as part of our Mastery of the Air class. They were powerful creatures who were both willful and obedient and strong. Each one I rode could easily carry my weight. What I loved the very most was when I could just swoop through the heavens at full speed, the wind in my hair. I became a goddess of the skies. No wonder so many feared us assassins when we had creatures like this on our side.

But these swans I was walking through were not on my side. They were wild, and if one mother grew angry, she could strike me dead with her beak. But Maestru Alesius had promised me I'd receive the points I needed to graduate. So, Corwin's plan was working.

Well, as long as I did my part.

I walked between the massive nests made of branches, mud, and feathers. I had drenched myself in a potion that made me smell just like a swan. And they smelled somewhat horrible. The swans had sharp eyesight, so I was also wearing the feathered costume of the egg gatherer. I'd used the feathers Thord had given me and pasted them to a rawhide outfit. The beak mask hiding my face was itchy. As stupid as I looked, it was enough to fool them. Now I just needed luck to give me a helping hand. Sometimes an egg would roll out of a nest. Or a mother would die, and the eggs could be brought back to the school to be incubated in the swannery.

One swan nesting next to the edge *squawked* loudly, and I froze, still expecting to be struck down. But she was only complaining to another mother.

I continued to pick my way over the twigs and branches and swan defecation (which had a horrendous stink all its own). Without meaning to, I walked directly into a swan. She batted me with her head, and I went flying. I skidded across the rocks and bird excrement and turned. The swan hadn't moved from her nest. I guess she had shown me who the master was.

Stupid, stupid me.

Then I corrected myself. No. It was my missing eye that had caused the problem. It made it hard to see things on my left. I had gotten into the habit of holding my left hand slightly in front of me in case I misjudged a wall or a doorway.

I'd have to be even more careful. I had read all I could about egg stealing in the library before heading out on this mission. There was no easy way to grab an egg and run. That would set off an alarm with all the swans, and they'd poke me with their bills until I fled or was dead. I tried to think of how I could reach under one of the swans without being caught.

And then I saw, along the edge of the nesting grounds, an egg that had slipped out when a swan had moved in her sleep. I tried not to run toward it.

I prayed to the assassin god to guide my steps. Bodies from small rodents the swans had dined on crackled beneath my feet. But I kept my eye on the egg, pausing only to look left to be sure I would not bump another swan. The farther I got into the nesting grounds, the warmer it became. The larger swans were in the middle. They were the ones who had fought to have the best place for a nest.

I crept past them and kept going until the egg was within my grasp. I leaned down. The mother swan next to me was a smaller one, and she snored ever so slightly. She hadn't even noticed the missing egg.

I glanced over the edge. A fall from these heights looked rather far, though it had been harder to judge depth since losing my eye. The egg had come far too close to rolling off the mountainside.

I reached down and set a hand on the egg. Oh, Maestru Alesius would be so pleased. I would pass!

The egg was warm. The swan inside was alive. I was sorry to take it, but it would be well cared for in our swannery. And, if I was lucky, it might even become my mount.

I stepped back onto the spine of a dead rat. It cracked.

There was a hiss of anger, and I turned toward the noise far too slow. The strike came from my blind side and hit me very, very hard in the chest.

I tumbled over the cliff, clutching the egg against me.

5

THE CURIOUS ECHO

The drop was only a few feet, but hitting the hard surface rattled every bone in my body. The side of the mountain angled sharply downward, and I rolled and spun and banged uncontrollably, feathers flying around me. Even in my fear, I knew I looked stupid. Thankfully, no one would see me in the darkness.

And no one would find me if I bashed open my skull. Maybe my brother or Maestru Alesius would remember I'd left the fortress and discover my broken body sometime after graduation.

I lashed out with one hand, trying to get a handhold, but continued to tumble head over rear. Down. Down. Down. I kept smashing my way down the mountainside. At some point, the egg came loose. It must have shattered.

Along with my hope of graduating.

I might as well give up. But the slant grew slightly less steep, and eventually I could dig my heels into the stones, grabbing at little bushes. Finally, I came to a crawling, skidding halt.

I sat up, ever so slowly, expecting my back to be broken.

It wasn't. And as far as I could tell, neither were my arms, legs, or ribs. There was little left of my swan outfit, and the moonlight showed me wounds that glistened all along my arms and legs, but none seemed too deep. The biggest wound was to my pride.

At least I still had one eye.

That thought made me laugh. Out loud. And the laugh sounded odd. It echoed.

But not through the valley or along the cliff walls.

The echo came from much closer. To my left.

I squinted until I spotted a half-hidden cave mouth. It was large, but the overhang would have made it hard to see from above.

Something enormous and rotten was inside that cave, or there were several smaller dead things. Either way, it reeked of death.

But my maestrus had trained me in the butcher's carcass pits near the town of Ogra, so the stink was nothing new. Part of my lessons had been to not gag when confronted by the odor of decomposing flesh. I had also learned what each smell meant, as well as how many days something had been dead.

I looked back up the slanted cliffside. There was no sign of the swan egg, not that there was any hope at all that it was intact.

I stood slowly and turned toward the cave. I lumbered closer, still aching, but I had enough strength to draw the dagger at my belt. The assassin smithies had forged it with black steel that didn't reflect light. I stepped into the cave, letting my eye adjust to the darkness.

You're being stupid, I told myself. *Don't go into the cave.* I nearly said it aloud. But I'd come out of the swan nests with nothing at all. And maybe if there was something dead here, there would be some interesting bones to be ground for potions. Or a partly decomposed bear liver that could be dried and sold to Akkadian soldiers for good luck. They worshiped bears.

Or the smell could just be from a herd of mountain goats who died of yellow sickness.

Two steps later I saw a glint of chain mail.

It was on a dead man. His armor looked to be of Truskian make, but there were no signs of a regiment, which was why I decided he was a mercenary. By the state of the body I guessed he had been dead at least a fortnight. Judging by the angle of his neck, someone had broken it.

Next to him was a woman in similar chain mail. Only the best mercenaries could afford chain mail of this quality. That alone might be something the assassins' smithies could use. The woman had been burned rather severely, and she smelled slightly of cinnamon. It made me think of Devil's Fire, which used a cinnamon-scented incendiary. Had an assassin used the flaming liquid on these mercenaries? It wasn't impossible. The fortress was quite close, so an assassin might have been wandering out on these goat paths. I tried to keep the hope down in my heart. If there had been some sort of battle between these mercenaries and an assassin, then there must be something in this cave worth fighting for.

And I really needed to bring an amazing object back to my maestru. I'd read about apprentices graduating with extra marks by presenting an ancient scroll or a magic ring.

The third body was not rotting because it had been burned to a crisp. No assassin could carry that much Devil's Fire at once. I leaned down and touched the corpse, my finger prodding the blackened and surprisingly hard face.

Then my finger poked clear though his cheek. Maybe his face wasn't that hard after all.

If not for my training, I might have thrown up.

I moved my gaze over the man. His robes hadn't burned, and that was very curious. They were likely the protective garments of an enchanter. But they still hadn't saved him from the heat of the fire. I knew most of the wizards were dead or had fled Ellos to the unknown lands. All because the emperor had put bounties on their heads. So seeing a magic wielder was a rare sight.

"You're too big to be a crow," a male voice said. It was deep. I had trouble placing the speaker's exact location, though it came from somewhere farther inside the cave. I hadn't heard a movement. Nor had I seen any motion. "What are you, my feathery friend?"

I held the dagger out in front of me, looking right then moving my head farther to my left.

"A one-eyed crow," he said. "Come for the pecking, did you? These idiots came for their pecking. And they got pecked."

I still couldn't see the man. He had to be huge judging by his voice—though small men could have big voices. If he'd killed these mercenaries, he had to be powerful too.

Yet, why was he still here? The mercenaries had been dead for weeks.

"You're a quiet crow. I hear the quiet crows taste better."

That made me shiver. Eating the flesh of fellow humans was completely against the laws of every kingdom. There were men who'd been lost at sea and cannibalized their companions. They'd been executed when they drifted back to shore.

Clink.

The sound of metal. Of something shifting. I'd heard

that sound before, recognized it from the prisons in the assassin fortress. They had chained me and my fellow students in a cell as part of our classes so we could learn to escape the various types of chains and to pick locks. Real bound prisoners had also occupied the cell.

They chained this person in a cave. And despite that, he had managed to defeat the mercenaries.

Why hadn't they just stood back and finished him with their bows and spells?

Clink. Clink. Clink.

Was he moving toward me? I stepped back, nearly tripping over the body of the female mercenary.

"Why so scared?" The man with the big voice *was* coming closer. Perhaps he still had the Devil's Fire in his hands.

I reached into my costume, found a handful of dust, and tossed it in front of me. It was an old mixture, and I prayed it would work.

The moment the sand-like substance hit the air, it glowed brightly.

And leering at me, not blinded by the sudden light in the slightest, was a dragon.

6

SCALES AND BONES

And it was not just any dragon, though of course a dragon of any sort was frightening enough. It was a Scythian dragon. They were rumored to be the most intelligent. The strongest. And they could regenerate. If you cut off a leg or a wing it would grow back in time.

This was not a huge dragon, perhaps not much longer than twenty-five feet. It was lithe and had black scales and long, leathery wings. The chain on its hind leg led back to...

The light failed.

Then light returned. The dragon had snorted out a flame, and a small pile of dried leaves and other filth began to burn. It smelled horrible but provided me with enough light to see.

"You look surprised, crow," the dragon said. A scar ran between his eyes and along his snout. "You were not expecting me?"

"No, I—I wasn't. What are you doing here?"

"Biding my time."

"For what?" I asked.

He moved his back leg, causing the chain to rattle. "For

freedom. To be out of this stinking hole and winging through the skies again."

Now that I looked at him, I could see that his ribs were visible under his scales. It had obviously been a long time since he'd eaten, but despite that, he didn't look like the hunger had weakened him. He could gobble me up in one or two bites.

And I was standing right in front of him.

His face was expressive, eyes gray, intelligent, and penetrating. I searched my mind for what I'd learned about this particular dragon. All dragons were rare, but the Scythians were the rarest. That much I could remember. There was a story you could get three wishes from a Scythian dragon.

My maestru had taught me to be observant. The chain led to the cave wall, where it was bolted into the stone. The chain also glittered slightly as though it had its own source of illumination. It had to be magic. I didn't think any normally forged chain could hold a dragon that long. There was a neatly piled collection of small bones behind him that I at first thought were the remains of children. I recoiled in horror. Then I settled my mind. No. They were of sheep and rabbits and other small animals. So, his captors had been feeding him. There was a stack of books next to the bones. Could this dragon read?

"You are spending a lot of time thinking," the dragon said. "I grow bored."

"How did you get here?"

"I believe the situation is obvious to any half-witted crow."

The sarcastic tone actually made me angry. He was talking down to me! Then again, he was a dragon, and I was only a mere mortal.

"These men trapped you in this cave."

He snorted tiny flames of derision out of his nose. "Any crow chick could come to that conclusion."

"The bones behind you suggest you've been here for many days—weeks, perhaps. And the books indicate that you like to read."

The dragon nodded. "Only fools hate reading. Plus, it passes the time. Keep going. Keep using your little bird brain."

I pointed at the body in front of me. "He was a wizard."

"He knew a few spells."

"He bound you here."

"He did."

"And even though he is dead, his magic persists."

"Correct!" He smacked his talons together, making a clapping sound. "He was a clever enchanter. He told me that his magic would continue for decades... but I had hoped it was a lie. If he wasn't dead, he'd be getting the last laugh."

"But how did they capture you?" I asked. I continued to breathe slowly through my nostrils. It surprised me how calm I was. All those years of meditating in a windowless room had paid off. But I also loved puzzles, and this was a fascinating puzzle. "They must have discovered you sleeping here."

"I sleep with one eye open. It's the only way to slumber in the human realms."

I gestured toward the bodies behind me. "Then these mercenaries lured you to this cave. But what could entice a Scythian dragon?"

"We do have our bad habits. And it wasn't a virgin sacrifice, in case you've come to that conclusion."

I shuddered at the thought of that. "Gold?" I said.

The dragon laughed. "I can get as much gold as I want at

any time. Just burn the guards off a treasure wagon and fly away with the treasury. Unlike you humans, I have no need for gold."

"Did they use sheep?"

"Oh, don't be stupid. I can eat sheep whenever I want. Crows are smart. I'm thinking you're not really a crow."

I glanced around me, taking measure of everything I could see. Bones. And books. And three dead bodies. I drew a blank. *Think, Carmen. Think!*

"You came here to learn," I said finally.

The dragon smiled, showing long rows of glittering teeth. "You are not such a dumb bird."

"Don't call me a bird. And don't call me dumb."

"Oh, you are a touchy little featherling. Yes, they lured me here because they promised me ancient texts that I had not yet tasted. I wanted to know more, to understand deeper truths so I could return to my land with new knowledge. New power. And they used that desire for knowledge against me. They doused some mutton with a sleeping draught, waited for it to take effect, and chained me here."

"But what did they want from you?" I asked.

"That, too, you should be clever enough to figure out."

"Three wishes?" I said.

This time the dragon laughed so hard flames snorted out his nostrils. "What do those idiot maestrus teach you in assassin school? Folktales? Lies?"

"You know I'm an assassin?"

He sniffed. "You all smell the same. Like almonds, if you must know. But no, it wasn't wishes they were after. That is an old, old story told by old, old men and women trying to scare grandchildren. It's not true. No one and nothing can give you three wishes."

"Then what was it?" I asked.

"I tire of this game, child." He raised his neck, so he was looking down at me. "What I want you to do is to pick the lock on these chains and release me. And in return, I won't kill you. Do it, now!"

7

ONLY ONE CHOICE

I recounted in my mind how many steps I had taken into the cave. Twelve. I was standing almost exactly where the enchanter had stood before the dragon had blasted him off his feet. Even the female mercenary behind me had still been in deadly reach of the flames. I would have to turn.

He would fry me the moment I turned.

I could slowly bend my knees and throw myself backward, hoping the flames would go above me. But I knew nothing about dragon flames. Did they come out in a straight line? Or spray in the shape of a funnel?

I went quickly through the few potions and herbs in my possession. Nothing. Not even an acid I could toss in the hopes of blinding him.

Jumping backward was my only option. I slowly, slowly bent my legs and tried to keep my nerves steady. "Why sh-should I help you?"

"Because you don't want to die."

I kept bending and hoping the few ragged feathers hid some of my motion from him.

"Well, I do prefer being alive," I said.

"I can tell. Despite being one-eyed, you risked those nasty swans. And you look old enough to graduate from the assassin school. Not an easy task, I've heard. So, you are a survivor. And despite my teasing, you are smart. What's your name?"

I hesitated. Had I read something about dragons and names? If he knew my name would he have power over me? I couldn't remember anything about it. "It's Carmen."

"Carmen. Carmen. A good name. A hard sound in your name. A hard stone in your heart."

"What does that mean?" I had managed to get halfway to a crouch.

"Something my mother used to say. I don't know what it means. Mommy loved her little sayings." He snorted out a little flame. "Well, Carmen, would you take some advice from a friend?"

"I—I don't know."

"I'll give the advice anyway. Don't leap backward. You are slowly bending your legs and thinking you can outdistance me. But you will be dead before you hit the ground. And then I will eat you. Medium-rare, in case you are wondering."

I stopped my slow movement and straightened a little. I swallowed. As long as he was talking, he wouldn't be able to turn me to ashes. "What's your name?"

"Braxas," he said. "Though you can call me Brax. Now, how about coming a little closer and seeing what you can do about this manacle and chain?"

"But you haven't had anything to eat for at least two weeks. How can I trust you?"

"I wish it was only two weeks." He began counting on his talons. "It's been thirty days, thirty-one nights, and twelve hours to be exact. You'll just have to trust that I don't want to eat you." He scratched at his lip with a talon. The front arms were rather dextrous, I noted. "Well, that's not quite true. I do want to eat you. You'll just have to trust that I won't eat you."

"It would be foolish to eat me." I was surprised I was talking so bravely and logically to something that might gobble me up for lunch. "You wouldn't be able to escape from here."

"Yes, that's a quandary. Plus, to be honest, humans taste horrible." He let out another of his laughs. "Now come forward, Carmen. Get closer to your new friend, Brax. You can trust me."

I took a deep breath. There really wasn't another choice.

I stepped forward.

8

THE LOGICAL THING

Each step made me tremble more. I misjudged and crunched down on the hand of the enchanter, which crumbled to dust. I kept going, getting closer and closer to the dragon. His scales had begun to sag a little—he really had lost weight. I also noted that each bone of the sheep and goats in front of me had been snapped in two and the marrow sucked out.

The biggest surprise of all was his smell.

I thought he would stink like death. Or have a swampy scent like a lizard.

Instead, he smelled like flowers. Familiar flowers, but I couldn't place the scent. There were several gardens in the Red Adept Assassin Fortress, and tending them was one of my biggest pleasures. I knew the flowers well. Of course, the garden was composed mostly of poisonous herbs and berries. But it was a place of beauty. I sometimes wished I could just become the maestru gardener and look after it for the rest of my life.

No one would bother me about my missing eye up there.

I ran through a list of flowers in my head before it came

to me: Brax smelled like chrysanthemums. It was more of an earthy, herblike smell. They were curious flowers that way because they really didn't have a sweet scent like tulips or roses.

"Why are you sniffing?" Brax asked.

"I'm not sniffing."

"Yes, you are. Humans and your sensitive noses! Every little smell is an affront to your delicate natures."

"It's just that you smell like flowers."

He looked shocked. I continued to be surprised at how expressive a dragon face could be. He raised one scaly eyebrow. "I smell like flowers? Do you want me to fry you where you stand?"

"Now look who's being delicate." The words were out before I could run them through my brain to decide whether or not they were offensive. I couldn't take them back now. I braced for a blast of flames.

Instead I was blasted by another gruff laugh. "You are a brave one, Carmen Crow. Please come around my right side. You will see the cursed chain that holds me."

I walked along his side, avoiding his foot. Very few humans would have ever stood so near to a live dragon. A dead one, certainly, for their hides made some of the best armor. And their brains could be dried and used for extremely strong potions.

"They were going to skin you," I said. The horror of it. Starving him so that his scales and skin were loose and easier to skin.

"Yes, they were, my dear friend," he said. "Oh, the money they would make on the market, even though I am not fully grown. A runt, if I'm truthful. Dragon claws. Horns. Scaled shields and scaled armor—all are worth big buckets of gold.

Plus, my brain is valuable too. Those schemers would have been rich for the rest of their lives."

"But to kill something so beautiful. That's wrong!"

"Are you trying to soften me up with your words, child? I will take the compliment. The mercenaries are dead now. They thought I was beautiful too, in their own way. I didn't really like their look though. Too desperate. They look a lot better to me dead." I shivered, for he said these last words coldly. "Now, examine my chain, child."

I went past his muscled haunches. The dark wings were flat against his back. They looked strong. Wings that would take him to the air. We had studied flight in class because we had been trained to use large kites to fly into high places.

The idea of flying on a kite seemed silly now. This dragon was able to ride every current in the air.

I went around to his back leg and saw that the long chain was not much thicker than my wrist. The only thing that made it look interesting was that it had a slight glow. The other end was hammered into the wall. Obviously, I couldn't pull it out of there.

"It's just a chain," I said.

"Look closer." A tight manacle was locked around his back-right leg and scrawled with runes. I had studied a few magic runes in class. Magic was unreliable, so assassins were taught to rarely use it. But it was knowledge we still couldn't ignore. It took me a moment to read the runes. "Binder," I said. "This is a binding spell."

"So, they do teach you something useful in that den of death dealers. Good. Good. Perhaps you'll be helpful after all."

I touched the chain. It was warm, and it pulsed with magic. The manacle had cut into his leg, leaving sores and worn-away scales.

"It has wounded you."

"It does burn. But I'm not one to complain. Can you undo the chain?" His voice actually went a bit higher when he spoke the last sentence.

The lock looked pickable, and I reached into the pouch on my belt and drew out two of my best picks. I was adept at picking locks, even better than my brother. I began poking inside the keyhole on the manacle, using the sharp edges like they were the ends of my fingers. I could find the smallest breach.

I poked. I prodded. But I found nothing. It was as if there wasn't a lock inside. Or at least no pins to move. Nothing. I kept forcing, pushing harder and harder until I snapped one of my picks.

"Oh, that is not a good sound," Brax said.

"The runes bind it. Perhaps another spell hides the actual mechanism."

"I thought as much. But one should try. Any chance you happen to have memorized any unlocking spells from your classes?"

I shook my head.

"Well, that's too bad." Brax sighed. "I guess the only logical thing to do is to eat you."

9

DEALS TO DREAM OF

I tensed and started to run, but Brax reached out quickly with his front claw and grabbed me by the arm. The underside of his talons was rough, and the grip was not painfully tight, though I still couldn't pull myself away.

"Let me go!"

"Now, now dear," he said. "I was kidding. You just don't understand my sense of humor yet. I'm not that hungry." Then he ground his teeth together. It was a horrible sound. "Actually, I'm very hungry. Maybe I should just eat your arm."

"What!"

He shook me. "Oh, don't be so jumpy. I'm being humorous again. Plus, your arms are too skinny."

"Well ... what if I gave you some food?"

"Do you have a cow in your pocket?" He lifted me, so I was directly in front of him. "No cow? Whatever scraps you carry in your pockets are of no use to me."

Despite my fear, I noted how much control he had of his talons—almost like human hands. He could certainly break my arm just by flexing his muscles.

"I'm good at figuring out puzzles," I said. "I'll find a way to feed you."

"Will you chase a herd of mountain goats into my mouth? Because I eat a lot."

"If I free you then you can get your own mountain goats." I did my best to hold his stare. "But you have to let me go. I'm the only one who can save you."

"I can save myself."

"You'll wither away."

He smiled. When a dragon smiled, they showed a lot of sharp, sharp teeth. "I can last a long time, Carmen Crow. Perhaps your whole lifetime."

I looked around the cave, my gaze settling on the three mercenaries. The rising sun was painting them red. They had wanted to kill this amazing creature! What horrible people. Then again, perhaps they had families to feed.

No, this wasn't like slaughtering a cow and using its hide for leather. A dragon was intelligent. It could speak.

"What thoughts are going through your tiny brain, child? What deals are you dreaming of?"

"I can go to the assassin library. There are plenty of spell books there. I can learn how to unlock that chain and set you free."

"You say that now. But my guess is you'll come back here with your maestrus and a hundred assassins, and I will be full of crossbow bolts in a heartbeat. Or perhaps just one blow dart and I'll succumb to one of your famous poisons."

"I wouldn't do that!" My voice went a little high-pitched.

"Why not? What do you owe me? Nothing. And I owe you nothing. All I have to bargain with is your life, and once you're out of this cave that bargain is forfeit."

"What ... what if I swore?" I asked.

"A swear word? Which one?"

"You know what I mean. An oath that I would return to free you."

"An oath from a human is as worthless as ashes." He was squeezing me very tightly now, and I wondered if he were thinking of some past betrayal. Likely his experience with the mercenaries was enough to make him not trust us.

"I swear on the graves of my parents," I said. "I, Carmen Dore, will find a way to release you."

Brax was silent for several seconds, staring at me. His eyes glowed gray with fury, as if he expected a trap. He had the same slit pupils as a lizard. It felt as if his gaze was stabbing right into me.

I hoped he could see the truth. Because I meant every word.

"I will take you on your word, Carmen Dore of the Red Adept Assassins. I release you." Brax let go of my arm. I stumbled a few steps, expecting treachery. Then I walked a few more steps and breathed in.

"Go. Go quickly, child. Before I change my mind. Run!"

I did run. Out of the mouth of the cave and into the sunlight. I paused only to shout, "I'll return, Brax. I will return."

He said nothing in reply.

10

A DAY OF LUCK

Belaz, the goddess of all assassins, was on my side, for I had only jogged a short distance from the cave when I discovered the black swan egg. It was still intact and somewhat warm. The egg had somehow careened that last bit down the side of the cliff and rolled to a stop in the open. No creatures of the night had cracked it in half to sup on the joys inside. I knew swan eggs were tough, but this intact egg was almost beyond belief.

"Thank you, Belaz," I whispered. "For this and for everything else."

I *had* just escaped from the clutches of a Scythian dragon. I had stood face-to-snout with it and survived. And I wasn't too humble to admit that it was my wits that had kept me alive.

I walked ahead, picking my way along the mountain paths. Soon the sun had risen partway in the sky and warmed me enough that I peeled off the last tatters of the bird suit, happy to be in just my ninja trousers and shirt. I used what remained of the costume to wrap up the egg and keep it warm.

It took most of the morning to reach the ten thousand steps that led to the Red Adept Assassin Fortress. The steps were curved back and forth so that an army climbing them would easily be brought down by a rain of arrows or hot oil poured from above.

A bell rang. Nine bells! I'd been out the whole night.

But it was worth it. Meeting Brax had been exhilarating. I should tell Maestru Alesius about the dragon. He deserved to know that such a powerful creature was only a short distance from the school. Assassins had a long list of uses for every magical creature, but I wasn't certain if that meant Brax would be unchained and then enslaved by some other means. Or if he would be bled out so his insides and exterior could become potions, armor, and tools.

Or if that would make me as equally horrible as the mercenaries who'd bound him.

I'd sworn an oath on my parents.

I found the thirteenth door and opened it with my lockpick—assassins never carried keys. I partly unwrapped the egg so that my fellow students could see what I had accomplished and strode into the school. I chose to walk down the middle of the hallway so as to lessen the chance of bumping anything. It would be stupid if I'd traveled all that way then broke the egg on a pillar.

The first person I encountered was Megan. Her red hair was tied tightly behind her, making her angular face look severe.

Ha! This will show her!

But Megan didn't look surprised at all; in fact, she didn't even give the egg a glance. "Have you heard?"

I adjusted my arm so that more of the egg was revealed. Maybe Megan didn't recognize what it was.

"Have I heard what?"

"The emperor prince is dead."

"Dead?" I pulled the egg back a bit as if the new information might somehow hurt it. "How?"

"He was given Abethaus poison. It leaves the scarlet marks."

"Abethaus poison?" My shock was making me repeat things, but I was unable to stop myself. "What assassin would dare poison a child?"

"It just takes one rogue assassin to taint us all." Megan did look worried, and it wasn't until she spoke the next sentence that I understood exactly why. "The emperor has declared a halt to all trade with assassins. And a Kellian knife was found in the room. There are rumors of war. Between the Empire and Kellia."

"Oh," I said. The students had spent so many hours memorizing the various treaties between the Five Realms and the Empire. We had also memorized the names and faces of every diplomat, every king and queen, and the entire royal line of every country. We also studied the senators of the city-state of Avenus, where they actually voted for two archons every two years.

A war between Kellia and the Akkad Empire would draw in the other four realms and be so large as to perhaps last generations.

"We won't have a place to ply our trade," Megan said. "It's horrible." And then she stepped past me. She still hadn't noticed the egg or the fact I was covered with bruises and cuts.

I sighed and carried the egg up the many steps to my maestru's chamber. I knocked gently on the door.

"Come in, Carmen," Maestru Alesius said.

The fact that he knew me from my knock and my approaching footsteps had ceased to surprise me. I'd stopped trying to fool him. I opened the thick wooden door and took a few steps inside his study. My maestru was standing at his table, a parchment in his hand. Scrolls, tomes and other papers were scattered across the table, indicating he'd been searching quickly for something. He was usually impeccably neat.

He had his hood back, so I could clearly see his dark-skinned face. His hair, always kept short, was looking grayer today. It matched his eyes. He turned and gave me an appraising glance. "You have succeeded," he said. "Congratulations. I will add twenty-five points to your totals. Barring any final surprises, you'll graduate." He reached out for the egg, and I handed it to him. "Ah, it is a male swan."

"You can tell that?" I asked.

"Of course. And since you have no way of keeping track of when the swan hatches, you'll never know." He smiled a little, though I did see signs of worry on his face. He handed the egg back to me. "It is in excellent shape, Carmen. You look like you had to fight for it."

I hadn't paused to glance in a mirror. I was suddenly aware exactly how much my clothes were torn and how numerous the scratches were on my arms. There were even still several feathers hanging from my hair.

"It was a long climb," I said. "And I did fall once. Or twice. Maybe three times."

"One must watch one's step near a precipice." He waved a finger in the air. "That's my wise saying for today." He then inhaled deeply, a curious look on his face. "Were you in the gardens before you came here?"

"No. I came straight to you."

"Well, you smell of chrysanthemums. But the scent isn't quite right. I can't place what's different."

He knows! I thought. *The dragon scent rubbed off on me.* I absently felt my arm when Brax had grabbed me.

"Let me see that." He gently took my elbow. The sleeve of my shirt was torn, revealing a circular bruise. "That's an odd-shaped bruise."

"I got it when I fell." I had only lied to my maestru twice. He'd caught me out both times.

"That's a contortion bruise. Did you have a rope with you?"

"Yes. Yes," I said. "I did. I used it to climb to the nesting grounds. I forgot. It must have wrapped around my arm as I was rolling down the cliff. It must have."

He looked me directly in the eye. "Well, then that *must* be what happened." He released my arm. I thought, perhaps, there was a glint of disappointment in his eyes. "Did you hear the latest news?"

"That the emperor prince has been poisoned? Yes. Megan told me."

"Gossip spreads on black wings. Especially in our school. His death bodes ill for our guild. Emperor Rima has sent several notices and official queries, demanding answers. He wants to see our records. Do you know why?"

It was always a test with Maestru Alesius. "Umm. To discover who was hired by the Kellians? But we can't show him our records."

"Correct on both counts. We have maintained over two thousand years of secrecy. No emperor or king has ever walked our halls, let alone been allowed access to our records. We do not give out our secrets."

"Then what do we do? He is an emperor, after all."

"You leave that to the maestrus to decide. Answer me this: who is now next in line for the throne?"

I paused only for a moment. "His nephew Sargon."

"Yes. Good. He is a ruthless man. He did such a fine job in hunting down the wizards when they were outlawed in Akkad. Though, I grieve for our part in winnowing down their numbers. The emperor has put Sargon in charge of the Immortals. Having such elite soldiers pursue this assassin means the emperor will leave no stone unturned. But we are hunting too."

"Why?" I asked.

"Because this assassin has killed a child."

"And what is the punishment for that?" The assassin textbooks had never given me that information.

Maestru Alesius grimaced. "A horrible death," he said somewhat sadly. Then he raised his hand. "I have work to do, Carmen. Please take the egg to the swannery. And congratulations. You will take your place with your fellow graduates and wear the official cloak of the Red Adept Assassins. You have exceeded all my expectations."

"I am pleased to hear that, Maestru Alesius."

But he was already reading his papers. I let myself out of his study.

11

A GOOD NAME

I was becoming attached to the egg. I liked holding it and feeling my own warmth keep it alive. I continued up the stairwell, again watching my step. This time a few of my fellow students in the main hallway did see me carrying the egg. And, I was certain, there was shock and perhaps jealousy in their eyes.

Good, I thought. And I couldn't prevent a smile from coming to my lips.

A few steps later, Thord came around a corner. He stopped and said nothing but bowed grandly as I passed. This time, I was the one who blushed. Why was someone with his looks being so kind to me? He had to see some advantage to it. But what could it be?

I had promised him a story, but now was not the time to tell it. And I couldn't let him know about every scaly detail.

I quickened my pace but nearly dropped the egg when a hand grabbed me just as I turned toward the lifts. The hand had come from my left side, of course.

"There you are," my brother said. He held me steady and gave me an up-and-down glance. "You look awful. But thankfully that egg distracts anyone from noticing." I'd long ago learned to ignore his harsh comments. Often, something nice would come out next. "I knew you could do it, Carmen. You have guts. That's one thing you're not missing."

"Unlike my eye."

"I didn't mean that as a dig—don't be so sensitive—it's just that you keep going, no matter what. Whoever hires you will be lucky." He put his hand on the egg. I resisted pulling it away. "It's warm. So much life in there. And power. Just think of how hard our assassin lives would be without the black swans to deliver us to our kills. Imagine an army of assassins on swans. Now that would be something!" He tapped the egg. "Amazing creatures."

"They are," I said, pulling the egg back. I had seen something even more amazing with wings. "But that's not the most wonderful thing I saw. I—"

I caught myself. I'd almost mentioned Brax.

"You saw what?" he asked.

"Nothing. Just the moon. It glowed over the mountains. It was just like a painting."

"Oh. The moon. How exciting," he said as drolly as possible. "The things that excite you are, well, cute."

"It was a beautiful scene." I didn't want to imagine what he'd do if I'd let it slip about Brax. Then I noted that he had a cut above his eye. It was a straight line, which I knew meant a bladed weapon. "What's that from?"

He grinned. "My juggling skills are not up to par." He mimed himself juggling then covering his eye. "I'll be more careful next time. You've heard the news about the emperor's welp."

"Yes. It's horrible."

"Horrible for us, you mean. It's a very precarious time to be an assassin. You be sure to take care of yourself. Keep an eye out." He slapped his forehead. "I don't mean that as another dig."

I spoke through gritted teeth. "It's hard to tell with you."

"Let it go, sis. The good news is that you and I will graduate in three days. And I'm sure all these problems with the emperor will soon be solved. After all, we wouldn't want to lose our best client." He patted my shoulder. "I'm so proud of you." Then he was gone.

I stepped into the nearest lift and pulled down the lever for the swannery level. There were rumors that students who broke school rules were forced to pull the lifts up and down, but I had read that the lifts were controlled by a series of underground pulleys, powered by watermills.

Soon I was on the second from the top level of the fortress. I went to the door to the swannery, opened it with one hand, and was hit with the overpowering stink of swan dung. There were rows and rows of stables, where black swans sat on their straw nests waiting for their riders. The best and biggest swans would be bound to their assassins by a process called imprinting, so they wouldn't leave even if the gates were left open. Other swans were trained to accept any human rider.

I had cleaned those stalls a thousand times in my lifetime. And I absolutely loved the feeling of warmth and closeness inside the place. And I was always impressed by the intelligence of the swans.

It was important, of course, to never anger them. Their beaks were sharp.

Maestru Arvid, the keeper of the swannery, was waiting for me, as if he'd known I was coming. He saw the egg and a wide, toothy smile split his bearded face. He gently took the egg from me. "Oh, this is a good one, an excellent one! We will raise her to be strong."

"Maestru Alesius said it was a he."

"Maestru Alesius is always correct, except with anything concerning swans. This is a girl. Now name her."

"Carnda," I said immediately.

"Oh. A good name! You chose it so quickly."

"It was my mother's name," I said.

"Ah, good, good. Well, you have brought Carnda to a wonderful home. Thank you; now you may go." Then, without even giving me a chance to say good-bye to the egg, he closed the door.

I was surprised that I felt so disappointed. *Were you going to kiss the egg good-bye?*

12

THINGS COME, THINGS GO

I took the lift down to the student dormitory level then followed the long winding hallways. I had no memories of my mother or my father. Both my parents had died in a fire, as far as I knew. I wasn't even certain what they did for a living or which country they came from.

"You are our children now," Maestru Alesius had explained once when I pressed him about my parents. "The past is wiped clean."

I only knew my mother's name because Corwin had snuck into the records office and saw that it was written down above our own names. My father was Ector Dore.

I went to the showers. No one else was there, which didn't surprise me since it was already midmorning. I was pleased to have the place to myself. The water was always cold, but I was able to clean off the sweat and wash out all the cuts. The bruise that circled my arm was growing slightly darker.

I thought I could smell the dragon scent being sloughed off. For some reason, that made me feel a little bit sad.

I actually relaxed under the cold blast of the shower. I

hadn't even taken a moment to enjoy the fact that I would be graduating and getting the red cloak of an assassin. I was not going to be at the top of the rolls as I had imagined years ago, but I would be an assassin. The gates would open in three days, and all fifteen of the graduates would walk out to start our own shops.

I knew that Banderius, the most famous of assassins, had his own palace in Trella. I bet the water was hot in his home. He was said to dine only on chocolate caviar, rare crocodile meat, and fine wines. The other recurring rumor about him was that he had grown soft.

I wrapped myself in towels and went back to my room, feeling quite refreshed despite the fact that I'd been out the whole night. There was still time to visit the library before attending afternoon classes.

After dressing and switching my eye patch, I made my way to the library. An impressive set of spiral stairs led down into a giant room with rows and rows of book-stuffed shelves. There were tomes on every poison and every creature in existence. This included the tracks they made, how to imitate those tracks, their smells, even their calls to fool our prey. There was even a chapter in one book on recreating fox droppings to throw suspicious soldiers off your trail. I hoped I'd never have do that.

I loved this room. All of those words waiting there for me to read. I had spent so much time here, often reading until my eye was dry. Today, I wandered the stacks, passing by *Weremonsters of Yore* and *Lore of Lodenstones,* until I came across *Here Be Dragons.*

I'd never seen the title before. I hefted the book from its shelf and brought it over to an empty table and carefully flipped it open.

The illustrations inside were startling in their detail.

The dragons were drawn from the tips of their snouts to the tips of their tails, with every talon and scale in between. I found a long list of dragon types, though most were only rumored to exist because dragons lived far away from human lands.

I finally came to a chapter about Scythian dragons. The image that had been drawn was much larger than Brax, which meant perhaps he was not full grown. But this beast had the same black wings and black-as-night scales. Ebony dragons were rare, according to the description. And they could release both a poison gas and a flame. *Here I was worried about being burned to death when I could have easily been poisoned.* I kept reading. The Scythians were perhaps the most intelligent of the dragon species.

I skipped ahead. The book went on for pages about the shape of their scales and included an article on how to skin a variety of dragons and use their organs for potions. Their teeth could become part of powerful ward spells. I was glad I hadn't told Maestru Alesius. I trusted him, but he would have done what was best for the assassin school. A good stock of dragon parts would be a treasure trove.

Finally, I came to a section about regeneration. The Scythians could grow back their tails, their talons, their ears —nearly every part of their body. Unless, of course, you cut off their head.

The regenerative blood of Scythian dragons had been sought by emperors and kings who wanted to extend their lives and their reigns. None had succeeded. There was even a wizard who'd removed a Scythian leg and attached it to his own missing leg. It was said to have grafted itself there, and so he attached another leg and an arm. It didn't explain what happened to his original arms. But the dragon blood eventually drove him mad, and he jumped off a cliff believing he could fly. He didn't magically grow wings on the way down, and he died.

That was insanity. But people would do anything for power. I kept reading and came across an interesting passage that I then read several times:

The Scythians are powerful magical creatures. But they are also oath bound—if they swear an oath, they will keep it until they are dead. There are rumors that these dragons can grant three wishes. These are not true.

Of course, they weren't. But—

"What are you reading?" a woman asked.

I shuddered. I glanced up to see Maestru Beatrix, the keeper of the library. She was a short, pudgy woman with the most amazing blue eyes. Her hair was gray and tied back by a black ribbon. "Oh, nothing. This book just caught my eye," I said.

"Books do that, don't they?"

I nodded. We'd had a thousand conversations about the importance of books. Maestru Beatrix was so happy that one of the assassin students was actually a reader.

"Ah, the Scythian dragon. An interesting topic. Are you writing a piece about them for extra marks?"

"No. I just picked the book up. I don't have a particular interest. I really don't."

"It's fine to be interested in dragons. As you know, I trade books with other libraries in the Five Realms. That book is a relatively new addition. One can never have too many books. Or read too many books."

"That's true." Normally, I would ask to see all the new books, but I held my tongue. I wanted to keep reading.

"You seem extra intense today, Carmen," Beatrix said. "Is it the news of the emperor?"

"Yes. Yes."

"Don't worry. These things come and go. Take that from someone who has read every historical text written. We'll find who is behind the murder of his child, and that assassin will be punished in a very public way." She didn't say this with any relish, only stating a fact. "And that will go a long way to correcting this matter."

"That's good to know."

"Now is there anything else I can help you with?" Maestru Beatrix asked.

"Yes," I said. "Do you happen to have any new books on spells?"

13

A FROZEN MOMENT

I read spell books until my eye grew dry. I was getting close to giving up when I found a short chapter on enchanted chains and bindings. At the very end of the description was a word and hand gesture that were often used together to unlock locks. The word was *enderos.* The chapter made it sound like even a beginning apprentice enchanter could master this spoken spell.

I wasn't an enchanter and had only been taught a few easy spells to erase footprints or scents. But I had a good memory and was always willing to try. Perhaps if I spoke the word aloud as I tried to pick the lock, I would succeed.

"Enderos," I said aloud. It did sound magical.

I wondered what Brax was doing with his time. Was he reading the books in his cave for the thousandth time? Could he use his own flames to see the pages? I knew that the smell of the dead mercenaries would keep anything but the bravest carrion birds away.

I closed the book and put it back in place, running my hands along the shelves as I walked back toward the entrance.

"You carry the library with you wherever you go," Maestru Beatrix had once said. I knew it was true.

The afternoon bell rang three times, which meant I would have to rush to get to Pressure Points class. Time always ran by far too quickly in the library.

I slid into my place at the table just before Maestru Olgra turned around to face the class. "Well, well," she said. "This will be our final class. I will miss your ugly faces." She had spent the last four years teaching us the various points of the body that would knock someone out, stop their heart, or collapse their lungs. We had memorized the exact locations of livers, hearts, spleens, certain vertebrae, and nerve endings. "For our final class I would like you to choose a partner and explore the various nerve points in each other's hands."

My heart sank. I hated having partners, especially since I didn't like any of the other assassins. Since there was an odd number of us, that meant someone always had to partner with Maestru Olgra. She was known to put students in pain with a thumb pinch for weeks—just to teach a lesson. I'd long given up trying to partner with Corwin. He preferred to be with Scyllia or Gregum.

Thord began walking toward me, and I sucked in a breath. He would be better than Maestru Olgra, though I didn't like the idea of exploring his hands for nerve points. Or even holding hands with him. It was just too personal.

My hands were suddenly sweaty.

Just as he was about to come close enough to say something to me, Megan sat down across from me, effectively blocking him. Thord turned away.

"Uh, hello," I said.

"I'd like to be your partner." Megan flipped her red hair back over her shoulder. She had what looked like a friendly smile on her face. At least she hadn't said *I'd like to be your partner, Cyclops.*

"Um. Yes. If you must."

"Good. Good." We joined hands, and I wasn't surprised to discover that Megan's palms were rough. She worked hard, especially at her hand-to-hand fighting. She wasn't the smartest of the graduating class, but she made up for that with tenacity. "I was not very observant this morning," Megan said. It almost sounded like an apology. "I was shocked by the news of the emperor princeling's death. Only later did it dawn on me that you were carrying a swan egg. That's amazing. How did you get it?"

"I went to the swan nesting ground in a swan outfit and stole it." I thought it best to keep the story simple.

"Oh, why?"

"To get points. To pass."

"Impressive!" she said. And she really did look impressed. "That's very brave. And did you get the points?"

"Yes."

"So, you will be the first assassin with only one eye to graduate?" She didn't seem to intend this as an insult. It was a genuine question.

"I don't know."

"I bet you are. That's something. You're in the historical records now. Congratulations!"

"Um. Thank you."

She continued to stare at me. "I was just thinking about how that eye patch makes you look."

I tightened my grip, but Megan didn't seem to notice. "How does it make me look?"

"Older. I mean not too old. But like you've done stuff. It makes you look experienced. I think we should be partners once we've graduated."

My mouth popped open in shock. I quickly shut it. "P-partners?"

"Yes. Partners. New assassins often team up. You have better scores than me on all the potions and poisons and stuff. And you will look good at the front."

"The front?"

"Yes," she said, now sounding very excited. "I've really thought it out. I'm so proud of myself." Her smile showed perfect teeth. She had a perfect face too. I kind of hated the fact that nothing was out of place. "You see, people will trust you. I mean not to do their missions, but you can speak to them about everything that an assassin does. And the way you look, that will be helpful for anyone who approaches our business. They talk to you, then they hire me to finish the job. We will make a perfect team."

"So, I don't work as an assassin then?"

She looked genuinely puzzled. "Of course not. I mean you've come to this conclusion, right? No one is going to hire a one-eyed assassin. Maybe a farmer who has a particularly mean chicken to kill." Her chuckle was punctuated by a couple of snorts. "Seriously, it's so perfect. You look the part. I look the part. And you keep twenty-five percent."

"So, you only want me for how I look?"

"Yes. Of course! And your potion skills, too. You understand. So, what do you say?"

I didn't think too long about my response. There was a nerve point between the thumb and forefinger that I had studied in class. It froze people. There was always a small chance that the person would never come out of the frozen state, but I was pretty sure I'd do it right.

"C'mon, Carmen. Give me your answer. You won't get a better offer."

I jabbed my thumb into the pressure point, and Megan

froze so that she could only move her eyes. A drop of saliva dripped from her perfect lips.

"No," I said. "I will not be your partner. I will be starting my own business, and I will find my own clients. Never will I ever work for you."

I pushed myself away from the desk and stomped out of the room. Maestru Olgra had her back to us, so she didn't see me leave.

14

AN IMPORTANT WORD

I stomped down the stone stairwell and into the open hallway and down another set of circular steps before I started to admit to myself that I probably shouldn't have frozen Megan.

But the offer is so insulting! I am an assassin. I deserve this. I was right to freeze her. To show her and anyone else that I have the skills. I will work twice as hard to be the best assassin in all the kingdoms. People will know my name.

I would never just sit as a prop at a table in someone else's shop. Never!

It dawned on me that there might be punishment for not finishing the final class (and leaving Megan in that state). I wasn't certain what form it would take, but the other students would remember not to cross me.

I returned to my room and yanked on the door, but it, of course, was locked. I reached for my lockpicks, then remembered what I had read about enchantments in the library. I had always been able to memorize pages, so I brought the spell page to mind. The instructions had said to speak the word aloud. So, with the thought of unlocking in my head, I said, "*Enderos.*"

Then I moved my hand in a circular motion.

My door unlocked.

I drew in a breath. I moved my hand again and the door locked. It was as if I could see the lock through all the wood. I should have learned this spell long ago!

There was no sense waiting around for punishment. I had to try this spell out on Brax. I dashed into my room, threw on my warmest cloak, picked my best boots for climbing, and then started the long walk down flight after flight of stairs to the three hundred eight doors.

It wasn't until I passed the kitchens that another idea crossed my mind. The cooks in the kitchen were already busy making the evening meal. I had spent plenty of time there as part of my training, because it was important to know how meals were prepared. Often assassins would have to disguise themselves as servants and kitchen staff to complete a mission.

It was relatively easy to sneak into the kitchen, glance around to see if any of the cooks saw me, then slip out, unseen, with the largest ham I could find hidden in a burlap sack. I continued on until I reached the thirteenth door.

I tried the spell, but the lock wouldn't move. There were incredibly ancient wards on the locks to prevent any type of magic user from entering. So, I picked the lock and went outside. The open air refreshed me.

By the time I got to Brax's cave, the sun was beginning to set. I passed the bodies of the mercenaries. They didn't smell any sweeter. Then I stepped into the darkness. Having come from the bright light, it took time for my eye to adjust, even though I often trained in darkness.

"Well, this is a surprise," Brax said. "I'd made a bet with my dead guests that you wouldn't come back. I lost the bet."

"I gave an oath." I still couldn't see him.

"I know. But you're human. And oaths and lies are often the same to you." He snorted out a small flame, lighting his face. He was grinning. I shivered at the sight of his teeth. Gods, what was I doing in front of such a fearsome beast? He licked his lips. "You've brought me a snack. Ham, by the smell of it."

"Yes, I thought it at least might stop you from eating me."

"For a few eyeblinks anyway," he said. "Toss it."

I pulled the ham from the bag and hefted it into the air. The chain rattled, his head appeared in the light for a moment, and I saw how sharp his teeth were, then the ham vanished down his throat.

"Salty," he said. "Just how I like it. Did you happen to bring any wine?"

"No. I'm not a walking market."

"A shame! Just remember that I do like wine." He made a sucking sound, which I realized meant he was sucking the pieces of pork out from between his teeth. "Well, that was a tasty morsel, at least. I suppose if you've come here, you intend to release me."

"I've learned a spell that might unlock the chain."

My eyes had adjusted enough that I could clearly see his look of doubt. "You've become an enchanter overnight?"

"No. But I am a reader, and I've done my research. I learned a magical word from a book of spells."

"Ah, book learning! So often it fails in the real world. What word was it?"

"If I tell you, then you'll escape and maybe eat me."

"I guess there is that possibility," he said. He'd touched a talon to his jaw, as if in thought. Such a humanlike pose. "I suppose you want me to swear something?"

"Yes. I know Scythian dragons never break their oaths."

"Not true, sad to say. But we do hold them as a high ideal, so you'll just have to hope I'm not an oath breaker."

I swallowed. "Promise you won't eat me or slay me."

"Now, just a friendly warning to be careful with your wording. I am rather gifted in misinterpreting oaths."

I clenched a fist, then held it behind me so that he wouldn't see how nervous I was. "I also want you to swear you won't do anything that'll knowingly bring me harm."

"Done. Any other terms?"

I hadn't thought much beyond my first request. What else could I ask? Then, without pausing to think it through, I said, "I want you to fix my eye."

"Fix your eye? I'm not a healer. Nor am I an optician. It's far too late for that eye."

"No. You can do it," I insisted, and the more I said each word the more I believed it. "You can regenerate it and give me sight. I'm sure you can do it. So, do it."

He chuckled. "You look and sound so serious. But Scythian regeneration doesn't work that way. I can only regenerate things on myself. And I don't control it." He wiggled one of his claws. "I lost this in a battle. It grew back. But not once did I say to it, '*grow back now, little claw.*' I can't help you with your eye."

It had been worth a try. "Then what do I get in exchange for releasing you?"

He made his wings ruffle, and there was something menacing about the movement. "Is there someone you'd like me to kill? An old boyfriend?"

"No! Besides, I'm an assassin. I could do that myself."

He lowered his wings. "Well, if you haven't thought it through, then I won't do your thinking for you."

"A ride on your back," I blurted.

"A what?"

"A ride."

He reared back, pulling himself to the top of the cave. "You want me to submit to having a human on my back. The degradation of it! I'm not a pack animal."

"I didn't mean to offend you. But I want to know what it's like."

"You might accidentally fall off."

"You promised not to hurt me."

"I can't control how tightly you grip."

"You can catch me if I slip."

He glared down at me, and I stared back. I put the most innocent look on my face, as if I wasn't aware of his anger. "Fine," he huffed. "One ride. At dark when no one will see it. And you will be safe. In return for my freedom. I guarantee it."

It didn't sound like very much to trade when listed that way. But I couldn't think of anything else to ask for, and I realized in my heart I just wanted to see him free. I decided to tell him so. "I really just want you to be free."

"That's sweet." I couldn't tell if he was being sarcastic. "Then be your most noble self and free me, Carmen of the Assassins."

I had brought a torch. I held it out and he lit it with a small puff of flame. Again, I shivered to be so near to something so powerful, so intelligent and magical and not human. You couldn't talk to the swans. I was tempted to run a hand along his scales but knew he might bite it off. He most likely didn't like to be touched.

I knelt by the manacle and propped the torch against the

wall so I could see. His leg looked even worse than it had the previous night. I wondered if a dragon could go septic.

I brought out my picking tools, laid them out one by one. Then I took a deep breath and spoke. "*Enderos.*" I felt a chill when I said it, as though it had brought a small wind into the cave. The manacle glowed slightly. *This is going to work!* "*Enderos!*" I repeated just to be certain. I felt that same chill, and the manacle was now glowing bright.

I had hoped the word would open the lock right away. I moved my hand in a circular motion, but nothing happened. This was a powerful lock. Perhaps I needed to help it along. I chose my strongest pick, which was made from andantium.

I poked it into the lock, searching for a catch to release. Nothing happened. I clicked left, right. I finally found the release and pushed on it.

Nothing.

"Well?" Brax said. "I'm not feeling very free."

"*Enderos,*" I whispered. "*Enderos. Enderos. Enderos.*" Nothing happened. Even the glowing had died away. There was no moving the lock.

And finally, my pick snapped.

"I don't like that sound," Brax said. "I am greatly regretting our deal."

15

ONCE MORE

I threw what was left of my pick against the wall. "It didn't work!"

"You have a gift for stating the obvious."

"Honestly, I believed that spell would open this manacle," I said. "It worked on the locks to my room."

"And was that lock enchanted?"

"Well, no. Though the one out of the fortress failed to work. But that's a very ancient enchantment."

"Ah, I see." Brax pointed a claw toward the dead enchanter. "That fried bag of bones over there was actually very adept at several spells—he wasn't a full blown wizard, or he would have been hunted down. Perhaps he knew tricks from his years of study that you couldn't learn to undo by reading a book for a few minutes."

"But I really wanted to get you out."

Brax laughed and, to my surprise, patted me on the shoulder. "You are so very strange, Carmen. You don't talk like an assassin. Perhaps your heart is too soft and too pure to really be an assassin."

"No!" I nearly shouted it, but it came out loud enough to echo. "I have done all the training and passed all the tests. I am an assassin. And assassins can be moral. We decide which missions to accept."

"Oh, I believe a nerve has been poked. I'm so sorry for doubting you." He didn't sound sorry. "You're an assassin. There, does that make you feel better?"

"No. You're just humoring me."

"I'm the one trapped in a cave, forced into a conversation with a child, and I'm taking the time to humor you. You had better appreciate that."

I stood up. "There must be another way." I stared at the manacle for several seconds. "I have it! Why not just cut your leg off?"

"Oh, ouch, how quick you are to remove my body parts."

"But it would grow back, right? I could sew the wound shut."

"You're a physician now too? Will wonders never cease at the hats you wear! But look closely at that leg and at the wounds."

I leaned in. The manacle had worn off his scales, and the skin below looked ragged and sore. "It isn't healing," I said.

"Right. As I said, that corpse was a clever enchanter. The spell isn't just cast on the chain, but on my leg too. My leg will not regenerate. So, if we follow your plan, I will bleed to death in a few heartbeats. It's a very clever spell from a clever and dead corpse."

"Oh," I said.

"*Oh* is right." He rattled the chain. I thought it must hurt to even move his leg. "Now I must say I am impressed that you didn't tell your maestru. I fully expected there to be twenty assassins here to take me down."

"I wouldn't break my oath."

"That, too, is impressive for a human. But we are deadlocked. You don't seem to have the ways or means to release me. There is no one you know in that den of assassins—and I mean that in a nice way—who you could trust to free me. Each and every one of them would want to mount my head on the mantle. So, your value to me is limited. Perhaps if I eat you, I'll have enough strength to survive until someone with a magic key stumbles across this hole."

"You do like to talk about eating me," I said. It surprised me how steady my voice was.

"I enjoy eating. But, I admit, I'd feel a pinch of guilt about it. I'm sure that would go away after the first couple of bites."

I glanced around the cave. There was a mess of bones surrounding the dragon. The bodies were just outside the reach of his chain. The books themselves were in perfectly tidy order. "Why are you here?" I asked.

"I told you, I was lured by the promise of knowledge. The enchanter summoned up a teensy-weensy bird that whispered in my ear and guided me here."

"Scythian dragons are from across the northern waters. Did you travel that far to end up in this cave?"

"You know where I'm from?" He shook a talon at me. "Oh, you have been doing your reading. I was already here in your lands."

I took a step back. He was almost fully revealed in the light of the torch. "Why are you here in the human lands?"

"I was outcast by my father."

"What could a dragon do that would get you cast out?"

He looked at the talons on his right hand and squeezed them together. "Murder. Of a fellow dragon. The books you've read do not likely delve deep into dragon politics, but

I was cast out because I killed a dragon before he could marry my sister."

"You did what?" I looked at the scar across his face. Did wounds caused by other dragons leave a scar?

"Yes. That scar is from our battle. Claw wounds, or any wounds for that matter, caused by a fellow Scythian won't regenerate. I imagine you've come to that conclusion already."

"And you killed this other dragon. In a ... a dragon duel."

"A duel makes it sound so civilized. It was *not* civilized. He was a prince. That meant my banishment. We don't kill our own kind. It is against our laws. We have enough enemies as it is."

"So, you have been surviving on your own in the human lands for how long?"

"Two years."

"And you can't go back?"

He shook his head. "Only if I kill the king. Or if he dies of natural causes. Oh, and I should mention the king is my father."

So, he was a prince too. I'd had no idea that dragons had kings and princes and other royalty. "Dragons are hunted by mortals in every kingdom, right?"

He gestured at the rotting bodies in front of him. "The answer is obvious. We are worth more dead than alive to your kind."

"So, banishment is a death sentence."

"I like to look at the banishment as a way to see the world. Meet other creatures. And eat them."

I managed a smile. "You're back to talking about eating again."

"The ham was more of a reminder to my stomach that it

needs filling. I must say the hunger is coming back rather steadily."

I put away my lockpicks and edged away.

"I can control my pangs, Carmen. Though I wonder if I'll always be able to? Anyway, I don't want to be here forever. Nor do I want to slowly waste away so that any wandering skinner could sneak up on me and remove my scales. So, I'll let you live if you promise to return."

"But how will I ever break that lock? I'll have to ask for advice."

"No. Tell no one. You are a smart assassin. I have the slightest glimmer of a hope that you'll find an answer. I want you to promise to come back."

"I will come back." I said this without hesitating. This was perhaps the longest conversation I'd had with anyone in years other than Maestru Alesius and my brother.

"Can you bring a wagon full of food?" Brax asked.

"I'll bring as much as I can carry."

He laughed. "Nothing salty. I get so thirsty."

"I will be back. I promise."

"You are an idealist. It's quaint. And very odd for an assassin. But when idealism runs into reality, something has to break." He stared at me for a long time. There was something about those gray, magical eyes. It was impossible to look away. He suddenly squinted as if in pain and shook his head. "You are going to betray me."

"I won't betray you!" I said.

He gave me a sad smile. "That's the thing about my eyes. They see things you humans cannot see. Other paths. Other futures. I see something about you that will lead to pain and bloodshed for me."

"What is it? What do I do?"

He shrugged, making his wings rattle. "That's the problem. It's not clear how someone as small as you can spill my blood. But I still have to let you go despite that. Return to me, Carmen of the Assassins. Free me, and I'll give you that which I've promised."

"I will return," I said. "I promise."

16

AN OUNCE OF SERVITUDE

I left the cave and followed the moonlit path back to the fortress. It rose above me as I neared, such an impressive building. I had no idea how the original masons were able to build it right along the top of the mountain so that all four walls seemed to blend into the cliffs.

With each step, I was growing more sluggish. There were ten thousand stairs, and I wasn't certain I could take them all without falling asleep.

Sleep. I hadn't slept for over twenty-four hours. Not a wink. I had been trained to go without sleep, but I knew I was at my limits. Too much had happened. It was at least four in the morning, I guessed.

It took several tries to pick the lock on the thirteenth door. No one was around. I stumbled up to my room, unlocked my door, and threw myself on my bed and promptly fell asleep.

It seemed moments later that someone pounded on my door. I struggled to wake, struggled to stand up, and then went to the door, not bothering with my hair. At least I was still dressed since I hadn't undressed last night.

I opened the door to find Thord standing there. He was holding a rolled-up scroll in his hand.

"What do you want?" It came out angrier than I intended.

"That story of the feathers," he said.

"You're waking me up for that?"

"It's twelve bells. You must have slept through the morning bells. But you can give me the story another time. I came here at the request of Maestru Alesius. He was in a rather severe mood. I—I don't think it's good news."

I took the scroll and unraveled it. The words were written in red, a bad sign because it meant that it was an order I would have to obey immediately. *Report directly to Maestru Alesius*. I'd never had a red-letter order before. It may mean I would lose marks. Or even my place in the school.

"What is it?" Thord asked.

"I'm not sure. But I think I may be in trouble."

"I have swannery cleaning duty. But I think I'd gladly choose that over an angry Alesius."

"Me too," I said.

"Well, good luck with it," he said, and then he continued up the hallway.

I couldn't ignore the order. So, I took a deep breath and left my room, closing the door behind me. I walked quickly up the several sets of stairs until I reached my maestru's study. I knocked on the door.

"Enter," he said. I couldn't read anything in the tone of his voice, but I had never been able to do that anyway.

When I walked into the room I nearly gasped. For, besides Maestru Alesius, both Maestru Olgra and Megan were there. Had they been waiting all morning? The fury on Megan's face was clear from across the room. I wouldn't have been surprised if she suddenly spun and threw a dagger. But the only dagger was in her glare.

"Where were you last night?" Maestru Alesius asked.

"I was in the stables."

"DON'T LIE TO ME!" The shouting made both Megan and me shudder. Maestru Olgra didn't even blink.

"I went outside. For a long walk. I wanted fresh air."

"Where did you go?" His tone was still angry.

"To clear my thoughts. That's all."

"You smell like chrysanthemums."

Was this what Brax had meant when he predicted that I would betray him? But I had sworn an oath. I had to lie. Again.

"I must have brushed against them."

"They don't grow anywhere near here other than at the gardens."

I drew in a deep breath. "I can't say why I smell that way."

He stared at me a bit longer. "You are playing with words. But where you have been and why you carry that scent, we will discuss later. I will get to the truth. I promise you. We have a different matter to discuss. Maestru Olgra, please tell us what happened."

Maestru Olgra cleared her throat. "Yes. The reason we are here is because your apprentice used Thaurug's pressure point to freeze this student. And she left immediately afterward."

"Is this true, Carmen?" Maestru Alesius asked.

"Yes, but I—"

"DO NOT SAY ANYTHING ELSE. DO NOT PREVARICATE. JUST ANSWER THE QUESTION!"

His voice was so loud and so angry it nearly brought

tears to my eye. I'd never seen him like this. "Did you use Thaurug's pressure point on a fellow student?"

"Yes."

"Are you aware that, if done improperly, it can paralyze the victim permanently?"

"Y-yes."

He leaned on his desk. "Can you, in a very few words, explain your motives?"

I glanced at Megan and felt a flare of anger when I saw that she was now barely hiding a grin. "Megan insulted me."

"Insults are an offense to idiots," Maestru Alesius said. "What was the nature of this insult that you foolishly took offense to?"

"She suggested I work for her as a greeter. Never to step away from the table. She suggested because I am missing an eye that I will never be a good assassin."

"She was stating a truth," Maestru Alesius said.

"But it's not true!"

"Do not argue with me." He tightened his hand into a fist. "You are missing an eye. Therefore, you are not as qualified as Megan. Though you have perfected the majority of your assassin skills, that eye will always be a detriment. It also makes you more memorable. It is only your ability to rise above this hindrance that allows you to graduate. But I would not hire you for a mission."

He had never stated these things so bluntly. He had always been so encouraging.

"So, it was not an insult," he continued. "It was an honest appraisal. And, on the last day of your last class, you lashed out at her. A sign of emotional weakness. Something you've rarely displayed in your years here. So, the fault is all yours."

I risked another glance at Megan to see that she now had a gloating smile.

"Normally, I would decide the punishment," Maestru Alesius said. "But I will pass that duty to my colleague since the transgression occurred during her class. Maestru Olgra, what punishment do you decree?"

Maestru Olgra's face had remained severe throughout the whole discussion. "I declare that for breaking the sanctity of the classroom, attacking another classmate, and risking that classmate's health, that immediately upon graduation Carmen will work with Megan as her assistant for no payment other than room and board for the period of one year."

I drew in my breath. I nearly screamed as I let it out. A year! A year! As a servant of Megan.

"That is fair," Maestru Alesius said. He turned to Megan. "Do you agree to these terms, and in so doing to be bound by the oath of the Red Adept Assassins?"

"Yes," Megan said. "I do."

"And Carmen, do you agree to these terms and in so doing to be bound by the oath of the Red Adept Assassins?"

Megan had a full grin on her face. To deny the terms would mean not graduating and perhaps being cast out. To what? Work as a sheep herder? I was not going to throw it all away.

But a year! A year!

"I agree," I said softly.

"Repeat yourself, but louder," my maestru commanded.

"I agree," I said.

"Then it is done," Maestru Alesius said. "Upon the date of graduation, you will perform one full year of servitude. It will be written in the charter books. You are both dismissed."

I lowered my head and turned, careful not to look at Megan. I'd be seeing that gloating face for a full year. No sense in staring at it any longer than I had to. I took a step toward the door, when it burst open without anyone knocking.

A black-robed assassin, hair slick with sweat, came rushing in. He smelled of the swannery. "Maestru Alesius, we have news. Urgent news!" He looked at me and Megan then back at the maestrus.

"Speak it. They will soon be sworn members of the guild."

"Emperor Rima is dead. Killed by poison. All signs point to another attack by an assassin."

Maestru Alesius actually went pale. That was something I never imagined I'd see. "You two—" He pointed at me and Megan. "Speak nothing of this. Go to your rooms and prepare for graduation. Leave this chamber now."

We did. When the door closed behind us, Megan's gloat was long gone from her face. "What can this mean?" Megan said.

"That things are going to get very, very bad," I answered.

17

LESSONS LEARNED

We left for our rooms. Megan said nothing about me having to be subservient to her for a full year. Instead, we silently parted ways, each still in shock from the news.

A figure in a red robe, face hidden by a cowl, strode past me. I could not tell whether it was a man or a woman, but I knew that graduation was upon us, and the three hundred eight gates of the fortress were being opened by the returning assassins. It might even be Banderius himself. The assassins were here to witness the fifteen new graduates. Sometimes they even offered jobs to graduates moments after they received their red robes. Several more assassins passed in their red robes. They were here early, since it was hours until the actual ceremony. But I guessed they had some sort of business to pursue. Or they were going to search through the archives for hints about who might have killed the emperor and his son.

When I was back at my room, I closed the door. The emperor's death was a major event ... made doubly important because his son had died only a few days earlier. The world outside those gates was now whirling with threats of war—and with a boiling anger toward assassins. Perhaps it was not safe to graduate tonight and step outside the fortress.

In time, I remembered the fact that I would be spending a year under Megan's control. I'd have to follow her every command and would help her to make money and become known. A full year! The punishment was worse than the crime.

I had heard rumors of other punishments. A trickster of a student had slipped flatulence pills into the meal of a maestru. That was two weeks of cleaning the swannery. Two weeks straight, that is, without being able to leave—sleeping and eating with the swans. Another student had been kicked out for poisoning another student, but since they were all immune, it hadn't led to a death.

So, this was one of the harshest sentences I'd heard of. For what was essentially freezing another student. Yes, there was that chance of permanent paralysis. But one thing I was gifted at was finding pressure points. I was certain no harm would have come to Megan. Unless someone had bumped her, and she fell over.

Maestru Alesius must have wanted me to learn a lesson.

Humility. That is what it was. That was why he said I would never be a full-fledged assassin. How could he say those words? He'd always had a layer of kindness beneath his actions.

Perhaps it was more than just humility.

But a year! A year! Under Megan's control.

A swift *knock knock knock* came to my door. I opened it, finding my brother there. Corwin pushed his way in.

"How goes the battle, sister?"

"It goes." I didn't want to get into the experience with Maestru Alesius. He might gloat.

"So, you had a run-in with the maestrus and with Megan."

"How do you know?" I asked.

"A little bird told me. Or a bat. I forget which one. I know most everything that goes on around here, sis. What penalty did you get?"

"So, you don't know everything?"

"I know enough. Now tell me."

I did so. He rubbed his chin. "That's a harsh penalty." He said this with a bit of commiseration, as though he understood what I was feeling.

I nodded. "It's horrible."

"Alesius has his ways, and he's set in them. A traditionalist through and through."

"It's Maestru Alesius," I said.

"Oh, yes, *Maestru* Alesius. Thanks for the correction. He thinks in the old ways, and thus you get punished hard for something that you really should be rewarded for. Using the pressure point to make a statement should have been rewarded."

"Then everyone would be using the pressure points that way."

"Bah. Only the best would, while the weaker ones cowered. Besides, you're defending Alesius." I didn't suggest he add "maestru" this time. "Do you ever wonder if your loyalty is misplaced? You've stuck with his every proclamation for years. Done every deed he's asked of you, and now look how he has rewarded you. A year of slavery."

I did pause to think about that. Perhaps if Maestru Alesius had only given me a fortnight or two. But a year. A year! He could have stepped in and adjusted the sentence.

"Do you want me to kill Megan?" Corwin asked.

"What?"

He examined his impeccable fingernails. "It wouldn't be the first time an assassin found a way out of a contract."

"But they would know it was me. And besides that, it's wrong."

"I was kidding, sister. I would never do that. It's against guild rules. Though six months into your drudgery and you might be tracking me down to see if I really was kidding."

"Never!"

He shrugged a perfect "I know better than you" shrug. "Anyway, the big news is that the emperor is dead."

"How do you know that already? Did Megan tell you?"

"Megan, how would she know? And how do you know?"

"We were both there when the messenger told Maestru Alesius."

"Well, I guess he trusts you enough to let you have that knowledge. But I learned through other means. As I said, I have eyes and ears everywhere."

He had such a huge view of how powerful he was. I couldn't imagine what he'd be like when he graduated. I sometimes wished I had half his confidence. Or maybe I did have it before he took out my eye.

"What do you think the emperor's death will mean?" I asked.

"Oh, it's very bad news for assassins. Word is that it was poison again. Sargon, his younger brother, is now the emperor. He really doesn't like assassins. His mother was poisoned a few years ago."

"Royal families never do like us," I said.

"Unless they need us. But what Sargon has is hatred of our kind. We are a weapon that he cannot control. I wonder where he will point his hatred. Perhaps it is a bad time to hang out your shingle as an assassin. We'll all graduate and then go directly into hiding."

I leaned against my dresser. "It's that bad?"

"You haven't walked the streets of the Empire. Do you ever get out of this rotting fortress?"

"Yes! And it's not rotting. And two trips to Akkadium do not count as much when you're there as your maestru's helper."

"It's farther than you've ever gone. Just the carcass pits of Ogra. My maestru had to sleep. I didn't. I walked the streets. The ill will toward us is very strong in the Empire. And in the Five Realms too. We don't have to worry while we're here ... no one has ever taken this fortress. But we do have to make a living out of doors, so to speak. So, we will have to tread carefully."

"That is how they teach us to tread."

"Well, that is true, sister. You are wise beyond your meager years." Again, that sardonic smile. "Meet me here tonight before the ceremony. I have a gift for you."

"A gift?"

"Yes, it's a new family tradition. When one does something wonderful, one gets a gift. Your graduation should be celebrated."

"You got me a gift?" I repeated.

"You hurt my feelings by being stuck on that. Yes, I did, and you will cherish the gift forever."

I opened my hands, palms outward. "But I have nothing for you."

"Your sisterly love is enough. Besides, once I've graduated, I'll quickly earn enough wealth to buy everything I need. So, promise to meet me here at seven bells."

"I promise," I said. Corwin kissed me on the forehead. It was a gesture of warmth. He turned and left my room.

18

A LITTLE READING

There were still three hours until graduation. The hallways were filling with more assassins in robes of several colors, though the oldest wore black. Not a single face was shown. All of the assassins gathered in the dining room and waited for the graduates to serve them the pre-graduation dinner.

Even as I took the steaming dishes—roast chicken, potatoes, and parsnips—to each table, I wondered who each assassin was. And if any of them were Banderius himself. It looked as if there were at least one hundred who had returned. Even while they were eating, they didn't show their faces. It was bad for business for people to know what you looked like. A few even wore masks made of thin gold.

The dining room was remarkably quiet. The senior assassins spoke softly and secretly. Only once in a while was there loud male laughter. But the rest were all hiding their features, their movements, even their personalities. All in all, it was the strangest dinner I'd ever seen.

When I went to a table to remove a dirty ceramic plate,

the assassin sitting there grabbed my arm and twisted gently, but with purpose, so that we looked eye to eye. Two dark eyes were all that were visible above the cowl. "I heard about you," the assassin said. It was a deep voice, but something about the timbre gave me the impression it was a woman speaking.

"Oh," I said. "I hope it was all good."

The assassin waved me away.

Does that mean I'm special? More likely, since there were only fifteen graduates, every student was studied and measured. The established assassins made note of each student's skill sets, to see whether they would be assets to their own businesses.

For me and my fellow students, it was our last night to show our faces to each other. Once we had finished the graduation ceremony, we would receive our red sashes, lift our hoods, and would disappear through one of the three hundred eight gates. Only to return, if we wished, for future graduation ceremonies or to consult the archives or the maestrus.

Soon the meal was done, and we were allowed five minutes to eat in the servants' room, gulping down our mutton and soup and the roasted turnips. I ate alone, though a few of the others were talking to each other. Megan laughed at something, then covered her mouth because her outburst was so loud. Even Corwin was subdued. He whispered to Gregum and Scyllia. It wouldn't surprise me if the three of them opened up a shop of their own. It would likely not be in the Akkad Empire, due to the current conflicts, but in one of the Five Realms. I made a note to avoid wherever they ended up. I could handle my brother. His two friends were venomous snakes.

Thord caught my eye and gave me a small wave from

across the kitchen. I immediately looked down at my plate, suddenly amazed by the greenness of the peas.

Tonight would be one of the last times I saw him regularly. And I did feel a bit of sadness about that.

Don't be silly! It'll be great once I see the last of them all.

Well, except Megan, I remembered. I'd be seeing a lot of her. But that was something I didn't want to think about right now.

As I gulped down the last of my turnips, I couldn't help but think of Brax alone in the cave. He would still be starving. There was time before the ceremony to hunt through the spell books. Perhaps there was an enchantment that would solve the problem of his manacle.

I washed my plate and rushed to the library. Within a few minutes, I was running my hands along the books in the enchantment section. I set a book on the table and it opened to a fertility spell—they all had fertility spells! I wondered if my parents had used one to get me and Corwin. Those types of spells were said to cause twins to be born.

I wasn't here to learn about magic and babies. I flipped through the book and found nothing about locks. I picked up another spell book and another, but only found curses, more fertility spells, and sleep potions. *I could search fruitlessly for weeks!*

I did discover a spell about regeneration. Maybe if I could somehow use that on Brax, it would cancel out the spell that affected his leg. Then we could cut it off, and he would be free.

I was pretty certain he wouldn't agree to that.

"Are you studying on the night of graduation?" Maestru Beatrix asked. It took all my will not to shudder. The librarian was the quietest of all the maestrus. "Have they added a new qualification that I'm not aware of?"

"No. I was just curious about spells. And I won't get to visit this library for some time after today."

"The door is always open. All students are welcome." I knew that was true. I had occasionally seen a cloaked assassin reading a book. "Is there anything in particular I can help you with?"

"Is it true Scythian dragons can be bound by oaths?" The curious look Maestru Beatrix gave me made me wonder if I'd let her know too much. "I'm just wondering, that's all. Or any dragon. I really do like dragons."

"Ah, you're not alone in finding dragons endlessly interesting. I went through that phase. I have read about arrangements with Scythian dragons."

"Arrangements?"

"Yes. There was a mayor in a Kellian village who arranged with a Scythian dragon to burn down a neighboring village in exchange for ten sheep. The dragon did exactly that. Alas, he came back and burned down the mayor's village the next day and ate all the sheep. You do have to be specific about any agreements. The Scythian dragons are said to be as clever as solicitors. Very, very intelligent, those ones."

I knew that firsthand. Brax would outwit me easily if I wasn't careful. "I have a different question. Has anyone ever made a magical eye that works?" The question surprised me. I hadn't been thinking about my eye.

"I'm not aware of such a creation. It doesn't mean it's not possible, but you won't discover that tonight. Especially in our meager spell section. Perhaps make that a long-term goal. You're formidable enough with one eye."

I blushed. "That is a kind thing to say."

"It was only an observation. Good luck with graduation tonight, Carmen. And beyond."

"Thank you."

I put away the books on the table and then went up the stairs and down the hallways to the dorm rooms, passing a few of my fellow students who were rushing to get ready for graduation. I went to my own room.

Through the slit window, I could see that the sky was growing dark. And I knew—because the knowledge of the heavens had been drilled into me—it was a night of no moon. Not the hunter's moon that soldiers would talk about. This was an assassin's moon, the reason assassins trained to have such effective night vision. For the last two thousand years, assassins had graduated on a night of no moon.

I removed my graduation cloak from the closet. They had been given to us three weeks earlier in preparation for this night. I placed it over my shoulders, surprised at how silken it was. The inside of the robe was black, because it could be folded inside out to become a travel cloak. I turned to look at myself in the mirror.

I did make a striking figure, I decided, with the missing eye and all. Maybe I would be intimidating.

Of course, I'd pay anything to actually see through both eyes again.

When I turned the third time, I realized I was being watched.

19

ADVICE AND A GIFT

I spun, instinctively reaching for my dagger, but the intruder caught my hand, squeezed a pressure point, and the blade dropped to the floor. My assailant laughed.

A far too familiar laugh.

It was Corwin. In black robes. He flipped back his hood.

"How did you get in here without me noticing?"

He wasn't yet dressed for graduation. And he had managed to blend in with the shadows in my room. His hair was slicked back. I wasn't certain whether he'd been standing there all along.

"Perhaps it's not just your vision you have difficulties with, but also your hearing. I picked the lock and strolled right in."

"Let me go then."

He did so. "You are fast, sister. I'm just a little faster and quieter and smarter, that's all."

"Did you come to taunt me?" I asked.

"No. Only to give you advice and a gift. Just like I promised. I am proud ..." He cleared his throat. Was he actually getting emotional? "I am proud of you. In some ways, I made you."

"What? I made me. The maestrus made me. Our parents made me."

He shook his head. "You are such an odd duck. You still feel loyalty to them even though they abandoned us here."

"Maybe they had no choice."

"They had a choice, Carmen. They abandoned us because our twin mouths were too much to feed. There is a lesson in that."

"How did you see the papers?"

"I am not as much a stickler for rules as you. So, I snuck into the archives and looked. Our parents were pig farmers. Imagine that! People as amazing as you and I sprang from pig farmers."

"What? You know who they are? Where are they now?"

"Dead, sadly. They died a few years ago. A porcine plague of some sort. Took our brothers and sisters too. It is only you and I left of our family. So that is why I'm proud of you tonight. And for all you've done. And I can guarantee you won't have to work for Megan."

"I don't want her killed."

He rolled his eyes. "Sister! As much as I joke about that, trust me, I won't kill her. But there are ways to be free of such deals."

"Let me handle that on my own."

He huffed out air in such a way that it made his dark locks move. "Ever the obstinate one. You don't have to stand alone all the time, sis." He waited for a heartbeat or two, but I had nothing to say in reply. "Well, as I promised, I brought you a gift. Two gifts, in fact." He presented, out of nowhere, a flag.

I took it, and the flag unfurled, showing the golden face

of a roaring bear. “A bear flag?” I said. It was so silky and beautiful.

“It’s a lucky flag that I bought at the market,” he said. “It will keep you safe. Tonight. Tomorrow night. For all the dark nights to come.”

“What does that mean?”

“I’m just being superstitious, sis.” He took the flag from me and walked toward the window. “But let’s hang it now in your window and see it unfurled. Maybe it’ll bring you good luck so you won’t trip during the ceremony.”

“I won’t trip,” I said.

He had already attached the flag to the curtain rod using a thin white rope and hung it out the window. The wind began to flip it back and forth, bringing it to life. “There,” he said. “A fine gift, I must say. And yes, I am being emotional ... well, as emotional as I get. It’s just that tonight is a night of endings. So many rituals, practices we’ve been doing for the last eight years, will be irrevocably changed. We will start our new lives in just a few hours.”

“You are sounding like an old man, Corwin. I don’t think I’ve seen this side of you before.”

“It’s important to remember that we are at the brink of greatness.”

“Greatness?” I asked.

“Well, you know what I mean, sis. We will become something great. And we don’t need a red cloak and a graduation scroll to prove that. I know it inside of me.” He tapped his chest.

I patted my graduation cloak. “I’ll be proud to wear the cloak,” I said.

“It is just cloth,” he said. “A true assassin holds that knowledge in his heart. Anyway, I did bring another gift.” He reached into one of my shelves and brought out a decanter. He must have left it there when he first sneaked into the room. I should have noticed it! I'd been trained to see things that are out of place. He filled two goblets.

"Is this wine?" I asked.

"Oh, you're too pure for wine, Carmen. It's cherry cider from the Heartbury Mill in Akkadium."

"How did you get that? It's at least twelve denarii per glass."

"I have contacts in the outside world. I've already made many influential and powerful friends."

"How have you had time to do that?"

"By starting years ago." He offered me a goblet. "Come, sis, let us drink to our health and to the memories of our pig farming parents. And, more importantly, to the future. A bright and bloody future."

"I'll drink to our future and to our parents," I said. "And our health." I took the cider. This was one of the sweetest drinks in all the Empire, and he had smuggled it into the fortress and was sharing it with me. Perhaps, at his heart, he was not so terrible. I took a sip.

It was like drinking a draught from heaven. A taste that tingled with life as it went down my throat.

"You know, you're not so terrible." I decided to say it out loud.

He grinned. "Oh, you may revise that statement after tonight."

The sweetness of the drink was swirling in my head, in my bones, in my blood. It took me several moments to clearly understand what he had said. "Why tonight? What do ... you ... mean?"

The words had slurred slightly. It had been a long day, and I had not slept properly for a very long time. Was I that tired? I still had a whole ceremony to sit through.

"I'm just saying there is a price to pay for having so many influential friends. So many gears are set into motion. But I don't want you to be harmed."

"Wh—" I couldn't finish the word. The drink fell from my hand, and the goblet rolled over to one side, spilling the cider. The waste!

But I cursed myself. I had trained for years to know the taste of every poison. I should have recognized this one right away, but it had been hidden by the sweet cherry sugary smell. He had poisoned me! I tried to move, but my body was locked in position. I attempted to open my mouth and accuse him of treachery, but my lips were frozen shut.

Corwin stepped behind me, pulled me into his arms, and lowered me onto my bed. I couldn't place the poison. It was freezing me like spider venom. Was it killing my organs one by one?

"I can see by your eye that you are panicking, sister," he whispered gently. "And I am certain you don't know the taste. It isn't poison, though. I wouldn't do that. It's just a paralysis tincture. It should last for twelve hours. You will be safe in this room. I will lock the door behind me. And the flag will keep you safe too."

A sad look briefly came to his face. He patted my cheek.

"I have hurt you enough, even if it was for my own gain. I don't want you to be hurt again. I don't need your forgiveness, but I will accept it someday. Now, as I said, my powerful friends are waiting. It's nearly time for graduation. Sleep well, sister. I love you."

Then he left me frozen on the bed.

I heard the door lock behind him.

20

TWO WARNINGS

I didn't sleep.

Nor did I die. My brother hadn't been lying about whatever he'd used. It was causing paralysis yet allowed me to breathe and my heart to beat. None of my limbs would move, but my eyes blinked. That was an impressive mixture. His skills went far beyond even what he had learned in class.

It was almost as if he'd had another teacher outside the guild.

There was a whistling outside my window—a sound that reminded me of hawks flying by, of wings in the air. Then a male voice spoke from outside my window. My room was hundreds of feet up the fortress and hung over a cliff. Who could possibly be out there?

"Leave this one," the man said. "It is marked by the bear."

I heard a soft scraping that slowly grew softer. Had I imagined the voice?

Time passed. Whether it was minutes or hours, I

couldn't be certain. My thoughts kept whirling around and around and around.

A bell rang. Once. From the very top of the fortress. It was the warning bell. We'd had drills many times to it. Each assassin would take their defensive station or disperse through the three hundred eight doors. But the bell only rang once, and it was supposed to ring three times for danger.

Several hundred heartbeats passed.

I next heard the ring of metal on metal outside my door. Something thumped into the wood, and then a cry of pain was cut off.

Despite the tincture in my system, my heart began to beat faster. Violence! Right outside my door! Had the assassins who came to the graduation somehow turned on the other assassins? The graduates? The maestrus? A long silence followed.

Then footsteps came skidding to a halt in front of my door and someone banged on it.

"Carmen!" It was Megan. "Carmen, are you in there?"

I couldn't move my lips. "Run," Megan said. "They're killing everyone."

Then she was gone too.

The only sound my ears picked up was my heartbeat. It was as loud as thunder. I concentrated on slowing it down and making myself calm.

I heard footsteps again. Heavier, but still quiet. "Carmen?" it was a whisper, but I recognized Thord. He attempted to pick the lock on my door but failed. He let out a groan. Had he been wounded?

"I—I didn't see you with ... with the others. If you're there, you must hide yourself. Or flee. But don't take any of the well-known gates. They are watched. I ... ugh ... I am going to fly."

If he intended to take a swan he would be killed. I was pretty certain the swannery would be the first place to be guarded by any attackers. I tried to warn him, but my lips were frozen.

"Find me if you live," he said. "I—I hope you're already gone."

Then came the soft sound of his footsteps going away from my door.

I lay there in silence for what felt like a millennium.

Very gradually I became aware that I could move my right leg. Just a little bit. Soon I was able to wriggle the fingers on my left hand. Perhaps, in all my years of building immunities to poisons and tinctures, I had developed an immunity to this one. Corwin had said it would last for twelve hours. But it had been no longer than an hour or two —that was my best guess. Time was hard to measure when lying so still.

I was able to slide my legs a few inches across the top of the bed. Eventually enough motion came that I could force both legs over the edge of the bed. The floor thumped as my feet hit the floor. There was now a little strength in my arms.

I tried to stand and immediately collapsed to the floor, banging my head into the dresser. I lay there for a few moments, feeling a sharp pain in my face. I'd not been able to put my hands out, but at least I'd managed to miss braining myself. I slowly used the cot to pull myself up to a sitting position, feeling woozy. Then I tried to stand again.

This time I managed a few steps, kicking the goblet on the way. I used the wall for support and limped to the door, only to discover I didn't have enough dexterity to pick the lock.

"Enderos," I said. My voice was slurred and ragged. But I repeated it and moved my hand in a circular motion. On my third try, the door unlocked.

I listened but couldn't hear any sounds from the other side. I ever so slowly opened my door.

A dead assassin lay right outside my door. He had a crossbow bolt in his back. His hood had opened enough that I could see the side of a scarred face. His gray hair clearly meant he was one of the older ones. The bolt had gone perfectly through his heart.

I crept slowly up the hall. Both Megan and Thord had told me to flee, but I chose the opposite way from the stairs that led to the three hundred eight doors. I didn't want to leave until I knew more about the situation.

But stairwells weren't safe, and hallways weren't safe, so where was the best place to walk? I did know whom I had to see. Maestru Alesius would know what to do.

I slipped into the kitchen. There were no servants remaining, but I did find another dead body with a crossbow bolt sticking out of his side. Since there wasn't a red sash, I was certain it was a student. I didn't want to turn the body over and see who it was.

I placed my hand on his neck to find no pulse. And it was squeamish of me to not see who it was. I needed all the information I could get, to know who remained alive. So, I took a deep breath and turned his head.

It was Maxen, one of the third-year students. I'd hardly said two words to him but remembered him as a hard worker.

I noted that the bolt was golden shafted, which was a sign the people who had invaded the fortress were from the Akkad Empire. They liked having their arrows and bolts glitter with gold in the air as they flew toward their enemies.

They liked showing what a rich and strong empire they were.

I stood straight and peered around the kitchen. It was odd to not hear a single noise, especially in a place that was usually bustling any time of the day or night. I couldn't take the hallway—they were too well lit. It took me a moment before I realized the safest way to go was right in front of me.

The potion had almost completely worn off. I climbed onto the cupboard and opened the door to the right dumbwaiter. There were several small lift shafts that ran up and down the fortress. It was cramped, but I was small enough to fit into the lift. The pulleys and rope system ran through the center of the wooden platform. It was just a matter of reaching out to the rope and pulling down without letting go of the tension. I wasn't certain whether me and the inch or so of wood I was standing on would keep falling to the bottom and break into a thousand pieces. I was a lot heavier than a plate of food. I hoped I'd chosen the lift that led to Maestru Alesius's study.

Bit by bit, I brought myself up—slowly so the pulleys didn't squeak. About halfway up, my arms grew tired, and I had to rest, though I still kept the tension on the rope. Then I started again, feeling the sweat form on my forehead. When I reached the top, I slowly opened the door to the lift.

My guess had been right. I recognized Maestru Alesius's chamber.

I recognized his body too.

21

A FINAL ORDER

His study was in disarray. Books had been torn, statues broken, and blood spilled. He had not gone down without a fight. A dead man in chain mail was on the ground a few feet from Maestru Alesius's body.

I listened, but my heart was beating too hard to hear anything else. So, I drew in a breath, imagining my heart slowing down. It took a few repetitions, but my heart returned to a normal speed, so I could hear properly again. The room was silent. I looked left and right, then forced myself through the small doors and down to the floor. I let go of the rope on the trolley, and the tray stayed in place.

I stepped around the pool of blood and the dead soldier. I saw a bear tattoo on his hand.

He was one of the Immortals—the emperor's elite guards. The same bear flag was flapping outside my window.

"It will keep you safe," Corwin had said.

I didn't want to accept what my brain was telling me. It was clear the new emperor, Sargon, had struck this blow against the assassins. And it was clear that Corwin had helped him.

My brother!

I drew in a deep breath. Now was not the time to scream in anger. Now was the time to observe and gather information before I made my next move.

I stepped over the guard and stood next to my maestru. He had fallen facedown and had three crossbow bolts in his back. He had died bravely.

"Carmen," he said.

He wasn't dead! I couldn't stop from sucking in a breath. He wasn't facing me, yet he recognized my tread.

"Turn me over," he said.

I knelt and slowly turned him, carefully holding one shoulder so the bolts wouldn't be pushed right through. I found a pillow nearby and shoved it behind him, helping him lean against a pillar.

His black cloak hid the blood he was losing. "Good. Good," he said once he was propped up.

"We have been attacked!" The moment I said it I realized how stupid I sounded.

"Yes, these are the emperor's troops. I should have predicted this and guarded against it. But I trusted too much in the security of our fortress and in our agreements. The Immortals came on gliders in through the windows. They have impressive skill."

"I heard them," I said. "They had help from inside. My brother."

"I know," Maestru Alesius said. "That, too, I should have seen. But I have failed my order. I have failed my brothers and sisters." He coughed a burbling cough. I was certain by the sound that his lungs were punctured and filling with blood.

"I'll get you out of here, Maestru. We can rebuild the order."

He shook his head. "No, Carmen. You would never make it out alive dragging me. And I am very close to death."

"No, you're not!" I wanted to shake him. "We can take a swan, fly out."

"They have already secured the swannery. Maestru Arvid is dead. I saw him fall. I made it here through a secret passage from the Grand Hall. The Order of the Red Adept Assassins has been destroyed in one night."

"But it's not destroyed."

"You were not in the graduation hall. Only a handful have escaped. You must find them, and perhaps there will be safety in numbers. Small numbers."

"We can strike back against the emperor."

He raised a hand dripping with blood. "Youth are always ready to fight. But the time to strike back is not now. Perhaps never." He pointed toward his worktable. "I want you to have a gift. It's an old, old artifact. Go to the top drawer in the table."

I stood slowly and walked over to the table where I had so often mixed potions.

"Open it."

The drawer was empty. "There's nothing here."

He gurgled. It took me a moment to recognize it as a laugh. "Press ... press the back upper left."

I felt for the back, and there was an indentation that I pressed.

"Now pull the drawer all the way out."

I did so, setting it on the table. A glitter below where the drawer had been caught my eye. I reached in and found something long and metallic wrapped in cloth.

"Yes, bring them out."

I pulled out a blue cloth. A gray handle was sticking out of it. I unwrapped the cloth to discover two sheaths of a plain gray pattern. Daggers! Longer than the ones I had been trained with. When I pulled one from its sheath, it made a *ssskt* sound. Even to my naked eye it was clear that the blade was sharp. There were runes written along the blades.

"Those are the Uriken blades," Maestru Alesius explained. "They have been warded and are over three thousand years old."

"They don't even have a nick in them!"

"That metal will not break. And it will cut through most anything."

I brought them over to Maestru Alesius and knelt. "Here they are, Maestru. You can defend yourself." Even as I said it, I wasn't certain if he could even lift them.

"No. They are yours." He coughed again. "Take them."

"But, Maestru, I can't."

"You must. I don't want them to fall into the hands of the enemy. You are my finest student."

"But I'm not. I—I don't deserve this, my ..." I was tempted to point at my patch.

"Yes, you are missing an eye. Despite that, you have risen to be a graduate. Only fifteen students across all the realms are allowed each year. Your pride is your only failing."

"But ..." I held the daggers. They were so perfectly balanced.

He grimaced. "Attach them to your belt now. That's an order. And reverse your cloak to the black side." I did so quickly. "You are officially a Red Adept Assassin now. And you must leave."

"I can't leave you."

"You will leave. That is another order. Search for any

survivors. And find Banderius. Of any assassins in the outside world, he has likely survived. He's ... he's a rough sort, but he has sworn an oath. He can help hide you and any other students you find. Promise me you'll find him."

"I will," I said.

"Good." He closed his eyes and seemed to sleep for a moment. Then he opened them again. He lifted his hand, which was shaking now. "There is a door behind that curtain. Push in the fish's eye, and the corridors will lead you to a way out of the fortress. Only I know of this door. Find safety. Then find your other students. Band together with ones you trust. And put as much distance between yourself and the emperor as possible."

"I won't run!" I held the daggers tight.

"The battle is over. You must recognize that. Revenge can be a thousand years in the waiting." He said this last part slowly. There was a sound of clinking armor and talking in the hallway. More of the Immortals were coming. "Go, Carmen. Go. Out that door and to freedom. Of all the assassins, you are the easiest to find because of your missing eye. So, you must go the farthest."

"I really can't leave you here!"

"You will leave me. That is my last order to you." He coughed and grimaced. "Actually, make that my second last order. I want you to hand me that crossbow. I will take one of them with me."

I handed him the bow and helped him crank the string and load a bolt.

"Good luck in the world, Carmen of the Red Adept Assassins."

I stood. "Thank you, Maestru Alesius," I said. "Thank you for everything."

I went to the wall and pushed on the fish's eye, and part

of the wall pulled away. I glanced and saw that he had propped the crossbow on his knee and pointed at the door.

I stepped into the passageway, pushed a lever, and the wall slid shut. It was completely dark. It took me a moment to find my light powder and spread it on my hand, holding it above my head to dimly light my way.

I followed the stairs that led me down and away from my maestru.

22

MAKING A DECISION

When I reached the next level, I had a choice. I could take another set of stairs that led upward. Or I could continue going down.

I went down, since I wouldn't find any way out above me. There was a short hallway, and I noticed that light was coming through a hole in the wall—a peephole. I stood on my tiptoes and looked through it.

I was looking into the library. Maestru Beatrix was gone. Several of the emperor's guards were gathering books under the direction of Scyllia. Her angular face was severe, except for a small smile that made her beady eyes shine. She was enjoying this work! She wore her graduation cloak, though a large bear pin clasped it to her neck. I guessed that was her way of letting the Immortals know she was on their side. It didn't surprise me that my brother had included his friends in his horrible plan.

I hoped Maestru Beatrix had escaped. Maybe there was another passage like this hidden in another library wall. There could be hundreds of secret passages; the fortress was certainly large enough for that.

One of the Immortals ripped a book in half and laughed. It took all my will to not try to punch through that wall. I was certain a nearby lever would make the wall shift open. I could sneak in there and kill the guard and his companions. And Scyllia too! Then I would sneak back out. In fact, it could be possible to do that in every room.

But they were Immortals and had just finished dispatching some of the finest assassins in the world. *And you only have one eye,* I reminded myself.

I had to force myself to turn away. I continued down the next set of stairs. I knew this level featured the Grand Hall that stretched out onto a large balcony overlooking the mountains. Another peephole sat waiting here, and I stood on my tiptoes but didn't look through it yet. This room was where my fellow graduates would have been waiting in line to officially be declared graduates. I hesitated to look. Would it be a horrible scene of destruction?

I swallowed and stared through the hole.

No bodies lay on the floor or spread across the benches. Several tapestries were ripped, and statues broken. The steps that led up to the stage where the graduates would have stood looked to be slick with a black substance. One of the Immortals was dragging something away, but the item was hidden from my line of vision by wooden benches.

I was certain many of my classmates had died in this room, but I was thankful to not see their remains.

What I saw next chilled me. Corwin was standing on the balcony, talking to an Immortal. My body went cold.

The guard was larger than Corwin, and the signs on his shoulder meant he was a commander. But he was nodding in deference as Corwin spoke. Then Corwin waved his hand, and the man walked away and down one of the halls.

It made me pause. My brother had that much power that he could actually command an officer of the Immortals?

But the sight of him now made my body vibrate with anger. There would be another lever somewhere nearby that would shift open this wall, I was certain of it. I could slip out, run straight at Corwin when his back was turned, and stick both of my daggers into him. He had killed my fellow graduates! My maestru! And many more. I began breathing harder, getting my rage up. My hands were already on the daggers.

But then I took a deep breath. Maestru Alesius had told me to flee. I'd be full of crossbow bolts before I got halfway across the room. Or I'd be cut in two. The Immortals were coming and going from the hall. Even with both eyes, I'd never be a one-on-one match with a single elite fighter, let alone my brother.

But he was standing on the balcony like he owned the Five Realms and the Empire itself. The wind rustled his hair. He probably really liked the feeling of looking down on everything.

And that meant he was vulnerable.

I just had to get to where he stood. I ran quietly up the stairs I'd just come down and took another set of stairs that led me higher. A peephole showed me that I had guessed right. This hallway led to where many of the maestrus had their private rooms. I pressed the lever, and the wall shifted open quietly. I turned my head from side to side to be sure I didn't misjudge the distance because of my eye. I cut across the hall and into Maestru Olgra's room. The door was already ajar. There was no sign of her, and I hoped she had somehow escaped too. I knew there was a balcony in these chambers because of her interest in the stars. She had taught us about the movements of the planets and the stars and how to use them to aid in our night hunting.

I nearly knocked over the spyglass in my hurry to look over the edge.

Corwin was below me, still standing on the Grand Hall balcony. He still looked completely full of himself. It was a long distance, but I was pretty certain I wouldn't break any bones.

Especially if I landed right on him.

So, before I could hesitate or get caught up in second thoughts, I launched myself over the edge.

23

UNDER THE STARLIGHT

The sound of my right foot hitting my brother's head was very satisfying. I could listen to it all day long. I'd meant to hit him with both feet but had misjudged. He collapsed to the ground, and I landed on one leg, jarring myself slightly, but was able to roll to a standing position.

Corwin was already standing, holding his head, clearly dizzy. Good!

I unsheathed one of the daggers and jumped toward him. So far, a crossbow bolt hadn't hit me. Also good.

I grabbed his cloak and twisted him around so that he was between me and the Immortals. Six of them had their small crossbows out, pointed at my head.

"Stay back," I shouted. "Or he's dead."

I realized suddenly that I hadn't thought this through. I had no escape path. I retreated until my back was against the stone balcony. The wind swept through my hair and Corwin's, the identical color moving in an identical way.

Corwin began to raise his hand, and I said, "Don't you move or I'll kill you." The dagger was right against his throat.

"I—I am just waving them away, sis," he said.

The Immortals were closing in. "Go ahead," I said. He made a signal, and the guards took three steps back.

"You're going to tell me why you're doing this," I hissed. "Then you'll die."

"Don't be so dramatic," he said. He turned his head enough that I could see he was grinning.

"Don't test me, Corwin. Why did you do this?"

"I'm just finding my place in the world."

"By murdering our fellow students? Our maestrus? Betraying our order and our oaths?"

He shrugged. "No one in that room was innocent."

"No, but they were your friends."

He shook his head. "My friends are the ones who I let live. And those who were struck off the board would have done the same thing if they'd been offered the same opportunity."

"No, they wouldn't." I jabbed the knife a little closer to his neck. "They had honor."

He let out a raspberry. "Our parents dropped us off to be raised by assassins. Where was the honor in that? None. We were only worth more because we were twins. Apparently, we learn faster. But what I learned right away is that we are all alone in this world, and we have to survive on our own."

"We can survive together. With friends and partners."

"That's hilarious coming from you," he said. I had to admit he was incredibly calm. "You're even more of a loner than me. Not a single friend in your years of school." He was right! But then an image of Thord drifted up. Why would I think of him? And was he even alive? "Be truthful, Carmen. You wouldn't weep for any of them."

"I didn't like every last one of them, but I would never kill them. What you've done here is horrible. It's … it's evil."

"Oh, sis. It was neither of those things. It was the right thing to do, and it was beautiful. So beautiful. If you could have seen the Immortals silently coming in on their flyers. All landing on the walls at exactly the same moment. It was glorious, I tell you. And brilliant, if I do say so myself. Every single assassin was surprised."

I couldn't help but marvel at the audacity of his plan. To attack the Red Adept Assassin Fortress while it was full of assassins. He had carved a place in history for himself. A horrible place. And it meant people I had known were now dead. "What did you do with them? Why did you drag the bodies away?"

"They are in the morgue to be identified. Emperor Sargon wants to be certain every assassin is dead. I'm just helping him with that little job. We'll hunt down any who escaped."

"But what about me? Why wouldn't the emperor want me dead too?"

"You only have one eye," Corwin said. I was certain he was smiling. "You're not a true threat. I promised him you'd become a pig farmer and take over our parents' farm."

"I'm more than you think I am."

He shook his head, even though it meant the dagger cut him a little. "You're just a half-blind girl, Carmen. You are nothing in this world. You have a few skills, and that's all."

I nearly stabbed him for that. "I have a dagger to your throat. You had better tell the Immortals to stop hunting for the others."

"Now you're being ridiculous. And you won't have that blade at my throat for long."

What did that mean? Several Immortals were standing twenty paces away, but they had their bows lowered. No one else had entered the room. Yet, he had a plan.

I needed to kill him now. He was my brother, but he had wrought such evil. Even if I were to die a moment later, at least I would take him with me. I pulled the dagger back an inch or two, willing myself to plunge it in.

He had turned his head slightly so that I could see he was smiling grandly. Then he chomped his teeth together, shaped his mouth in an O and blew his breath toward me. Some sort of gas came out of his mouth.

I plunged the dagger toward him.

Well, I tried to. But I was frozen. Standing on the edge of the balcony.

One by one, my brother gently unlocked my fingers from his cloak and stepped back. The Immortals came running up with their bows aimed at me, but Corwin barked, "Stay back!" They stopped in place.

"I keep a metal shell with basilisk powder in it in a hollow tooth. Twice tonight I've frozen you, sis. That's what a failure you are as an assassin."

Again, I tried to move, but not a muscle responded. I stood like a statue.

"You will pay for this," I said, surprised that my mouth would work.

Corwin looked surprised too. "Well, that's interesting. Perhaps you're a little immune to this powder. But not immune enough. And I may pay for all of this," he gestured around him, "in the future. But it won't be you demanding that toll. You shouldn't have gotten out of your bed. I tried to save you. I really did try. And, in my own way, I care for you, Carmen. You're blood of my blood. So, I will give you one more chance. Join me and live. I'll make sure you are well taken care of. I was kidding about the pig farm. You'd have a house in the capital with a garden. I know you like gardens. You'll even have your own servants. Join me."

He actually put out his hand.

I hesitated. Not because I had a thought of joining him. But I decided that maybe, just maybe, my freezing was wearing off. My toes were tingling. Just a few more seconds.

"I ... maybe ... I will, but ... just give me a moment. It's a big decision."

Corwin let out a quick bark of a laugh. "Do you think I'm stupid? You're just hoping the dust will wear off. You had your chance, sis. I love you, but now you're of no use to me. Give my greetings to Mother and Father."

And then he booted me in the lower ribcage, smashing the breath from my lungs.

And knocking me over the balustrade.

24

THE FALL

The Fortress of the Red Adept Assassins had been built on one of the tallest cliffs in all the kingdoms. The fall was such a great distance that I knew I'd be shattered to a thousand pieces when I hit the sharp stones below.

And I was still frozen, not able to even grab at the wall, not that it would save me. Then I moved my arms a bit. It did surprise me that I wasn't panicking as much as I could. Perhaps it was the freezing, or maybe I didn't quite believe that my brother had just kicked me to my death like I was nothing more than a bag of seed. A carcass.

But my right hand still tightly gripped the dagger. I didn't want to let it go, which was laughable. What use would a dagger be to a pile of flesh and bones?

I thought of Brax. Of how he could swoop up here and save me, but he was chained to the wall of the cave.

It also impressed me how quickly I was thinking, how in moments of battle and danger, my brain slowed things down.

My body began to turn and twist in the wind, and I was getting farther away from the wall now. There was nothing I could do. I might as well just face it all with fearlessness. It had been a hard life. But I wasn't going to go out with a whimper.

No! I thought. *I'm not going out at all.*

At least I could control how I shifted through the air. I remembered our jumps over the cliffs and into the water. We'd performed thousands of them, learning to control how our bodies moved through the air.

An idea came to me. I had fallen the full length of the fortress and was now passing the cliff walls.

I was able to move my arms and legs. The powder had worn off enough. I adjusted my angle, so I drifted closer to the wall. Then I grabbed the other dagger.

I reached out at speed, both knives in my hand.

Maestru Alesius had said they would cut through anything. I hoped he wasn't exaggerating.

I stuck them both into the rock wall, and they jerked in my hands, but I held tight. The daggers began sparking.

And they cut through the stone with sparks flying, lighting the darkness, leaving two trails in the rocky cliff. I was able to slow myself by digging them deeper into the rock. My hands sweated, but I grabbed them even tighter, praying to Belaz.

I slowed. And slowed. I eventually could place my feet against the rock, burning my boots as the soles wore away.

But the daggers cut and cut and were perhaps getting duller.

I eventually came to a stop.

I had fallen nearly the whole distance down the mountainside.

I moved one arm, cut into the stone, then twisted so the blade was flat and didn't cut downward. Then I did the same again lower. And was able to climb down a few feet.

It took me hours to travel the remaining distance to the ground. When I got there, my robe was torn, and my boots were mostly worn away, and there were scratches along my arms and body.

But I was alive.

And angry. So very angry my body shivered with it.

A blood-red plan hatched itself in my head.

25

NEVER

It was an arduous journey to Brax's cave. I didn't want to stop, in case I had broken bones. I didn't want to think about my classmates and maestrus who had died and that my brother—my blood—had caused so much destruction. I concentrated on getting one foot in front of the other. Ignoring the pain. Ignoring the voice that said, *Lie down. Sleep. Surrender.*

I climbed a short cliff wall using the dagger. All those years of training, the push-ups, the running for leagues, the rope climbing had helped me become strong. I was testing every last bit of that strength.

When I came to the cave, it was almost dawn. Light was outlining the mountains behind me. I strode past the first body of the mercenary without even looking at it and past the second, then stopped where the enchanter had fallen. My eye had adjusted just enough that I could see the outline of Brax. His gray eyes glowed in the darkness.

"You look horrible," he said.

"We have to make a deal," I answered. I had been

running my words through my head for the last few hours. "It's a deal you won't like."

"Oh, how exciting. Do tell me more." He clasped his talons together.

"I will release you from your bonds, but in return I demand three things from you."

"Three things? Why not ask for the world in a bauble?"

I narrowed my eye. "Do you want to hear them?"

He pulled back a lip in a half grimace, half smile. His teeth caught the little bits of light and glittered. "You are all business tonight, Carmen Crow. What has happened?"

"I don't want to talk about that now. I want to discuss our deal."

He set his front feet on the ground as if preparing for a charge. "Then give me your offer. I am all ears."

"First, you will promise not to harm me or do any action that knowingly results in harm coming to me."

"You sound like a barrister. You sound cold. Good. Good. You were innocent before. My guess is that you've been blooded."

"Do you agree to that term?" It came out harshly.

"Yes. I agree. Please continue before I grow angry."

I pointed at my eye patch. "Secondly. I am blind in one eye."

"That's not news, Carmen."

"I want you to remove your left eye from your head and shape it so that it can be placed in my eye socket so I can see again."

A puff of flame came out of Brax's nostrils. His eyes were wide. "What? What sort of madness is this?"

"It is not madness. You can do this. I'm certain of it. Certain!" I nearly shouted the last word. "Your eye will grow back, and I will see again. I will be whole."

"You've gone insane, child. I see the blood on you. Something horrible has happened, and it has broken your mind. This is absolute madness."

I drew in a hard breath. "I want your eye. I must have it."

"You ask too much, mortal. I have no idea how long it takes for an eye to grow back. And you will not like looking at the world through a dragon's eye."

I stamped my foot, hitting the body of the enchanter. His legs smashed into ashes and dust. "Will you agree to that term or not? I don't want to hear the reasons why it won't work."

Brax snorted out another flame. "You have me caught in a hole, child. Starving. I may have a week left. Maybe two. What choice do I have? I agree to that term. Now tell me your last term before I change my mind and kill you where you stand."

I swallowed. I knew the last request would be the hardest. So, I spoke it quickly. "I want you to surrender yourself and allow me to become your rider. Until such a time as we have hunted down and killed my brother, Corwin. After that moment you will be free."

"What? Me become your winged pack animal? Never!" He pulled hard at the chain and reared up. He shot out a blast of fire, and the flames went past me and into the air. It made me sweat, the cave suddenly hot. "I will never, ever submit to you. To have you shout orders from my back. Never!"

"It is the final term of our deal."

He pulled on the chain and unfurled his wings. They filled the cave, the air from them pushing me back. "You ask too much, Crow Child! You ask too much. It's slavery!"

I set my feet. Put my hands on the hilts of my daggers.

"Yes or no?"

I could see his ribs clearly and was certain a dragon usually wasn't that skinny. He lowered his wings. "I have let the snake into my den," he said. "You have betrayed me just as I said you would."

"This isn't a betrayal. It's a deal. Your one chance for escape."

He was silent for several moments. "I have a counter request. A deal must go both ways. First, you will become my servant immediately following your brother's death for the space of one year."

"Done," I said. It surprised me that I didn't hesitate.

Brax smiled. "And you will kill someone for me. No qualms. No backing out."

I hesitated, running that through my mind.

"Who?"

"Who? Or what? Oh, the answer is a secret. Part of our deal."

"Yes," I said. "Yes. I will do it!"

"Then Carmen of the Red Adept Assassins, we have a deal. Don't make me regret it any more than I already do."

"I won't."

I strode to the chain and pulled out one of the daggers. I lifted the chain and the blade went through it like it was soft flesh.

The chain fell. Brax shook his leg.

"Just like that? That is quite the dagger you have there."

"Yes, it is."

"What about the manacle?"

"One moment." I leaned over and cut carefully until I could break the manacle away from his leg. It clanged when I threw it down, but I was surprised at its lightness.

"I am free," he said.

"Yes, you are," I said. "Now, may I please have your eye?"

26

MY WORD

"I am a dragon of my word," Brax said.

Then he reached up toward his eye. I couldn't watch the rest and looked down, shutting my eye. But I heard the screaming, the horrible sound of absolute pain, and it made my bones shake every moment. It would be something I'd hear in nightmares for the rest of my life.

Then the screaming stopped.

I still didn't open my eye. Brax was moving toward me, and he gruffed, "Look up, Crow."

I did, opening my eye. He had only one eye. The other was bleeding. He was holding his left eye in his hand. It was larger than I expected.

"Lift the patch," he said. "And hold steady. This is going to hurt, and believe me, I take pleasure in it."

It took a millennium for him to place his eye in my socket. And I, too, screamed. I was shamed.

It was a time I wanted to forget. A pain I never wanted to feel again.

"Well, you stayed on your feet. Impressive," Brax said. And he did sound impressed. "The eye seems to have shrunk to the size of your other one. Even I didn't expect that. But dragon magic is clever."

I blinked. Once. I saw him with only one eye. Twice. Again, with only one eye.

The third blink I was looking through both eyes. There was a glowing around the dragon. He was clearly visible in the dark now. *I can see in the dark!* I looked past him at the books, the bones. Around the cavern.

"Yes, you have night vision now. So, it has taken, good." When I turned my head and looked out at the landscape, the distant cliff seemed closer. By focusing, I saw details I couldn't have made out before. A tree growing out of a crack in a mountain. A goat on a path. It was an amazing distance.

Then my vision went black and flashed. I saw a palace for a moment, and I was jumping, daggers in hand into a courtyard. I saw my brother's bloodied face. And a young woman had fallen at my feet.

I rubbed my eyes. "What was that? What was it!"

"Oh, that. Just a bit of witching blood in our dragon line. You may have seen the future. Or you saw something that will never pass. You'll grow to hate it."

My vision had returned to normal. I took off the patch and looked at it. How many years had I worn a patch? And now I could toss it away. I pulled back my arm to throw it but paused and placed it in a cloak pocket.

"You look older," Brax said. "And the dragon eye makes you appear more intelligent."

I drew in several breaths. It was still amazing that I could see. But I had to put that amazement in a compartment inside me and lock it away. It was time to plan.

"I'm hungry," Brax said. "May I feed, Master?"

"Don't call me that," I said. "Yes, let's get you some food." I walked to the edge of the cave. The fortress was visible from here, and I could make out smoke coming from several windows. Would Corwin even still be there? Even if he was, he'd be surrounded by at least a hundred Immortals. A starving dragon and a half-broken assassin would be no match for them.

"I do see a goat over there," I said.

"Yes, there are several. I can smell them."

"Then let us go. And once you've had your fill, we'll begin to look for my brother so I can kill him."

Brax lowered his head, and I slid onto his back and took hold of one of the bony spikes that ran along his neck. We took to the morning sky.

PART 2: SHADOW HUNTER

1

FOOTFALLS IN THE SHADOWS

I slipped off the back of the dragon and landed softly behind the guard. He stared over the parapets of the tower toward the city of Myra. Perhaps he was watching the torch-lit merchant ships sail into port. He had not expected anyone to touch down behind him.

And so he fell easily when I slid out my dagger and smacked the hilt into the side of his head. I caught him, making sure his chain mail didn't clatter, and lowered him to the ground. Then I crouched beside the guard and felt his pulse. From what I'd learned in assassin school, he'd be out for at least two hours.

Plenty of time to complete my task.

Brax was already high in the air. It was amazing how such a large creature could travel in silence. He'd promised to circle high above the walled mansion, being careful not to come between it and the crescent moon. No sense letting anyone spot a dragon flapping around in the mortal realms. I had practiced a Whiskered Screech Owl hoot to summon him.

Two guards patrolled the grounds below along with four

large dogs. I'd observed their movements over the last week and knew they'd be on duty for the next three hours before being replaced by another set of guards.

I adjusted my mask. I'd made it from a moveable wax—a skill I'd picked up under the tutelage of Maestru Alesius. The mask gave me the appearance of a middle-aged man. It would be bad if my brother knew I was still alive.

Worse than bad, in fact. It would be deadly.

I had also painted a left eye in the mask that I could peer through. As long as no one looked too closely, it would hide the fact my dragon eye glowed.

I needed to know Corwin's plans and to figure out how to track him down. The mansion belonged to the Horus family. They had a son named Gregum, and he was one of my brother's closest friends.

I'd spotted Gregum coming and going from the mansion at all hours of day and night. I was sure he was doing my brother's work. And I was pretty certain I knew which room was his.

The tower door was open, so I crept down the stone stairs. The stairwell torch had burned itself out, but with my dragon eye that didn't matter. The faintest bit of moonlight was enough to see the outline of the steps. Even my balance was better.

I still wasn't certain what to make of my new eye. The fact I could see such a great distance was sometimes alarming. And there were moments where I felt I was looking into other spaces, other worlds.

"It's just the witching blood in my Scythian veins," Brax had explained. "Guess you have it now. It only makes sense since it's my eye."

He didn't elaborate. He continued to be angry about the deal we'd made.

I was glad to no longer wear an eye patch. And, at the same time, I missed it. Which was an odd reaction.

The tower stood in the courtyard's center, and the mansion had been built around them both. I came to the bottom of the steps and edged open the door, revealing a lush garden: there were grapes, apples, lilies and other fauna the country of Trella was famous for. This interior yard was where the Horus family would have massive parties. And the tower was where they'd flee if they were ever threatened.

Obviously they were a very, very rich family.

My dark assassin's cloak hid me from any watching eyes. I crossed the courtyard and entered the house through a servant's door. There would be guards in the mansion itself and I had no idea of their patrol patterns, so I'd have to be completely silent.

I went down a hallway. Paintings of Trellian gods hung on either side of me. Their gods wore little in the way of clothing. I thought I recognized Gregum in one painting and I nearly tittered out loud. An artist had painted the whole family into the scenes as if they were gods, too: eating, drinking, fighting. Oh, how highly they thought of themselves!

I was so busy smiling that I nearly bumped into a servant girl clutching an armful of towels. At the last moment I threw myself against the wall and stood still.

She walked right by, humming a jaunty song.

The mind should never wander, Maestru Alesius had often said. I missed him. I missed our long conversations. I even missed how he would correct me.

His death was yet another reason to find Corwin.

And to kill him.

I padded up a set of stairs and came to an open window.

It was a warm enough night to keep the windows open. I hopped out onto the windowsill and climbed hand over hand along the gutters, thankful they were strong.

I made my way to Gregum's windowsill. It was open, the curtains moving slightly. I knew when I crouched in the frame I'd block the moonlight, making myself more visible, but there was no way around that. *Thank the gods the Horus family is so rich!* I thought. Being that rich meant they hired the best masons who didn't make ledges that crumbled easily. I knelt and peered in.

Gregum was asleep in his bed.

Just the sight of him made me shudder in revulsion. He'd always been coiled like a massive snake next to my brother. His eyes coldly watching me and the other students like we were something to devour. He was the largest of our graduating class, and he relied on his brute force.

He slept soundly, making the slightest snore. Obviously, he felt no guilt about the students and maestrus he'd killed.

I thought of skipping the questions and just stabbing him. They trained me for killing, though I'd never taken a life. But tonight, I wanted information. I'd very much like to know what work Gregum was doing for my brother.

I drew in my breath, searched for any trap and then lowered myself onto the floor. First one foot. Then the other. Another advantage of an expensive stone house was that the floors didn't creak.

I grew warm. Glowing embers in the hearth were still casting out heat. I sweated at once.

The mask on my face slipped slightly. I could still see fine, and there was nothing I could do now to secure it. I just had to hope the sticky sap on the underside kept being sticky.

I noted a desk against the wall with a few scrolls on top,

and beside them were several dolls. Why would Gregum collect children's toys?

I took a step. And another. The carpet was thick. I didn't make a noise.

Then: *tinkle.* The sound of breaking glass under my foot.

He had hidden glass balls beneath the carpet. Now that was clever! I glanced over to see him move in his sleep, rolling so one hand lay over the far edge of the bed. I did my best impression of a statue until I was sure he was still asleep.

My dragon eye spotted several other small lumps in the carpet and I avoided them.

As I neared the hearth, sweat dribbled down my face and the mask slipped enough to block my vision. I fiddled with it. Maestru Alesius would mock my mask-making skills. Was the wax itself melting? Perhaps I hadn't made a strong batch.

I pushed the mask back into place and shuddered once I'd lined up the eyeholes. Gregum was sitting up, glaring at me, a small crossbow in his right hand. He must have had it hidden at the far end of the bed.

"What's your name?" he asked. "I like to know the name of the person I kill."

2

POINTY THINGS

Gregum was a gifted, loud braggart. After any school trial where he'd emerged victorious, he'd thump his breast and roar like a demented lion. He'd do the same when he finished an exam at the top of the class (which wasn't that often). His confidence was second only to my brother's.

He was also pointing a crossbow at me. And I was far too close to even think of dodging. His hand was steady.

"So, dead man, who are you?" he asked. Gregum gave me a great big toothy smile.

"Um.. Uh," I said, keeping my voice gruff and as manly as possible. "I... I have information for you. As a gift."

"I don't need gifts. You're here because I'm killing the other assassins, aren't you? You came to save yourself."

It took a moment to understand what he'd said. He was hunting assassins?

"Yes," I said, thinking it best to keep my answers short. "A deal. For my life."

"No deals. Sorry. I get paid too well to make deals. But it's obvious that you are from the Red Adept Assassin

School. It's where the best are trained. I'm right, aren't I?" He shook the crossbow a little as though urging agreement.

I nodded slowly.

"Of course I am." He licked his lips. "We are wiping out all the assassins. They're just too pesky to have around. And cleaning the slate is my little project. Now, I am curious about how you found me, since no one knows my name."

"A bird told me."

His eyes narrowed and glinted as if they were made of polished stone. "I don't like games. Unless they involve pointy things being stuck into my enemies. So tell me who you are and how you found me. Now!"

"But don't you want the gift?" I asked again, gruffly.

"You have nothing of value but your name. I will draw a line through it when you're dead."

"But I have the gift, here." I gestured at my cloak.

"I told you not to move! Not even a finger." He spat a little as he spoke. It was clear I had to give him something to think about, or he might just put a bolt through me.

"The surprise has to do with Scyllia," I said, still speaking gruffly.

"How do you know her name?" There was a dangerous tone to his voice. "You know far too much." He got out of bed and I was glad to see he was wearing undergarments. His aim, as he moved, was directly at my chest. "That's a mask, isn't it? You're hiding your face. But you spoke the names of my classmates, and there are only five of us alive. And I know you're not Scyllia or Corwin. So which one are you?"

I'd made a mistake! I wanted to smack myself upside the head. Why did I let him know I knew so much about him?

"In fact, I am not sure if you're a girl or a boy," he said.

Damn. Gregum looked dull-witted, but behind that thick skull was a clever brain.

"I'm a boy," I gruffed.

"Prove it!"

How did he expect me to do that? And then a thought came to me. A dangerous thought.

"I'm Corwin." I tried my best to copy my brother's voice.

"Corwin?" His grip on the crossbow wavered. "Is that really you, Corwin? Is this another test?"

"Yes," I said. "It's me. And yes, it's a test. The emperor told me you would betray us."

"That's not true!" He still hadn't lowered the bow. "You sound like Corwin and you're about the same size, but why would you risk your life to test me?"

"You know my jokes, Gregum," I said. "I'm just playing with you."

"I've passed all your trials. I even broke oaths for you. Why more tests?" He whined.

"It's—it's not a test," I said. "I lied." I had perfected my brother's snarky tone. "I have a gift, remember? I gave Scyllia hers, now I'll give you yours. It awaits inside my cloak."

"What sort of gift?" he asked.

What did Gregum want? Gold? No, look at where he lived. Nor would he want gems or books. Would he love a sharp blade? Or the beating heart of a princess?

"It's a crown," I said. "I am giving you a whole province. Well, me and the emperor. Take it, Greggs." I also knew that was my brother's nickname for his friend.

Gregum was still for a moment, then he reached out with his left hand and felt the inside top pocket of my cloak. I didn't move.

"It's a box," he said. "It's too small for a crown."

Squeeze it! I wanted to shout. *Squeeze it.* I'd put a venom needle on my coin box. Not enough to kill, but it would really, really sting.

"There's a gem inside the box," I said. "For your provincial crown."

He held his fist in front of him and opened his palm. The box was sitting there. Why hadn't it stung him?

"It's so small." He sounded disappointed. He prodded at the lock with his thumb. "Ow!" he shouted, dropping the box.

At that same moment I swung my fist into his elbow so the crossbow bolt flew into the wall. He was disoriented and clutching his hand, so I slammed into him and reached for my dagger. Then I thought better of it and ripped a pouch from my pocket and threw a handful of dust toward his face. I held my breath.

He said, "What the—"

Then he fell to the ground. The knockout powder had done its work. I knew the effects wouldn't last long; in fact, I was lucky that he wasn't immune. But I wasted no time tying him up.

When he was properly bound, I went to his desk and shuddered. The dolls were clad in assassins' robes. At least half of the dolls were stabbed with a pin each: one in the head, another through the heart, or jabbed in the neck or in the stomach.

This was Gregum's way of keeping track of those he had hunted down and how they'd died.

What type of animal would remember his kills this way?

I unrolled one scroll and saw a list of names. Many of them had lines through them. I rolled it and the second scroll on his desk up and stuffed them into the long pockets of my cloak.

The dolls made me sick, but I paused long enough to count them. There were twelve. If each represented an assassin, Gregum had killed eight in the four weeks since we graduated. Each assassin who had escaped the graduation night massacre was being hunted down one by one. And those who hadn't attended that night were no safer.

I wanted to twist his neck until it was broken. I grabbed a doll—a girl doll with red hair—and stuffed it into my pocket.

"You aren't Corwin."

The voice made me shudder. I turned. He was awake already! If he'd been extra clever, he would have hidden that fact until he could wriggle out of the ropes.

"No. I'm not." I kept my voice deep.

"You tricked me. For that I'll eat your liver."

I chuckled at his threat and kept the chuckle deep. "You'd find it bitter."

"How do you know Scyllia and Corwin?"

"I studied all of you. In fact I was going to hire you after graduation."

This gave him pause. "Truly?"

"You are the strongest. The best."

He smiled, showing large white teeth. "Well, perhaps I won't eat your liver," he said.

"And I won't eat yours," I replied. "We have a deal."

"I still must kill you. Corwin's orders." He shrugged those massive shoulders. "I'll make it quick since you think so highly of me."

"How kind of you," I said. "Corwin will betray you. You can't trust that one. That's why I wouldn't hire him."

"You're wrong. He rewards his kin."

I was his kin! I nearly shouted.

"He rewards those who have the same heart," Gregum

continued. "And he has so many plans, and there is a place in those plans for me. A big place. I wouldn't want to work with you. Ever."

I hadn't concluded what to do with him. He had been involved in the massacre of the Red Assassins, and he would continue to sow destruction if I didn't kill him. And to kill him would also stop him from passing anything he had learned about me to Corwin.

"Why would you hide your face?" He raised an eyebrow, clearly visible in the moonlight. "I know you. That's why you're wearing a mask. If you took it off, I'd recognize you."

There was a corporthium pill in my third pocket. It would put him in a coma. The people who came out of that deep sleep lost their memories. Forever.

He had a family. He had riches. They would care for him as he became someone else.

It was just a matter of pulling back his head and shoving it down his throat.

"We're done here," I said. I took a step toward him, preparing to do a juji move that would leave his mouth open so I could drop the pill on his tongue.

Gregum launched himself upwards, the ropes falling to the floor.

And then his fist connected with my jaw.

3

A SHATTERED MASK

The blow sent me flying and shattered the right half of my mask. I managed to smash my head against the desk leg on the way down. I had fought hand to hand many times at school and had taken many blows, but none as powerful as that.

It was important to stand right away and fight back, but my thoughts were slow and dizzy. My body was not responding to my commands. *Get up! Get up!*

"You're a girl," Gregum said. His voice came through the mist and I shook my head. "Is that you, Megan?"

The vision in my dragon eye cleared first. The room was black and white and Gregum was a moving bundle of red energy jumping toward me.

I pushed away with all the speed I could muster, somehow rolling across the floor and out of his reach.

"You're a quick one," he said.

I was too fuzzy to speak. And I still couldn't see clearly out of my human eye. The red shape stalked toward me.

"I like my prey dazed," he said. "And I will eat your liver. My cooks downstairs will fry it up."

It was hard to convince my body I was in danger. I was certain my mask hadn't come off completely or he would have recognized me.

"Wait," I said. But it came out, "Waaah."

"'*Whaaa?*' You sound like a baby. No, don't move."

I blinked several times. He was leaping toward me with a dagger in his hand. He must have hidden weapons all around the room.

I thought about breathing fire on him.

No! You're not a dragon, I told myself. The blow had scrambled my brains. At the last moment, I reached into my robe, grabbing the first thing I came across and throwing it.

He parried with his dagger. Glass shattered. My hand began burning as liquid drops hit it.

Acid! I'd tossed my acid globe at him.

The rest of the liquid hit his face.

He screamed in pain and anger, grabbing at his cheek. He crashed down next to me and I stumbled away.

"You will die a thousand deaths for that!" He lurched to his feet, his face seeming to bubble flesh.

Gregum barreled himself right at me and I dodged. He hit the wall so hard I thought he'd go through it.

The path to the window was clear and so was my vision. I ran toward that square and jumped. He flailed at my legs, grabbed a pant leg, but failed to catch hold. I landed a wobbly landing on the windowsill and, without pausing, leapt toward the roof.

Then I grabbed onto the edge of the roof and held myself over the window.

"You'll pay! You'll pay! You'll pay!" he shouted, each word getting louder as he charged toward the window.

I let go and came down like a bag of bricks, just as Gregum stuck his head out.

I connected with his skull, but didn't hear any bones crack. He smashed against the windowsill though and I kept going, down to the ground.

I landed hard. I wasn't certain whether I had broken my ankle. A quick glance over my shoulder showed me he was moving slowly, holding his head and groaning. He'd be fully awake in moments, but at least I'd have more time to get away from the mansion.

The problem was that Brax couldn't just swoop down to pick me up. The guards would see him and discover there was a dragon.

I ran into the mansion and out through the nearest door and into the front courtyard. The guard dogs were already barking and a warning bell rang behind me. It was dark enough, and I was fast enough, to make it to the wall without being spotted. I took the steps three at a time, barely keeping my balance. My hand was aching, but I didn't want to look at it. It felt like I'd burned a finger or two right off.

I made it to the top of the wall and turned to run along the walkway. A guard threw himself in front of me, his sword in hand. I dodged him, but slipped to the ground using my burnt hand as support. I let out a yell of pain, then kicked him in the knees so he clattered down the stairs.

I stumbled along the wall walk. I was glad I'd chosen the side that faced away from the city.

"Boo! Boo! Boo!" I said, my best approximation of a Whiskered Screech Owl.

Nothing appeared in the sky.

I made the noise over and over and over again, running at top speed. I would soon run out of wall walk.

Was Brax deaf? I sounded like a bleating goat, my voice getting higher and higher pitched.

A crossbow bolt stuck into the wall next to me. The guards were all on the ground, aiming their bows. Another bolt grazed my leg. A third went right through my robe.

And there was no sign of Brax yet. Not even a distant shape in the sky.

Then I saw a blur below me on the opposite side of the wall.

I jumped toward it.

4

WORDS ON A MOUNTAIN

"That wasn't a Whiskered Screech Owl," Brax said. The wind whipped his words back to me. "It sounded more like a sick cow. So I wasn't certain if you were calling me."

I clutched a spike on his back with my left hand. My right hand wouldn't close because it hurt too much. Brax had timed it perfectly by flying below the wall and out of sight. I'd made a desperate and lucky jump.

"You could have been here a lot faster," I said. We were speeding away from the mansion. It wasn't until the first branch hit me that I realized we were not going skyward. "What are you doing?" I asked. We were winging and smashing right through a grove of olive trees.

"I don't want them to see me," Brax said. He sounded a little snarky. "The next thing you know there'll be soldiers and dragon hunters and, well, it gets messy. So we're staying low."

"We're flying through the trees!" I shouted.

"Yes, we are. And it will only hurt one of us."

Another branch smacked my head, and I lowered myself

even flatter against his scales. Smaller branches scratched along my back.

"Oh, do watch your head," he said, perhaps knowing he was too late. "This will get tricky. If only I had both eyes, I might avoid a few branches."

A branch as thick as my arm bounced off the top of my skull and almost knocked me into the air.

"You're hitting those branches on purpose!" I shouted.

"I am not!" Brax said. "Never would I do that! I'm saving us. It's not my fault they keep reaching for you."

We continued to smash our way through the grove. At times we glided only a few inches from the ground. Brax weaved and wove to avoid the trunks. After what seemed like hours we came out the other side. We were now a great distance from the walls. Brax slowly ascended. "See," he said once we were level with the clouds. "That worked out."

"For you." Branches and leaves filled my hair, but I didn't want to let go to brush them out. My head ached, and I still didn't dare look at my injured hand.

In time we came to the lone mountain that had been my home for the last few weeks. We landed on a high ledge, and I was pleased to see my tent hadn't been blown away by the winds. A pile of sheep and ram bones were next to the tent and a few scavenger birds took off, squawking, as Brax settled his wings.

I slid off and collapsed on the stone I'd turned into a bench with a few blankets.

"You look like you've been through about seven different hells," he said. "I take it your well-planned plan didn't go so well."

"Gregum is still alive," I admitted.

"No surprise. You don't have the guts to kill your enemies."

"That doesn't take guts!" Shouting made my hand hurt more, as if the anger was sending the blood there.

"Your kindness will be the death of you." He stared down at me, his one remaining eye glowering.

"It's the last thing I've got," I said, not even certain what I meant. Why couldn't I be more like my brother?

I peeled away the tatters of the leather glove on my right hand.

"Oh," Brax said. "You really hurt yourself. With what?"

"Acid." It had burned two holes right through my palm. There was very little blood, and it seemed the acid had missed melting away my bones. So Belaz had been watching over me.

But just moving my hand caused such pain. I dug around until I found my waterskin. The mountain-cold water cooled my flesh and flushed out what remained of the acid. The pain lessened to the point my thoughts became clearer.

"You'll need something colder," Brax said. And without another word he flapped his wings and vanished into the darkness.

What to do for acid? I tried to remember what I'd learned in class. It wasn't like I could walk into the library and ask Maestru Beatrix for a book. Just the thought of that made me wince and feel a sense of longing for that room full of books. And for her calming presence.

One more reason to kill Corwin.

I knew that water diffused acid. More cold would take away the pain, but I'd need to put a salve together with the few herbs and materials I had on me. Already, my hand was throbbing to the point it became hard to think.

A chunk of snow hit my shoulder. I looked up in time to see several more large chunks rain down around me, hitting my head and shoulders and forming a pile on the bench.

Brax landed silently across from me, snow caught in his wings, his snout and his paws. "It's not clean, but it's the best I could do. Sorry for dropping so much on you."

I scooped up a handful and pressed it against my hand. The numbness took the edge off. "Thank you," I said.

"Just fulfilling my side of the bargain," he said. But he seemed to have what passed for a smile on his face. "You have a high tolerance for pain, Carmen. Most humans would be screaming their heads off by now."

"I'm good at gritting my teeth," I said through gritted teeth.

"Brush off the snow," Brax said. I did so, and he poked his nose near my hand and said, "It's not so bad. Once it's frozen enough be sure to clean out the wound with your good water and use a salve of mincegus."

"I have nothing that fancy," I said. "But I'll make do."

"Good," he said. Then he looked me directly in the eyes. "You should have killed him."

"I am not my brother," I said.

"Well, your brother is living in a palace in Akkadium and you're here freezing on the side of a mountain covered with bird droppings. One of you has the wrong attitude."

"I don't kill people without good reason!"

He made an exasperated motion with his talons. "One does not argue with the mad or the insane. That's something my mother used to tell me." He moved a few feet away. He was nowhere near as skinny and wasted as he had been several weeks ago. Eating a sheep or two a day and whatever deer and elk he could catch had brought meat into his stomach and back onto his bones. "I need my breakfast. May I go eat now, Master?"

If my hand didn't hurt so much I might have punched him. "Don't call me that. I'm not your master."

"I know. I know," he said. "But the title aggravates you so."

"You're welcome to eat whenever you want. I need to rest."

"Ta ta," he said. Which, coming from something of his size, sounded ridiculous. He dived off the edge and winged toward the valley below us.

I leaned against the rock wall behind me. The sun was rising, but I knew it wouldn't bring a lot of warmth to these heights.

I washed the wound out as he had suggested and then packed it with my salve and stretched cotton bandages across. I scarfed down a few biscuits I had bought several days ago, pausing to brush off the bit of mold that had grown on one. They were rock hard and tasted horrible, but I needed something in my stomach.

Then I went through the folds in my robe and took out the things I had recovered from Gregum's room.

Two paper scrolls and the doll.

When I opened the first scroll, I saw the name *Banderius* at the top. Banderius! I had promised my maestru I would find him. Below his name was a paragraph of writing in Oldtongue. We hadn't been taught that ancient language, but the scroll must be important or Gregum wouldn't have it.

I put it away and unrolled the second scroll. It was a list of names, locations, and descriptions of assassins. There were lines drawn through several. Thankfully, I didn't recognize the first bunch of names.

But in the second group I saw Maestru Xerithus. He had cared for the garden and he'd always kindly and patiently answered any questions about herbs or poisonous leaves. A line cut through his name.

I didn't see the names of any other maestrus or students in the next group. These must only be the assassins who escaped the fortress or didn't attend the graduation. The ones who were killed on graduation night had to be on another list, for I also didn't see Maestru Alesius. Maybe Corwin had divided up lists of the remaining assassins and given them to Gregum and Scyllia to hunt down.

At the bottom I saw a name I knew.

Megan. Red hair. Scar on cheek. Thespian Way Avenus.

My classmate Megan. Being on this list indicated she had lived through the red graduation, but it also meant that Gregum and Corwin knew where she was hiding.

Her name didn't have a line through it.

They would soon be traveling to kill her.

5

A LOYAL CREATURE

By the time Brax returned, several hours had passed. I had packed all my gear in my knapsack and used it as a pillow, getting a few minutes of sleep here and there. I scanned the names on the scroll several times. Thord was not on the list. I didn't know what that meant. Had they caught him before he could escape? Or was he on a different list? There were likely agents from the emperor combing every part of the Five Realms and the Empire to find the last assassins.

My hand continued to hurt. I had used the snow to freeze the pain several times and dressed the wound again. I didn't know if it would ever heal.

"Leaving so soon?" Brax asked as he landed on the ledge. "I was beginning to like this place. The muttons are plump. The farm women are plump, too."

"You weren't eating humans!"

"No." He smiled a big smile. Chunks of meat and sheep hide were stuck between his teeth. "Just making mention that creatures are well fed in this valley."

"We have to fly to Avenus," I said. "One of my friends—a fellow student, I mean—is there. She's in danger."

"That's a long way to go just to visit a classmate. I'm sure she's aware of the danger she's in."

"She doesn't know they have discovered exactly where she is," I said. Megan had been cruel to me, calling me Cyclops and not even bothering to say the nickname behind my back. She had wanted me to be a showpiece of her business—the girl with the eye patch who took all the orders and did nothing. And yet, Megan had come to my door on graduation night and warned me about what was unfolding.

"I owe her," I said.

"You are a loyal creature," Brax said. "It's admirable."

"Are you being sarcastic again?"

The look on his face surprised me. It was almost as if he had respect. "No. You are admirable, Carmen Crow. Loyal and conscientious. You're loyal to an assassin guild that no longer exists. I find it confusing. My own loyalties made me an outcast, but here you are with only the clothes on your back and an old knapsack and you are thinking of a classmate."

"I do have a dragon on my side," I said.

"A pitiful dragon, if there ever was one. A dragon ruled by a human. But I see you are packed and your eyes and mind are set. You won't even give me time to digest properly."

He went down on all fours. I grabbed my knapsack and tied it on my back, then slid onto Brax and held on with my left hand. It still didn't feel natural to be there.

Without another word, we took to the sky.

6

TOO HOT FOR THAT

We flew east along the Trellian coast. The sun set and the Aldric Ocean looked endless under the moonlight. Brax was tireless. He chose the right air currents, so the wind pushed him even faster. It was a smooth ride, and I almost forgot to hold tight. I was too busy looking at the land, the stars, and as far as I could see along the ocean. We passed near the occasional boat. The fishers would be petrified if they knew a flame-breathing dragon was this close to them.

Being in the air, on Brax's back, made my soul sing. I'd never tire of this view of the world or of the feeling of power I got. We could conquer anything. I was one with him.

Of course, with a flick of a wing or shrug of a shoulder he could send me to my death.

We turned south and crossed the Aven Strait. For a time there was only water below us, then land appeared again. The city-state of Avenus sat on the west end of a large island. Being on an island had helped keep them out of the clutches of the Akkad Empire and turned them into the best sailors in the mortal lands.

When we reached Avenus itself, after at least seven hours of flying, my jaw dropped. The city was the second largest of all the cities in the land of Ellos. There were lamps lit all across the avenues so from above it looked like a burning jewel. They had built the walls surrounding Avenus in the shape of a pentagon with one point reaching over the water to protect the harbor. They said the walls were the thickest made by men.

The citizens of this city were not ruled by a king or an emperor. Every three years, the population gathered in a natural amphitheater called *Grekois* and cast cards for two Archons to lead them. The laborers elected one Archon, and another was elected by the merchants. The merchants had voted in a man named Perkan. The workers had elected a woman named Thena. I was glad I'd paid attention in class.

"Whenever you're done staring, you should tell me where to land," Brax said. "I have no desire to fly over Avenus. There are ballistae batteries at every wall to keep winged invaders away."

I had read about the massive bolt-throwing bows. They had been installed after an elite regiment of Immortals had attacked the city using gliders. Ill winds called up by a sorcerer had sent them into the ocean to drown. "Those are not meant for dragons," I said.

"Dragons or a man in a kite, they'll go through either. And I don't like having holes in me."

"Then let's find a quiet and well-hidden place to land," I said.

Both of us searched. Even though it was still dark, I could see a great distance with my dragon eye. There were no high mountains, but the hills were tall. That was perhaps where the Empire had launched its failed glider attack.

"There," I pointed.

"There," Brax said at the same time. Then he laughed. "Ah, I forget you have my eye. Well, I don't completely forget because there's a horrible itching pain where my eye used to be. I may still have a pinch of bitterness about that."

We landed on a hill thick with trees. And the trees were thick with broad leaves—the foliage would provide cover for Brax. "It's a good thing you're not a Quant dragon," I said. "They are gigantic. It'd be impossible to hide."

"That's right," he said, gesturing at his body. "Good thing I'm a scrawny Scythian."

"I didn't mean it that way."

"Well," Brax continued. "Since Quants can't speak and have no control over their appetites, he'd have gobbled you up right away. That would have saved you and me a lot of time and effort."

"You have such an interesting way of looking at life."

He turned his palms upwards. It made him seem almost human. "I am a curious and strange beast." He pointed at me. "Be quick with your mission, Carmen. Find this *friend* of yours, warn her and depart. Hiding under leaves and branches is no noble pursuit for a dragon."

"I'll return," I said. "As fast as my feet can fly."

I turned away. He was already pulling branches and leaves over himself. I jogged down the hill. My legs were sore from the hours of riding and it was good to stretch them out.

After about twenty minutes I realized my right hand no longer hurt. This surprised me since two holes had been burnt in it just over twenty-four hours earlier. I pulled at my bandages.

I nearly tripped when I saw what had happened.

The holes had healed! The skin was still red where the

acid had burned me and when I squeezed my hand, it did send a spark of pain. But the holes had come together. It was as if a fortnight of healing had taken place in a few hours. What strange magic was this? My poultice hadn't been that strong.

I kept moving, still staring at my hand. I eventually put the bandages back on.

It was two hours on foot to get to the city gates. The sun was rising in the East and painting the walls of the city red. The ocean here was the lightest color of blue I'd ever seen.

I pulled my cloak around me and, remembering how odd my eye looked, retrieved my old patch from a pocket and put it on. With my dragon eye covered I felt more than half blind—I wasn't as steady on my feet. In the few weeks of having that eye my body, my balance and my brain had gotten used to seeing everything through it.

There were already merchants and other travelers lining up to go into the city. I joined a crowd, each of them speaking in the same tongue as me but with an Avenian accent. I chose not to converse with anyone. Even the patch over my eye was too memorable. If I'd had time and enough material, I would have made a mask.

Soldiers guarded the gates. They were clad in bronze armor designed to make it look like they had perfect chest muscles. The female guards wore the same type of armor, and I felt a bit shy looking at either male or female soldiers. It was like they were walking around half-naked.

"You there," one of the female soldiers yelled. She pointed at me. "Off wit your head."

7

THESPIAN WAY

"What?" I said. I threw myself back a step and bumped into a woman with a basket of eggs. None of them broke, but that didn't stop her from swearing at me.

"Off with your head!" the guard shouted.

I reached for my daggers.

"It's too wurm a day to 'ave one on!" Now she was pointing a spear at me. "Off wit your 'ead."

I suddenly smiled and relaxed. The woman's accent had confused me. She'd said, "Off with your hood."

I pulled back my hood, and she stared at me for a long moment then nodded to indicate I could pass. I wasn't certain whether her command was just a show of power or a rule about entering Avenus with your face uncovered. Either way, both soldiers had had a good look at my face.

Soon I was walking along perfectly laid cobblestone streets. The houses and other buildings were made with white sandstone bricks and had tiny gardens out front. Everything looked neat, not the same as in Myra. That city had slums. Perhaps Avenus had slums too, but I bet even the refuse was piled in a tidy manner.

The scroll had said Megan was on a street called *Thespian Way*. I knew thespians were the actors who entertained the people of Avenus. I had expected to find a stage with some rooms attached. Maybe she'd even become an actress herself! Though that seemed an odd way to hide.

Instead *Thespian Way* was an inn. And it was the oldest, most unkempt building I'd seen so far—a gray-stoned two-story structure that leaned to one side as if it were a little drunk. The garden outside was long dead—a collection of vines and stalks of plants that stunk like pee. My guess was that those inside the inn didn't stumble very far when their bladders were full.

I pulled up my hood and stepped inside. It took a moment for my eye to adjust to the darkness. If my dragon eye hadn't been behind a patch, it would have been instant. All I could see at first were shadows, and all I could smell was the stink of burnt food. And with it came that stench of belching, which made my stomach turn a little. It reminded me of how Corwin would often belch in my face as a child.

Come to think of it, he did that even a few weeks ago.

Just another reason to kill him.

There were about twenty patrons sitting around tables and benches. I'd arrived early enough that several travelers were having their breakfasts. The nearest man was using his hands to scoop food from a metal plate covered in hard-boiled eggs, burnt ham and pickles. All I'd had in the last few days was a handful of hard crackers. I wanted to steal his food.

I marched up to the counter. The innkeeper looked like he'd spilled half the morning's meal on his apron. He ignored me as he regaled a few of his guests with a tale about his champion fighting dog. When he was done his gruesome story, he quaffed a beer and came over.

"What can I get you for?" he asked. His beard was gray and flecked with foam.

"I'm looking for a young woman," I said. "I believe she's staying here."

"My clientele are the private type," he said. "Who might you be to her?"

"I'm—I'm her cousin," I said. "I haven't seen her for two years. She wrote a letter to my mom and said I could find her here."

Maestru Alesius had taught us that mentioning a mother would often disguise a lie. Even the most bitter man likely had fond thoughts about his mother.

"And what is your cousin's name?" the innkeeper asked.

"That's the thing. She changed it and I've forgotten the new one. It's a stage name."

The innkeeper let out a gruff laugh. "Many a patron has changed a name. It's part and parcel of what thespians do. One name doesn't work to drum up money... try another."

"My cousin owes my mother coins," I said. "And she's paying it off by teaching me the craft."

"Ha, good luck with that. You only have one eye, so you'll be stuck playing the one-eyed goddess." He scratched at his mushroom-shaped nose. "What does this cousin look like?"

"She has red hair and is about as tall as me. She may go by Megan or Mary or Mandra."

He nodded, and it looked like he was about to say something, then he stepped back and shouted, "We need more bacon, darlin'." A hag of a woman came through the kitchen door and nodded, then turned around and went back. At the same time he reached for a goblet on a shelf behind him.

I noted that he also pulled a string attached to the wall. Was that how he got more bacon? I was again aware of how hungry I was, but I didn't want to eat until I'd found Megan.

"Do you know her?" I asked.

"Know who?" His grin revealed brownish teeth. He tapped the counter with one finger.

I realized what he was asking for. I retrieved two coins from my cloak and softly set them on the counter so they didn't clink.

His smile widened. Then he looked at the ceiling. He looked at me, then at the ceiling again. Clearly he didn't want his patrons to know the was giving up the location of one of his clients. Being a snitch was not a good characteristic in an innkeeper.

"Thank you," I said. I turned away and walked toward the stairs. Obviously the man was aware people would come looking for Megan, or he wouldn't have been so reticent to tell me her location—and yet he'd sold her out for two coins.

I reached the top of the stairs. There were two doors in the hallway ahead of me, but the innkeeper had gestured directly above him. So I went down the hall to the room at the end.

I listened. There wasn't a noise.

"Megan," I whispered. I knocked lightly. "Megan?"

There was no response.

Then I remembered the innkeeper had pulled a string. I thought it led to a bell in the kitchen, but perhaps it went directly up to this room and sent a warning to Megan. She might be fleeing at this moment. He likely charged her extra to keep an eye out for any pursuers, and now he would pocket both of our coins.

I said the word *Enderos* and made a motion. The door unlocked, too loudly. But I pushed it open, not foolish enough to step right in. It revealed a small room; the covers on the cot were thrown off and the window was open. She had fled!

I dashed through the doorway, intending to run to the window and see if I could spot her.

But when I'd crossed the threshold, I knew I'd made a mistake.

Because something heavy—very heavy—smashed into my back and slammed me to the floor.

8

MEETING A TRAITOR

How *stupid!* was my first thought. The room had been set up to lure me in and someone had been hiding above the door. That someone had knocked every last bit of wind out of my lungs and was squishing me into the floor. I slid to the side just as a dagger was jabbed next to my face, cutting off a chunk of my hair.

My hair! I'd never been that fond of it, but I preferred to have it on my head.

I rolled away, making the next stab miss me and jumped to my feet, daggers out. My right hand barely had the strength to hold tight.

Facing me was a woman with short dark hair and such anger on her face it distorted her eyes and nose. "You!" she said. "You. He sends you to kill me!"

I deflected the next blow, and my mind caught up with what I was seeing. It was Megan. She'd cut her hair and dyed it black. Her eyes were tinged with rabid madness. "You betrayed us." She lunged, and I dodged, but as she brought the blade back, it cut along my ribs.

"Oww!" I said. "I didn't betray anyone."

"Liar!" This time she feinted to the left then came in from the right—my blind side. I still had the patch on and didn't have an extra moment to remove it. I only guessed at the angle and was able to guide her arm away with a punch. "All of our friends! You helped Corwin kill them, you witch."

She took a moment to slap the hilt of her dagger against the wall. "Get up!" she shouted.

I was standing, so I didn't know why she'd yell that. Perhaps she was going insane.

"I didn't kill anyone!" I shouted again.

I blocked her next diving attack, but she surprised me with a kick that jarred my innards and knocked me into the middle of the room. She had always been good with her legs. I was better with blades if I had both eyes, but when I reached for my patch, she saw that as an opening and drove me backwards.

"I'm going to pay you back for their deaths," she seethed. "I've made a list. Every friend dead. Every maestru. You will suffer."

With each word she was forcing me to retreat, and it was all I could do to deflect the blows. I tried a disarming move with my right hand, but when our blades collided mine went flying. My hand, not quite healed, was just too weak to hold it.

That got a chilling smile out of her.

"For Maestru Arvid," she said. The blade sliced my ear, leaving a small cut. "For Maxen!" This stab missed my face. He was one of the fifth years. I'd seen his body.

Megan had forced me to stumble back against the wall, and she hit it with her hilt. On purpose. Then redoubled her attacks.

My only choice was to run. And so I made a feint which she reacted to, and I then slipped past her and charged toward the hallway. The patch over my eye made me misjudge and I slammed into the doorway, spun around and hit the opposite wall. I was up in a heartbeat, but Megan was on me and swinging her blades, driving me back.

Two things happened. The first was the door beside me opened and Thord stepped out. We both had the same look of shock on our faces. He swung out with his sword and blocked Megan's blow, saving me.

"Thanks," I said. "I can't believe—"

Thord punched me square in the side of the head.

All went dark.

9

A STEP BEHIND

The light eventually returned. I opened my right eye. Two foggy but familiar faces were floating in front of me. The walls swirled behind them. They'd left my eye patch on and, when I tried to move, I discovered they'd bound me tight enough to pinch the skin on my arms.

"I'm not a traitor," I whispered.

Megan was a step behind Thord and aiming a one-handed crossbow at me. The bolt had a very glittery and sharp point. They weren't powerful enough to go through armor, but would put a hole in flesh.

Or my forehead.

"Ha! Lies! Lies! Lies!" Megan shouted. I expected the bolt to be loosed with every word. "We discovered your list of kills in your cloak." She shook the scroll at me with her other hand. "You're a murderer."

"I'm not!" My thoughts were coming together far too slowly. "I stole that from Gregum."

"More like you work with him," she said. "Is he soon to arrive? Or do you let the Immortals finish your prey?"

"I'm here to warn you." I looked at Thord. His face

was unreadable, though if I was to venture a guess I would say he was angry. "And what do you believe, Thord?" I asked.

"You survived graduation night," he spoke as though thinking about each word. "You being in league with your brother is the most likely explanation for that."

"It isn't!" I said. "I'd never join him. He's evil."

"You had me fooled." Megan was aiming at my head now. "All those years of being standoffish and arrogant. I thought it was just the whole *I'm missing an eye* thing. But you and your brother were planning to betray and kill everyone."

"Look at that doll," I said. They'd plucked the doll from my cloak and left it on the floor. It had red hair. "That doll was you, Megan. Gregum had dolls as trophies for all his kills."

"More like you collected them," Megan said. "Or you made them while you were locked away in your room planning all this."

"I would never collect dolls!" I shouted.

"Poking holes in dolls does seem like Gregum," Thord said. He was holding the doll now and his big hand made it look small.

"Don't you take her side." Megan pointed the scroll his way but kept the bow aimed at me.

"I'm not. I don't mean she's not working with him."

"Did you learn nothing of me in all the years we studied together?" I asked.

"I thought I knew you," Thord said. "But you are a lone wolf. Plus, you aren't the friendliest girl in the world."

"I—I... " My thoughts were caught in molasses. I must have been friendly once in all those years.

"Why are we even discussing this?" Megan asked. "We

should stab her through the heart and flee. Her helpers could be along at any moment."

"Stabbing me would be a mistake," I said. "I can prove that I'm on your side. I really can." Though the moment I said it, I had no idea what proof I could offer.

"How?" Thord asked.

"With logic. Just like Maestru Alesius taught us."

"Oh, this I have to hear." Megan looked tougher with her hair short. "Impress us with your logic, Cyclops."

I ignored the fact she used that name. I breathed in and said, "First, I am here on my own. No Immortals at my side. No Gregum or Scyllia or Corwin." I spat each of their names. "Why would I attempt to kill you without help?"

"You like to work alone," Thord said. "So that's not surprising."

"Yes, but look at that list of dead assassins. Do you recognize any of them?"

"Some are familiar," Megan said.

"They were seasoned men and women." I wasn't certain where I was leading them. My logic was failing me. I closed my right eye, hoping to block the pain of my headache and to clear my thoughts. With that eye closed and the patch over the other, I couldn't see a thing. But doing that gave me an idea. "It is Corwin's great plan to kill the rest of the assassins and win favor with the emperor. Do you honestly think he'd trust me with that work? His sister. The girl with one eye. I can't even aim straight. He teased me mercilessly about my missing eye." I wanted to shout "and you, too!" at Megan, but held back. "And furthermore, do you believe I could work with him? He's the one who cut my eye out of my head."

Thord's face had changed—it didn't appear so set in

stone. When I looked to Megan, I was surprised. There was a hint of remorse in her eyes.

"Explain something." She continued to point the bow at me. "How did you escape?"

"My brother gave me a paralysis tincture that night. He wanted to save me. He didn't see me as a threat, in fact said I could retire on a pig farm. That potion was why I couldn't answer either of you when you came to my door to warn me. I thank you for that." I meant those words. Then I told them about my escape, including seeing Maestru Alesius and facing my brother. I skipped the part about falling down the mountainside because that would let them know my daggers were enchanted. And I certainly didn't mention Brax. "Once I'd dodged the Immortals, I used the tunnels Alesius had shown me and escaped through an unguarded gate. Then I hid in a cave for three days and walked to Bekon, and then took a wagon to Myra to hunt Gregum."

They both stared at me. After looking me up and down, Megan lowered the bow. Her gaze lingered on my eye patch. "I believe you," she said. "Your brother wants everything to be perfect. And you, missing an eye, are not perfect. He wouldn't trust you with anything."

"You don't have to make it sound like I'm useless," I said. I tried to keep my tone light but failed.

"Oh, you are far from useless," she said. "I have great respect for you, Carmen."

I'd hate to be someone she didn't respect, I thought. But before I could reply Thord said, "I'm sorry."

"Sorry? That you didn't believe me?"

"No. We were right to come to that conclusion. And Megan is correct: Corwin wouldn't trust you because of what you lack. His mistake. I don't want to repeat it, so I'm willing to trust you." He rubbed at his chin. "I am sorry I punched you."

"That was a punch?" I said. "I thought a butterfly had brushed my cheek."

That got a chuckle out of both of them.

"Besides," I said. "We wouldn't be having this lovely conversation now if you hadn't punched me."

Megan knelt down beside me and untied the ropes. Then she rubbed a healer's sap onto my cut earlobe and ribs. Her touch was actually gentle.

10

IT'S SURVIVAL

I shook out the tingling from my limbs. The bandages on my hand flapped in the air, but didn't come off.

"How did you hurt yourself?" Thord grabbed my arm and turned it so he could stare at my palm. His hand was warm.

"Oh, that? I threw acid at Gregum and it spilled onto my hand."

"When did all this happen again?" Megan asked.

"A day ago," I said.

"It healed quickly," Thord noted.

I pulled my hand away and peeled off the last of my bandage to reveal pink skin. There was no sign of a wound.

I hid my hand. "I'm a quick healer, that's all. Or it was a bad batch of acid."

Thord frowned and looked like he would pursue that line of questioning, but instead he asked, "Why are you here, Carmen?"

"I saw Megan's name on the list. I wanted to warn her that my brother is after her."

"Well, that's not news," Megan said somewhat haughtily.

"That's why I'm hiding out in Avenus. We got as far and fast away as possible from the emperor and your snake of a brother." She was hooking her bow to her belt. "But thanks. I appreciate you traveling all that distance to get here."

"Of course, you knew Corwin is after you," I said. "What I wanted to warn you of was that Corwin knows *exactly* where you are. That's what the scroll means. It lists this inn as your location."

"But how did he know I was staying here?" Megan asked.

I pointed at the floor. "My guess is the innkeeper sent a message. Perhaps he's making money from you and from informing the emperor."

"The innkeeper was to warn us if anyone came looking," Megan said. She pointed at a small bell in the ceiling. "That's why I knew you were coming to my room."

"Yes, he rang that bell," I said. "I saw him pull the string. But he also took my bribe, so I guess he didn't care where his money came from. And I'm sure the emperor's underlings are paying a rather hefty fee."

"I'll kill him," Megan said.

"We can't just go killing innkeepers," Thord reminded her. "That'll draw attention."

"Well, I'd settle for a good maiming."

"Just hold your temper for now," Thord said as he took the scroll from Megan. She looked like she was on the verge of lashing out at him. "How did you get these papers from Gregum?"

"I walked into his family's mansion, evaded his guards, fought with Gregum, and stole the scrolls."

"You did that on your own?" Megan said. "With... with one eye?"

"Unlike you, I paid attention in class. I only needed one eye for that." I was tempted to whip my patch off and reveal my dragon eye. I imagined that would make them stagger back. But it was better to keep as many secrets as possible. That was another thing Maestru Alesius had taught me.

"And you didn't kill Gregum," Thord said. Why did everyone ask me that?

"No. I intended to use the corporthium pill and wipe out all his memories. But failed."

"You aren't like your brother at all, are you?" Megan sounded a little disappointed. "I'm surprised the same mother birthed you two."

"It's a surprise to me, too." I felt a moment of sadness when I thought of the mother I'd never known.

"And all this happened two nights ago." Thord tapped the scroll on his open palm. "How did you get here so quickly? It's two weeks by cart, five days by ship."

"I—" I tried to think up a lie that would work and then decided lying would only add more suspicion. "That's a secret."

"It's a secret I'd like to know." Thord continued tapping the scroll on his other hand.

"If you trusted me," I said, "maybe I'd tell you."

He now tapped the side of his head with the scroll. "You must have a swan, because it's the only thing that could travel that far that fast. You somehow got it from the swannery. Maybe one of the younger ones that wasn't imprinted yet. Is that how you got out of the fortress?"

"The swannery was heavily guarded," Megan said. "Stealing one would be almost impossible."

"Nothing is impossible," I said. I had to work to make my voice sound confident. "I may have stumbled across a swan when I was outside the fortress." It was better to let them think that was what happened. "I've shared my story. Now tell me how you escaped."

"No secret tunnels for me," Megan said. "I got lucky, that's all. I went down to the gates. Every one of them was being watched by Immortals with crossbows. But the assassin who had gone before me had fallen in such a way as to hold the door open. And I could see was which direction the bolt in his chest had come from. I jumped out with a shield on my arm, and it deflected the next bolt. The Immortal had made the mistake of standing too close. I ran toward him, and the next bolt came right through the shield and clipped my shoulder. But he tried to fix a third bolt. He died with that bolt still in his hand."

She had killed an Immortal? This impressed me. They were legendarily skilled.

"And you." I pointed at Thord. "I know you had wings."

"Yes. I flew with the wings I'd made as a project. That was pure luck. And I happened to see Megan as she was dashing toward the ten thousand steps. Which, of course, were also watched. I swooped down and—"

"—scared the devils out of me. But it didn't take long to convince me not to take the stairs."

"And, well, we tested my wings to the fullest," Thord said. They were completing each other's sentences, I noticed. "I was very pleased with how well they worked."

"And you both came here?" I asked.

Thord nodded. "Yes. We agreed it was a far enough distance to give us some safety. But apparently not safe enough."

"Well, I have a suggestion," I said. "A plan, in fact."

Megan crossed her arms. "If it's taking on the emperor and getting revenge on your brother, count me out. I plan on catching a ship and making my way to a fishing island. Maybe even hunt for the unknown lands. Wherever it was the wizards disappeared to."

"I would rather face our enemies," I said. "But you would rather run away."

"It's not running away! It's survival. Your plan sounds like charging straight toward certain death."

I grabbed the doll from the floor. "Gregum poked a pin through each of the dolls to remember how he stuck a blade in each of our friends."

Megan took the doll from me and stared at it. "You already told us about his poking habit."

"It's a sign of the lengths they will go to hunt you down," I said. "Both of you. I don't believe we'll be safe anywhere in all of Ellos. And we'd kind of stick out on a tiny island."

She was still rolling the doll around.

"I'm not saying we should face them directly," I said. "But Maestru Alesius suggested one person who could help us: Banderius."

"Banderius?" Thord asked. "I'm sure he, of all assassins, would be in hiding. Or dead."

"In hiding, yes," I said. "Dead, no. We'd know if he was dead. Corwin would gloat about it by paying every town crier to bleat out the news. Banderius is the greatest of all assassins."

"Are they after you, too?" Thord asked. I wasn't certain if there was a tone of accusal.

"They think I'm dead," I said. "There was an... an accident with the swan."

"So they aren't hunting for you?" Megan said. "But what, and excuse me for saying this, can a one-eyed assassin and two barely blooded assassins with death prices on them do?"

"Oh," I said. And I relished the moment as I reached up toward my face. "I'm not one-eyed."

I removed my patch.

11

THAT THING

Megan's eyes bulged like they were about to pop out of her skull. Thord's jaw dropped open, and he blinked several times.

I enjoyed their shock. Every second. I may have even chuckled.

"What is that!" Megan pointed.

I winked with my dragon eye. "It's my new eye."

"Absolutely amazing!" Thord said. "It glows. Can you see through it?"

"Yes," I answered. "In fact, I see farther and clearer through it than I do with the eye I was born with."

"But what is that thing?" Megan had edged further away from me as if my dragon eye would leap out of its socket and strike her.

I hadn't thought this moment through. How many lies was I prepared to tell? "Maestru Alesius gave it to me," I said. Oh, the falsehoods slipped off my tongue so very smoothly, but to explain where the eye really came from would let them know about Brax. And I didn't trust them with that information. Yet. "It was a graduation gift."

“Did he have it in a jar full of eyes in his study?” Megan asked.

“Yes,” I said. "Yes! Good guess." I nodded, trying to convince her and myself this was true. “But there was only one eye. He took it out of a small jar full of brine and helped me put it in. It burned at first, but then I could see light for the first time in years. And then I saw shapes, and finally my vision came clear. He said I was stronger because I'd graduated without the help of two eyes.”

“It’s so gray.” Thord stood close enough his apple-scented breath wafted over me. Living on a mountaintop and not having had a bath for two weeks meant I likely smelled rather ripe. I certainly didn’t give off the scent of apples and cinnamon! I stepped back, but he followed. “It’s not the same as your other one. The pupil. It’s... it’s like a lizard’s.”

“It’s not a lizard’s eye!"

"Well, where did Maestru Alesius get it from?" Megan asked. "Or did he form it out of some sort of magical, glowing clay?"

"He didn't tell me. He probably saw it in some bazaar during his recruitment journeys. You know how he liked to collect oddities. Helpful oddities, that is."

Megan had lost her fear, and both she and Thord were right up in front of me now like I was a bug they had just discovered. “It’s an interesting look,” she said. “It makes you stand out, though.”

“Yes, it does.” I had backed right into the wall. “I need to find a way to hide it—I mean other than the patch. That's too memorable in case someone is looking for me. And it blocks my vision.”

“There are charmers in the market," Megan said. "They’ll sell spells to change your eye color, so that might work. I can't even hazard a guess how long a charm would last, but the more you pay the stronger the charm."

"That's a good idea," I said. They were both leaning far too close. "Enough about my eye." I stepped to the side and got away from the wall and them. I pointed at the window. "Outside that window is a world full of people who would capture or kill us for a bounty. We are much stronger together than we are apart."

Megan looked at the doll in her hand. "He was really going to stick a pin in this once I was dead?"

I nodded.

"It would have saved me a lot of work if you'd killed him." She was squeezing the doll tightly now.

"I'm sorry. I messed up his face. So that's a start."

She stuffed the doll in the pocket of her cloak. "I'll keep this. And you might be right about Banderius; perhaps he'll be able to tell us how to avoid the emperor. I'll go as far as finding him and getting his advice." She winked at me. "There is one more reason to see him: I've heard he's incredibly handsome."

"I do hope that's true," I said. I surprised myself because I rarely made comments like that. Then again, I really didn't have any girl friends to share those sorts of thoughts with.

"He's old enough to have fathered either of you," Thord huffed. "How are we going to find this incredibly pretty assassin?"

I grabbed the second scroll. "Someone wrote his name on top of this, but the rest of the writing is in Oldtongue and none of us can read it. Even Maestru Alesius didn't know very much Oldtongue. The only person I know who could read it was Maestru Beatrix. But..." I let my answer hang there.

Megan and Thord glanced at each other. It was as if they knew something I didn't.

"What's that look mean?" I asked.

"She's alive," Thord said. "Librarians are surprisingly hard to kill."

"She survived?" My heart was thumping hard.

"Yes," Megan said. "That's what he's telling you. And she's in the safest place of all: she's hiding at the Library of Avenus."

"She's right here in the city!" I nearly shouted this. I wanted to clap with joy.

"Apparently librarians have a code that is even deeper and older than the assassins' oath," Thord said. He pushed a lock of his hair to the side of his forehead. "So they are protecting her. That protection doesn't extend to us. I asked."

"But how did you find her?"

"She found me," Thord said. "I went to the library to research islands."

"Islands?"

"We've spent the last few weeks dreaming up every imaginable way to hide from the Empire," he said. "I was digging into some older map scrolls, hoping to discover where the wizards fled to. Maestru Beatrix came right up and said, 'Thord, that's ten points off for a bad mask.' I never got high marks in disguise class."

"You barely passed," I said.

"Well, you don't have to rub salt in the wound." His laugh made his eyes light up. "Maestru Beatrix escaped the Red Fortress with only the clothes on her back and one book in her hand."

"Which book?" I practically spat the question out. "There

were thousands of books in her library, some of them amazingly rare. Which was the one she would save?"

"Only you would ask that question," Megan said. She had curled up her lip in a snide manner.

"I didn't ask her," Thord said. "We didn't talk long because it would arouse suspicion. But she promised to help in any way she can."

"We must see her. At once! At once." I couldn't keep the joy from my voice.

"Yes, yes," Megan said. "We'll go right now, but put your patch back on. We don't want people staring at you."

It only took a few moments for them to pack. Then I followed my classmates out the door.

12

TWO DROPS OF BLOOD

Megan charged down the stairs ahead of us, stomping the whole way. She wanted to be heard, and it worked: the noise drew the glances of several patrons. The innkeeper's eyes widened, and he stopped shining a brass goblet. He grinned, perhaps thinking of how he'd gotten money from all of us. Then he spit into the goblet and continued shining it.

He nearly spat again when Megan threw a dagger at him. It stuck below his right arm, making him drop the goblet, and pinned his shirt to a support post. His jaw flapped open, hiding his double chins.

Megan was over the counter in a heartbeat, her second dagger poked under his jaw.

"One word about us to anyone," she said, "and this blade will slide between your ribs and tickle your heart while you're lying in your greasy bed. I will wake you up for your death. Understand?"

He nodded very carefully, not wanting to cut his chin on the blade. Sweat was already dripping down his forehead.

She yanked her other dagger from the post, slid over the counter and led us out of the inn.

"Was that wise?" Thord said. "You displayed your skill with a dagger. People will guess you're an assassin and someone might come snooping after us. There's a lot of coin on our heads."

"It wasn't wise," she said without a pinch of regret. "But it sure felt good."

Thord shrugged, and I wondered if he'd been frustrated by dealing with her attitude for the last few weeks. "The library is this way." He pointed down the street.

"We're going to the market first," Megan replied. "Carmen needs a charm to hide that ugly eye of hers."

"It's not ugly!" I said, putting my hand up to my patch.

"I mean that wonderful, strange magical eye that attracts attention wherever you go." She gave me a grin as she spoke it.

"That's better," I said. "Charms can be dispelled, though. One warding cast on a doorway and the charm will vanish."

"Only the richest can afford a warding on their windows and doors," Megan said. "And we won't be going where the richest frolic. So the charm should hold. You have a few coins?"

I nodded and we walked briskly down the cobblestone street. Megan kept in the lead, and her whole demeanor suggested she wanted to get everything over with as quickly as possible. The street was so clean I assumed they hired night sweepers. After a few minutes of hard walking we came upon the market.

Even this area had a sense of order to it. The tents were in straight lines. Wagons filled with vegetables and herbs and a variety of wares had been carefully stationed beside each tent. Smoke wafted up from a few hundred cooking pots. It wouldn't have been shocking if even the smoke rose straight in the air in perfect columns.

I glanced around, taking in the sights. The smells made my stomach grumble, and I thought about finding a food wagon but Megan said, “Here’s one.” Without another word she pushed me into a tent decorated with a circled eye.

I was suddenly out of the bright sun and in a darkened smoky space, standing before an ancient crone with tan skin. She sat in a wooden wicker chair. “Both of you are welcome,” the woman said. I turned and saw that neither of my companions had followed me. Perhaps she was seeing double.

Or even more than double. Because as my vision adjusted, I noticed she had seven eyes. All of them were staring at me. I blinked and blinked again. No, I realized, the extra eyes had been tattooed on her cheeks, forehead and chin. Her real eyes glittered as if she were holding back a laugh.

“What brings you here, daughter?” Her voice was soft.

“I need a charm for this.” I removed my patch. She didn’t react at all, only beheld my dragon eye. She was quiet for several moments.

“It’s beautiful,” she whispered. There was a tone of awe to her words. “It’s the most beautiful eye I’ve ever, ever seen.”

“That’s kind of you to say.” I had only seen it in a looking glass on two occasions, and both times I got a chill. The eye began to hurt and my vision flashed for a moment, then I covered it with my hand and the pain went away. “I need a charm to disguise it. People will stare at it and in turn stare at me.”

“Yes. Yes. A charm,” she agreed. “That is exactly what you need: a powerful charm to hide such powerful magic.”

“It’s not magic,” I said.

"You know nothing," she answered. She made a motion and spoke a word in another language, then a befuddled look crossed her face. She gestured with her hand again, holding two fingers up, and spoke another word. She followed this by frowning, which made her face seem even more wrinkled. She closed her two real eyes, but the other five stared at me.

The hag reached into her shawl, came out with something sharp and, before I could move, stuck it in my arm.

"Ouch!" I said.

A large pin was quivering in my forearm.

"Needed and necessary," she said. She waited until drops of blood formed. She swiped one on her finger and placed it in a small metal bowl. The second drop she tasted.

"Its blood is in you," she said. "It's part of you." I wasn't certain what she meant, though I was beginning to suspect she knew this was a dragon's eye. "It's a burden for you, too," she added.

"It's not a burden. I need to cover it up and get on my way."

"You do, daughter." She mixed the other drop of blood with a powder, and when she was finished she traced a circle around my eye. She spoke a magical-sounding word: "*Oranu.*" And then she smiled and held up a mirror.

Both my eyes looked exactly the same. I hadn't seen my eyes like that since I was thirteen. "It worked," I said. "It really worked."

"Of course." She chuckled. "I am not a fraud, daughter. I am the thing that is real."

"Yes. Yes, you are. Will I need the ashes and blood every time I renew the charm?" I asked.

"Just speak this word: *Oranu*. It will bring the charm back and send the charm away."

"Thank you," I said. "Thank you." I reached into my pouch but she put up a withered hand.

"No. You have paid enough," she said.

"But I should pay you. It's proper!"

She shook her head, and her bristly long hair moved on her shoulders like twigs. Her neck was sinewy. "No. The gift was seeing your eye. Now go, daughter. Go."

Confused, but thankful, I stepped out of the tent and into the light.

Megan and Thord both examined me. "She did a wonderful job," Thord said. I liked the look on his face.

"For once I agree with Thord," Megan said. She smacked my shoulder hard enough to make me stagger, then looked me in the eye again. "And it doesn't come loose."

"It's a charm. It shouldn't!" I said, rubbing my shoulder.

"I was just testing." She then smacked Thord on the back, and he winced. "Now lead us to the library, bookworm."

13

HIDDEN IN MAPS

The Library of Avenus was an impressively large building with massive columns on either side of the doorway. A green garden thick with vines and walnut and olive trees surrounded the structure. Men and women were sitting on stone tables outside, drinking coffee or tea in steel mugs and reading bound books. Children were poring over scrolls with illustrations. Someone had created books for children!

Libraries were sacred to the Avenians. The citizens were said to be obsessively in love with stories and wrote down every tale they heard from all corners of Ellos, including the Akkad Empire. They stored them in this library.

"I could die here," I said.

"Don't be stupid," Megan gruffed. "It's just a big building for books. It's not like we'll find any good weapons inside. Now if it was a weaponry museum, you really could die there."

I wasn't certain whether she was attempting to be funny, so I gave a half chuckle.

"I don't know if Maestru Beatrix is here every day," Thord said as he led us through the open wooden doors.

The inside of the building was twice as impressive as the outside. The tall domed ceiling was made of transparent stone that let in light and brightened the rows and rows of books. Avenians in ragged togas and others in finery browsed through the selections or sat at reading tables. There were even more children inside. Three women and two men in gray robes sat behind a long round wooden desk in the library's center—the librarians.

"I really could die here," I said.

"This is why you had no friends in school," Megan said, though she smiled to let me know she was teasing. "Crazy statements like that scare sensible people away."

"But think of how all of our books at the Red Assassin School were locked away from the world," I said. "And here anyone can read them. Anyone can learn."

"I'm not certain you'd want everyone to know how to mix poisonous potions," Thord said. "Might put us out of business."

"Then again, it's not like we're in business anymore," Megan said. "Where's Maestru Beatrix?"

Thord glanced around. His hair was longer and a little unkempt, but that somehow complimented his face. He had a perfect nose.

I stopped staring at his nose.

"Well, last time I was in the maps section looking for islands to escape to and she just appeared. Let's try there." We followed him over to a section where the shelves were wider and the books much larger. I opened one giant book to discover it was jammed with full-color maps of the Akkad Empire. They were hand drawn and beautiful and represented hours and hours of labor for an artist. It still amazed me that anyone could pick any of these books up and flip through the pages. I found maps of the Akkad Desert, of the western mountain regions and stopped at a street map of Akkadium itself, the capital. Just knowing Corwin was in that impressive city, standing beside the emperor Sargon at the center of power for the Empire, made me shiver with anger.

And fear.

Because what were three assassins to the power of an empire? No more than pesky fleas. Vast resources were being used to hunt us down.

Maybe Megan was right about fleeing.

"The color comes from the pigment of the Beck cherries," a voice said beside me.

A familiar voice.

"Maestru Beatrix," I whispered and turned with a grin on my face. The grin faded when I saw that a man stood beside me. He had short dark hair and was clad in an Avenian-style gray toga.

"Oh, I'm sorry," I said. "I thought you were someone else."

"I am that someone else," he said; his voice continued to be familiar and feminine. "Look closer."

The face was rough, with a bulbous warty nose. There were no telltale signs I was staring at a mask. The eyes were green and twinkling with humor.

"Is... is that you?" I asked. "Maestru Beatrix?"

"Yes," she said. "I took ages to create this face and to perfect my man talk." Then she said, in a male voice, "These are the finest and most detailed maps in all of Ellos. I believe every outhouse in every country has been marked. That kind of detail can save your life and your bowels."

My eyes widened, and I barked out a laugh, then cut it

short, not wanting to attract attention. "I—I'm so happy to see you. To know you're alive!"

She grinned and her mask moved with the smile. "You are alive and you have two eyes," she said. "There must be an incredible story there."

"Yes, there is," I replied. "And you—you have a story, too."

"Oh, I have thousands," she said. Then, as she saw Megan and Thord step closer, she pointed. "You want to read the Grindenium Cycles," she said, using her male voice again. "Such good taste for such young minds. Follow me."

She led us through the stacks to a side room with what looked to be a special collection of books along the walls. Next to that was a pile of older, smaller books with a sign that read: THESE BOOKS ARE A GIFT FOR YOU. TAKE ONE. Did that mean I could just walk out with a book?

Maestru Beatrix closed the heavy oak door.

"All three of you, alive," she said. "I am so very thankful." She hugged me first, her short arms tight around me. It made me realize that she was a head shorter than me. She gave off a pleasant scent of sandalwood. She then squeezed Thord in a similar hug, and he made her look even smaller. And finally she wrapped her arms around Megan, who returned the hug, albeit stiffly. "The three of you are such a wonderful sight to see. Please have a seat."

We sat at the rectangular wooden table in sturdy wooden chairs. There were several piles of loose stalk paper in front of us for note-taking. This was some sort of study room.

It was still odd to see Maestru Beatrix with a male face, and I marveled at the detail and how alive the mask looked.

"You keep staring at me, Carmen," she said. Then she stuck a finger in the air. "Oh, this!" She peeled off a mask of such thin material it was almost impossible to see. Her face —her real face—was a comfort. I had grown up visiting the library, and she was the closest I'd had to having a mother figure in my life. I relaxed as though part of me hadn't believed it was her until I saw her real face.

"That's a marvelous mask," Thord said. "What's it made of?"

"My own special mixture. It feels like a second skin and sweat goes through it. The best part is you can eat with the mask on. I have to wear it almost all the time, so it needed to be flawless."

"What's in the mixture?" I asked.

She gave me a great big grin. Her smiles always magically made me smile, too. "You are consistently inquisitive, Carmen, but we librarians have our secrets. Someday, if you're good, I may teach you."

"It's so wonderful to see your face again," I said.

"And to see all of yours." She stared at each of us in turn, and the look of warmth and caring she gave us was almost overwhelming. "The fates have been kind. Do tell me how you escaped."

We told our tales. She nodded, looking thoughtful and not interrupting with questions. She'd always been gifted at listening. And as I spoke, I felt this sense of protection, as if a warm blanket were being lowered over me. She would know exactly what path we should take.

"I learned a bit of Thord and Megan's story," Maestru Beatrix said. "Thord was kind enough to relate portions to me. But you three have survived the greatest blow our guild has ever been dealt, and you should be proud of that." She tapped the table. "And you should flee as fast and as far as your feet will carry you."

"Flee?" I said. "But they killed so many of us. Our fortress was sacked. And they—they burned your books."

"Books can be replaced," she said solemnly. "Knowledge can be rediscovered. But the dead cannot return to life." She shook her head. "Three young assassins can't face the might of the Akkad Empire. The wizards tried and failed partly due to our pursuit of them. I am lucky that the librarians of Avenus will hide me, but they can't hide you. And no amount of money will keep you safe."

"Just before he died, Maestru Alesius made me promise to find Banderius and ask for aid," I said.

"Truly?" Her face was hard to read. "That braggart did not spend much time in my library. He believed he already knew everything."

"But would he aid us?" I asked. "To set things right. To perhaps somehow restore the guild?"

"Restoring the guild is a hundred-year project. Let it go. What you need is to survive, first and foremost. And I am puzzled by Alesius's suggestion. Why Banderius? I admit I am biased against that man. He burned a library book."

"He did?" I nearly spat, I was so shocked.

"What's so bad about that?" Megan asked. I shot her a glare, but she was smiling. Oh, another attempt at a joke!

"Yes. He burnt it. Though he was thirteen at the time, so I should forgive him. One day I might."

"Then why would Maestru Alesius suggest him?" Thord asked.

"Alesius rarely gave up on any of his students," she said, looking directly at me. He hadn't ever given up on me, despite the fact I was blind in one eye. I wondered if he'd had to fight hard to keep me in the school. "Banderius is a strong supporter of the guild, and despite his bravado he's saved more than one assassin from the gallows. He also is likely the only assassin who could out-think your brother." She let out her breath slowly, as though not certain how to say the next words. "Perhaps he is your best chance at survival."

"As long as we stick together we have a better chance," Thord said. And he put his hand on my shoulder as he said this. His palm was warm and my skin began to tingle there. But then I saw he had his hand on Megan's shoulder, too. She gave him a frown and he removed both hands.

"Every country in Ellos would be afraid to anger the Empire by harboring you," Maestru Beatrix said. "Killing an assassin is a way to get on good terms with Emperor Sargon."

"We'll do our best to associate only with people who hate the Empire, then," Megan said.

"Our problem is finding Banderius," I said. "These are the scrolls I stole from Gregum." I showed her the list of assassins that included the crossed-out names.

She read it and tears filled her eyes, though none ran down her cheeks. "Ah, one is too many. Several of these were students I taught. The emperor is finding us so very quickly."

"Well, he does have my brother's help," I said. "But I think this scroll might hint as to where Banderius is hiding. We can't read it because it's in Oldtongue."

I handed her the scroll. She opened it and read the old words with what looked like ease. Then she started at the top again.

"What does it say?" I asked when she seemed to be reading it a third time.

"It's a recipe," she said. "A very peculiar recipe. Here are the ingredients: Eye of Hokum Flower, Skull of Bardur Fox, Berry of Black Lotus Vine. It's not clear what it makes—a potion, a poison or a hearty soup. And at the bottom are the words: *the messenger has one arm. The blade will come.*" She frowned. "It's nonsensical. I've solved every riddle of the Stone Lions, but this is a puzzle I can't fathom. It looks like a random list."

"Perhaps if we get the ingredients, we somehow will find Banderius," I said. "It could be..." I faltered. "I'm not sure how."

"Do you think Gregum understood what it meant?" Megan asked.

"Never," Maestru Beatrix said. "He was horrible with languages. But Corwin was gifted at languages, and perhaps he could have read it with the help of the emperor's translators. But even if they could translate it—it makes no sense."

Thord cleared his throat. "It makes perfect sense," he said. We turned our gazes to him. "It's not a recipe—it's a map. And I know exactly where Banderius is."

14

EVEN FURTHER THAN DEIRA

"Don't just stand there gloating." Megan gave him a shove that nearly knocked him off his chair. "Tell us."

He playfully rubbed his shoulder. "I'm very familiar with each of those ingredients. And they only come from one place: my homeland of Woden. The Hokum flower, the Bardur fox, the berry of the Black Lotus vine. They are all from the fields around the city of Gudheim."

"You come from Woden?" Megan asked. "I thought there were only sheepherders up there."

"There's nothing wrong with sheepherders," he replied. "Be sure to thank one next time you sit down to a plateful of mutton. And don't ever make fun of my home country."

He said this last line with a hint of menace. Since I never knew where I came from, I never felt an allegiance to any kingdom. My allegiance was to the place I grew up. "What do these ingredients have to do with Woden?"

"My mother ran the gardens of Gornia." He paused as if he expected us to recognize this supposedly famous place. "Well, they are well known in Gudheim."

"I'm sure many boring things are," Megan said.

This got a frown out of Thord. “Anyway, I believe this list is showing us where Banderius is.”

“It’s a complicated way to find him,” I said. I leaned on the table. "Very few people would know where those ingredients were from."

“He was a master of riddles,” Maestru Beatrix said. “And he had an odd sense of humor. Though the berry of the Black Lotus vine and the petals of the Hokum flower are used in soporific potions. So it is a riddle that many assassins might figure out. He also knows every nook and cranny of Ellos, so it doesn’t surprise me he'd be familiar with Gudheim.”

“So you think he sent this out to fellow assassins?” I said.

Maestru Beatrix thought for a moment. “Yes. This ‘recipe map’ could have been retrieved from the home of a dead assassin—someone Banderius knew personally. And Corwin is trying to decipher it right now, or he has deciphered it and is hunting for Banderius. His death would be a prize kill, like when Sargon had the great wizard Davak crucified on an oak tree. That was the final blow to any strong wizard resistance. Banderius’s death would be the end of hope for any living assassins.”

“Then we have to get to him before Corwin,” I said. “It's our only chance to receive his counsel and perhaps the help of his sword. Plus, who knows how long he'll wait in Woden. If no one comes, Banderius might choose to vanish forever.”

“But Woden is a full month’s march northwards,” Megan said. “And that’s only if we don’t stop to sleep.”

I knew it wasn't a month's march for me. But Brax couldn't carry three passengers. He didn't even want to have one.

“Maestru Beatrix, what should we do?” I asked.

“I am not your maestru any longer,” she said. “You could

follow the wisdom of the remaining wizards who hired boats and sailed away to the west."

"None of the wizards returned," Megan said. "No one returns from those seas."

"Yes, there's that," Beatrix answered. "Your best course is to gather information. Banderius is an egotistical man, perhaps the most egotistical I've known. And I'm including your brother when I say that." She looked at me. "But Banderius is brilliant and if there is anyone who can uncover secret places for you to hide, he would be the one. He swore the Red Oath to aid guild assassins, so I'm confident he'll help you."

"We still have the problem of two months' travel," Thord said. "If Corwin is looking for him, he'll just fly there on a swan in a few days."

"I may be able to solve that problem," Maestru Beatrix said. "At least for two of you." She pulled her mask back on again. I was amazed at how quickly it changed shape to make her look like a man. An ugly man! She even broadened her shoulders. "Come with me, it's a walk."

The three of us followed her out of the room. I was last, so I paused and took the top book from the pile. It was titled *Bartum's Revenge* and was small enough to fit into one of my cloak pockets. I knew nothing about it or the author, but it felt good to be carrying it near my heart.

We followed Maestru Beatrix out of the library. She was in a secretive mood and she led us through the streets without telling us a word about our destination. She stopped to buy a fresh and wonderful-smelling loaf of bread and four sausage pastries. Then we left Avenus by the same gate I'd entered. One guard nodded at Beatrix, and I wondered what contacts and bonds she had formed. He already knew her by this face. Would she have to wear that mask for the rest of her life?

We walked on and when Megan and Thord had fallen a few steps behind, Beatrix said, "I wasn't aware that Maestru Alesius kept a magical eye in a jar."

I blushed. I didn't want to lie to her, so I said, "He didn't. But I can't tell you where it's from."

"I'm just glad you have it," she answered.

In time we came to a large white stone farmhouse. Behind it was a two-story manger made of the same impressive stone—the barn must have cost more than many of the homes in Avenus! They had made all the fencing of similar alabaster stone.

"One librarian owns this." Maestru Beatrix gestured around her.

"A librarian is this rich?" Thord said.

"There's no law against librarians becoming wealthy," Maestru Beatrix replied. "And we do know how to invest our meager pay."

She removed her mask and led us into the barn. There were several impressively muscled horses inside eating at a bale of hay. They had that horse smell to them, which I always had enjoyed. It meant travel. There was very little manure in the barn. Perhaps the Avenians did not want a single drop of mud or manure to hit the floor. It was almost an obsession.

"These are racehorses!" Megan said. The look on her face was of such shock. "There is more wealth inside the building than outside."

"Well, they are champion horses," Beatrix said. "They won the Green Dome Races three times in a row."

Megan's eyes grew even wider. "And, and we will get these horses?" she said. "They must fly like devils."

"Never, by Belaz!" Maestru Beatrix said. "Your mounts are waiting up above us." She easily climbed a wide ladder on the wall that led into the loft. "Ah, there you are, my sweeties."

Something stirred at the sound of her voice and made the boards creak, and I got the odd feeling that there was a dragon up there.

I was the next up, and once I stepped off the ladder and turned, I shuddered. There were four black angry eyes staring at me and two razor-sharp beaks pointed my way.

Two giant black guild swans. They glared at us with their intelligent dark eyes. One lifted its wing and scratched at her side with her beak, all the while keeping an eye on us.

"I was able to rescue these from the fortress," Maestru Beatrix said. "I escaped on Bolt here while Maestru Arvid battled the Immortals." This swan had a white grouping of feathers on his chest that looked like a lightning bolt. I remembered him from all the time I'd spent mucking out the swannery. "Master Arvid was supposed to leave with me. But... well, he died defending his swans." She pointed at the second swan. "Naga followed me. I also saved two eggs that Arvid had packaged."

"Where are those?" Thord asked.

She smiled, showing wrinkles. "In a very safe place."

Thinking of Beatrix escaping on the back of Bolt reminded me of an unsolved puzzle.

"Thord said you brought only one book with you," I said. "I really want to know which book out of your whole library was the most valuable."

"Ohh..." Beatrix blushed. "*The Mountains of NeverNone.*"

"What?" I said. "An adventure story?"

"I wasn't finished it. In fact, I was reading it when the Immortals charged into my library. So I had to bring it with me. The ending was worth it." She gestured toward the swans. "Anyway, the important thing is that Bolt and Naga are here. Neither was imprinted as a youth and so they will welcome any rider." I took a step closer and Bolt snapped at me. "Well, most riders. I guess there's something about you that upsets them." She looked me over. "It surprises me. They've been friendly, well as friendly as swans can get."

"Perhaps it was something I had for breakfast," I said. I guessed they could smell the dragon on me.

Maestru Beatrix gave a chunk of the loaf to Megan and another to Thord. Naga lowered her head so Megan could scratch it and feed her. I stayed out of beak range. Thord began feeding Bolt.

When the swans had finished their bread, Maestru Beatrix offered each of us a sausage pastry, and I swallowed mine in seconds. I could have eaten twenty.

"So you are offering these to us, to fly to Gudheim and then return them to you?" Megan said.

"These will belong to you from now on. A librarian has no use for a swan. I don't know what Carmen will do if they don't allow her to ride double." She looked at me.

"Well," I said. "I may have the answer to that. But I think I should show you."

15

THE SURPRISE

We bid farewell to Maestru Beatrix, who hugged each of us in turn. I didn't want to let her go. She had been one of the first people I could remember hugging me when I was a child. And our hug lasted longer than the others, though I finally released my arms.

"Safe journeys," she said, patting my shoulder. "You know where I am now, which is dangerous for me, but I don't believe I'm being hunted. The librarian is not as important as the trained assassins. Foolish that they think that way, isn't it?" She tapped her forehead. "There is nothing more dangerous than knowledge. I trust you will not betray me even under torture."

"Never," I said, sounding much more convinced than I felt. We had taken classes on how to keep secrets under duress, but that was far different from actually being under duress.

"I am glad you found each other," she said. "You are worth a lot dead, so be careful who you talk to."

"We will," Thord said. "Thank you for everything."

"You are welcome, and do come visit me anytime you want. I'll always have a book for you. And time."

And then she was down the ladder and gone. We waited until nightfall to open the loft gates, and both Thord and Megan mounted their swans and flew out. I closed the gate behind them and made my way outside.

As I walked toward the hills Thord and Megan followed me, high in the air, their outlines visible against the stars. Even with my dragon eye they were hard to see. The swans were perhaps the most powerful tool an assassin had. It meant we could strike a target at any location. And, as long as the moon wasn't full, we could hide in the sky.

I climbed one incline then another, getting sweatier and dirtier and a little more tired. The darkness had altered how the landscape looked so that I wasn't certain which copse of trees Brax was hiding in. I searched until I saw a familiar smaller hill and signaled for my companions to come to me. The swans swooped down silently and landed without even snapping a twig. Thord and Megan dismounted and staked the reins to the ground. There wasn't even a squawk from Bolt and Naga.

"Where is this secret you've hidden?" Megan asked. "Is it some sort of chariot?"

"Come along," I said, staying ahead of them to avoid any more questions. Even with their night vision training they would only spot half the things I could with my dragon eye. I ducked under several branches, crossed a gulley and stopped before the pile of leaves that Brax had hidden under. "There!" I said with a flourish. I gestured like a magician at a traveling show.

"There what?" Thord asked.

"There!" I said again. And pointed at the pile, which

refused to move. Was he asleep? What happened to those famous dragon senses?

"I didn't tramp out here for nothing." Megan had crossed her arms. "What kind of game are you playing?"

"But... But..." I said. I kicked at a few of the leaves. "It's not a game."

"It's a stupid game," she corrected. "We are—"

"Have you brought me food?" His voice was deep and echoed in every direction. I stared at the leaves.

"No, Brax," I said. "You're not being funny."

"I am hungry," he said. "I want food. They smell rather scrumptious."

"What is this!" Thord said. "Tell us? Who is your friend?" Both looked way more frightened and angry than I had intended. It was supposed to be a grand revelation.

"I'll eat the boy first," Brax said.

"These are my friends, Brax!" I took a few steps toward the pile of leaves.

"I only promised to protect you. Everything else is food."

"Enough!" I flipped the largest branch out of the way.

He wasn't there.

Both swans hissed in anger. I turned and saw what was bothering them. Brax was behind the three of us. He had somehow snuck up on us and was bending down, looking like he would pounce on my friends.

Thord and Megan, seeing my alarmed look, both spun around. Thord reeled back, reaching for his short sword and shouting, "Sweet mother of Hecab!"

Brax opened his mouth and plunged toward him. I rushed to get in between them but knew I'd be far too late.

Thord tripped over a root and fell just as Brax snapped his jaws only an inch from his face. Then Brax grinned.

"I was just toying with you," he said. "With all of you. I've already had a deer."

Thord was up on his feet and backing away. "Is—is that what I think it is?"

"It's a Scythian dragon," Megan said. She had not put her daggers away. "And it talks."

"Oh, look, it's an assassin girl-child and it talks," Brax said. "Of course, I talk."

I stood between my friends and Brax. "That was not funny."

"I laughed. That's all that matters. My guess is you wanted to surprise your friends and show them your pet. So, being a good pet, I surprised them."

"He—he is talking like he knows you," Megan said.

"These are not the smartest assassins, are they?" Brax waved his wings, and the swans made another hiss of fear but they did not attempt to fly away, so strong was their training. "I guess they killed the smart ones first."

"This is Brax," I said. "And he's right—I meant to surprise you."

"Oh, it surprised me," Megan said. She still was pale, and it wasn't just the moonlight. "I think I aged ten years."

"I may require new underclothing," Thord added.

"You have a lot to explain," Megan began, then she pointed at Brax. "He's missing an eye." She looked at me. "You've gained an eye."

"Oh, this one is smarter than she appears," Brax said. He clapped his talons together.

"Yes. I have his eye," I answered. I was about to launch into the story when Brax interrupted.

"Let me tell them. She found me in a cave where I was bound by a magical chain. She freed me with her daggers in exchange for my eye and the right to ride on my back until her brother is dead. Then she will be my servant for a year. So, if you are here to help her with killing her brother, I am your newest, closest and dearest scaly friend. Does that about sum everything up?" He looked at me.

"Yes," I said.

"How did you free him with a dagger?" Megan asked. And here all this time I'd thought her looks meant she wasn't a quick thinker. Another stupid assumption on my part.

"The daggers were warded Uriken blades," I explained. "They were the actual gift I received from Maestru Alesius." I took a dagger out and cut through a six-inch-thick branch. It fell to the ground.

"If we are to work together there will be no secrets," Megan said. "At least not ones like this." She gestured toward Brax.

"Yes, I agree," Thord said. "No secrets. No more hidden dragons or daggers. Anything you've forgotten to tell us? How about your eye, is it special?"

"I can see in the dark."

"Is there anything else it can do?" Thord asked.

I drew back. I didn't want to talk about the visions I'd seen. Or the sense that I sometimes saw other worlds. "No. Not that I know of."

"You are not the same person I knew at school," he said. There was a ring of wonder to his voice. "You have changed a great deal in a short while. I almost don't know you."

"I think," I said, "we are all getting to know each other for the first time. And, if you are ready, I suggest we begin flying and then we can continue this discussion."

16

AN IMPORTANT QUESTION

The swans would not fly near enough to Brax so that the three of us could talk, so we took the lead. Thord and Megan fell in a long distance behind us, but only a few wing lengths from each other. I couldn't hear their discussion, but whenever I glanced over my shoulder, they were talking.

"I found a book for us," I said, deciding to start my own conversation.

"A book? You got a book?"

"Yes," I said. "Don't sound so surprised. I like reading, too. It's from the Avenus library."

"You stole a book from the library?" Brax said. "All of Avenus will hunt you down and skin you alive for that evil crime."

"No, they won't," I said. "The book was free."

At this he was silent for several moments, though by the way his head moved I guessed he was trying to make sense of what I'd said. I wished I could see his expression. "A free book! The Avenians are wondrous people. For humans, that is. Show it to me at once."

I pulled it from my cloak and leaned ahead, keeping one hand tight on his neck spike. I held it in front of his right eye. "*Bartum's Revenge*? By Ptolemak! There is not a better adventure writer in all of Ellos. This is wonderful news."

"I thought you'd like it," I said, though I actually had no idea what his tastes in reading were. I slid the book into my knapsack.

"Well, life is worth living again," he said. He cleared his throat, which made his body rumble below me. "When you were in Avenus did you see a witch with stringy white hair?"

"Yes," I said. "How did you know?"

"Oh, it was a guess," he answered. Apparently winging through the air at a good clip didn't tire him out, as he could talk easily. "A good guess, that's all. Plus you have a charm on your eye and the spell still hangs about you. I recognize that type of stink."

"You can smell magic?" This dragon ability wasn't in any of my books.

"Of course. I can smell a number of things."

I didn't know if he was hinting about my smell, which I hoped wasn't that bad. I'd said the word that removed the eye charm because there was no use in having it on while we were in the air. "But how did you know what the witch looked like?"

He laughed. A dragon laugh is so throaty, and his long neck echoed with the sound. "They all look like crones. Probably they have charms that make them appear ancient and decrepit. A comely young woman could only sell spells and knickknacks to men. An old witch can sell them to everyone."

"That makes sense," I said. I was pretty certain she was as ancient as she'd seemed. One thing assassin school taught was that eyes could be easily fooled. But my dragon eye? I didn't think so.

"Do you trust these other two?" He motioned with his head toward Thord and Megan. I looked back, wondering if his question would be carried along the wind to them.

"Yes," I said. I wouldn't have had the same answer a few weeks ago at school. Not that Thord was someone I couldn't trust, but I had been suspicious of his motive for being kind. But now that I'd had time to reflect, I saw that it was just kindness. That was all. Did I feel more trusting now I had two eyes? And Megan had been a viper toward me, toward everyone sometimes. But she didn't seem to be the type to betray me.

Again, I wondered if it was just having the dragon eye that made me confident enough to trust them. Or was it having been deceived so horribly by my brother that I knew what true betrayal was?

"You are thinking deep thoughts," Brax said. "You're not good at that."

"I'm beginning to see why you were banished from your country. I have a feeling it was your snarkiness."

He laughed again, though it sounded hollow.

"And I do trust them," I said. "Both of them came to warn me the night our school was attacked. They could have fled without doing that, but they risked their lives to see if I was safe."

"That's something then," Brax said.

"I do have one more question," I said, realizing I was using my left hand to hold on to his spike. "My hand healed incredibly quickly. But only hours ago acid had burned right through the flesh. Do you know why this would be? You heal quickly, too."

"I don't know exactly why that would happen. And my

only answer is that you are very, very lucky to have my eye in your head. Now, let me concentrate on which direction is the shortest to Gudheim."

We flew for hours. It was such a perfect and smooth flight. It still didn't feel natural to be on a dragon's back and viewing the world from such a height. It was like being a god. It was more exciting than anything I could imagine.

But I eventually yawned. I couldn't remember the last time I'd slept or even rested properly. But sleep was not in the cards for me, because we had to go as far and as fast through the night as we could.

As the sun rose the world below became more visible. We found a landing spot in a copse of trees that had been cleared in the center. The swans were still not comfortable around Brax, and he looked at them and spoke, "I don't eat swans. They taste horrible." Naga hissed at him but they settled down after that.

"They really do taste worse than horrible," he continued more softly.

"You ate a swan?" I asked.

"Shh." He lifted a talon to his lips. "Not so loud. They're sensitive about being eaten. Like I said, they're not worth the crunching, and those little wing bones stick in the throat. Now mutton—I can eat mutton all day long and will do so soon. But first I sleep."

He lay down and pulled a wing over his head to shade his face and was asleep within moments.

"He is quite the creature," Megan said when I joined her and Thord. The way she was looking at him made me think of the mercenaries who had viewed him as something to chop up, skin and sell.

"He's more than just a creature," I said.

"I see that. Don't get too sensitive about it."

"He's changed you," Thord said. "It's very curious how much more confident you are."

"I was always confident." I felt like standing up and shouting that. Thord and Megan exchanged a glance as if I was going mad.

"He's also an incredible asset," Thord added. "We're lucky to have him on our side."

"I'm an asset, too," Megan said. She sounded upset that Brax was getting Thord's attention. Or was I reading that wrong?

"You do breathe fire, that is true," Thord said.

She flicked fallen leaves at him. They had clearly bonded in the last two weeks. I wondered what else they had done?

"This incredible asset has to sleep." Megan stretched out on the mossy ground using her knapsack as a pillow.

"I'll unsaddle the swans and feed them the last of the bread," Thord said. "And keep first watch."

I stretched out beside Megan, who was already snoring. She snored! At least she had that tiny imperfection.

It was not long before I joined her in sleep. I didn't know if I snored. I'd have to ask Brax later.

17

THE COLD OF WODEN

The land of Woden was the furthest country to the north, and it took five nights of hard flying to get there. We stopped on the third night near a stream, so we could wash ourselves while the swans fed on trout and salamanders. Brax contented himself with an otter. Thord wandered further down the river to give Megan and me privacy.

"You don't smell as bad," Brax said once we were up in the air again.

I didn't talk to him again for at least an hour.

As we crossed the border between Trusk and Woden the air grew colder and the land rockier. After a few hours of shivering and staring down at mountaintops, I began to dream about diving into any hot springs I spotted. The country matched Thord. He was as strong as this land.

"The mountain goats are stringy here," Brax said. "This is an ugly place."

A skinny bearded goat was standing on a mountain path a great distance below us. It likely hadn't seen fresh grass for months.

"You'll just have to eat three," I said.

Thord gave a shout to tell us he would take the lead, and we followed him for the next few hours, passing over torch-lit villages and darkened farmlands. It looked like a stoic land with stoic people. I wrapped my cloak tighter around me. They would have to be stoic to put up with this cold.

Thord pointed down several times then went into a steep dive. At first I thought he saw something and was aiming toward it, but after a few loops and further dives, I realized he was showing off.

"He is a man of little brain," Brax said.

"Don't say that!" I said.

"Sorry." There wasn't even a pinch of contrition in his voice. "You're right. I shouldn't say *man*. I should say *boy*."

We landed on a large hill topped with a gray stone barn-like building. A stone fence surrounded it and outlined several pens. On the other side of that fence was a flock of sheep—all of them ran as far away as possible from Brax until they reached the end of their enclosure. They turned to face him, watching nervously and staying still. One let out a meager *baaa.*

"Oh, food," Brax said. He rubbed his talons together. "They look fatter than the goats."

"Eat none of them." Thord walked up to Brax and came close to pointing right up his nostril. "Those belong to my father."

"This is your family's land?" Megan asked.

"Yes, I grew up here with my eight brothers. Last born means last to inherit." He stared into Brax's eyes. "If you are going to eat sheep, fly over to Oin's farm." He jabbed a thumb over his shoulder.

"You dare to tell me what to do?" Brax drew himself up so that he dwarfed Thord. But Thord didn't back down.

"I'm not telling," Thord answered in a voice that very much sounded like he was telling. "I'm asking politely as your friend."

"We aren't friends." Brax snorted out a small flame as he said this.

"As your companion, then. As someone who has the same goals as you. Please don't eat my father's sheep." Thor jabbed his thumb over his shoulder again. "Oin deserves to lose a few sheep. I hear his great-great-grandfather killed a dragon."

Brax held his face stern, then smiled. "I'll eat his sheep first, but don't leave me here too long. I have a big stomach."

I gestured to the tall barn, hoping to distract both of them from their *I'm tougher than you* display. The building had what looked to be living quarters on the top. "Is this your home?"

"No!" Thord said.

"I didn't mean to offend you," I said. Megan laughed. Was I missing something?

"I guess you wouldn't know, since you grew up in the Red Fortress," he said. "This is our sheep hutch. My brothers and I would take turns staying here in winter to feed the sheep. Our family home is much, much larger and warmer, and it's in the valley below us."

"Oh, I see," I said. "I don't know a lot about sheep herding."

"Why would you?" he said. "The swans and Brax can hide in the barn. It'll be big enough for them, assuming Brax can fit through the door. He can have one side and the swans the other and maybe they won't fight."

"It wouldn't be a fight," Brax said. "It'd be a feathery massacre."

Bolt and Naga hissed at him and he grinned.

"You be good." I wagged a finger.

"That's not in our agreement," he replied. His grin didn't fade.

Brax did fit through the door. I followed him into the barn, which was surprisingly pleasant smelling. Well, if one liked the smell of straw. Each of us bunked down near our mounts and fell asleep.

An hour or two later Thord shook my shoulder. "It's time to get up."

I rubbed the sleep out of my eyes and nodded. The dragon eye was always the first to focus, and it outlined him in a red glow. I stretched.

"Just to make this clear," Brax said without opening his eye. "You're going down into a dangerous city populated by smelly barbarians, and you're leaving the fire-breathing dragon behind. Is that wise?"

"There isn't another way," I said. "You can't flap around there during daylight. You know that. They'd put a thousand bolts through you. And it's hard to sneak around with a dragon hanging over your shoulder."

"Yes, but I wanted to point out that I won't be able to hear your sad hoots for help."

"The three of us should be safe enough together." I made sure my daggers were held properly in their sheathes. "But I appreciate your worry."

"I'm not worried. If you die, our contract is broken and I am free." He still hadn't opened his eye.

I didn't want to say anything else so I snuck out of the barn, following my companions. Thord led us down a long grassy hill, pointing out landmarks as we traveled. He and his brothers had spent most of their youth hunting and playing among these hills and rocks. All the other assassins had memories of the places they'd grown up. Megan had

Allessaria and stories about the endless waves of the eastern coast. But Corwin and I only remembered the fortress. It was the only place we had called home.

And he had burned out its insides and left the walls covered with student blood. I put my hands on my daggers.

“We can’t visit my parents,” Thord said as he pointed at a long house nestled between two hills. "But that’s my home. I'd give my left arm for another bowl of her mutton stew." I could see why he’d been offended when I thought he'd been living in the barn. This place was large enough to house a small army. He came from what counted as wealth in Woden. There were torches lit out front, and it had a chimney that rose high into the air. The place looked so warm and inviting. It wasn’t hard to imagine some breakfast porridge bubbling in the hearth. “Corwin may have figured out who our families are and where they live," Thord continued. "The Empire's agents are likely watching for my return.”

He glanced longingly as we strode by. When we were over the next hill, the city of Gudheim stood below us. It was not anywhere near as impressive as Avenus or Myra. The protective wall was high and wide, but it was constructed of wood. It guarded a massive collection of huts that looked like a giant had plucked them up and popped them down any which way. I didn't know if there were actual streets in the city. “We are getting close—prepare yourselves,” Thord said. He pulled a wax mask out of his pocket and placed it over his face, waiting for the heat of his body to make it stick. “Someone might recognize me,” he said.

"It looks like you have a pimple," Megan said, and she pressed her finger against his face. "There, got rid of that air bubble. That mask is a big improvement on your real face."

"You said that last time," Thord said. "But thanks."

Megan didn't bother with a mask, and I whispered my charm to make my eye look human.

The sentries were at a lookout point on the wall. By the way they were chatting with each other and sharing what I assumed was warm mead, they didn't seem to expect any type of attack. We waited until Thord gave a signal and then we scaled the wall easily, threw ourselves silently over the ramparts and climbed down the other side into a backyard pen of one hut. A pig, completely nonplused, watched as we stepped through the muck. "Oh, wonderful! Pig poop," Megan said. "People will smell us before we can sneak up on them."

She was right. The gloop we'd stepped in was thick and stuck to my boots. It made it hard to walk.

"We'll fit right in," Thord said. He put his hand on her shoulder, and I did feel a moment of envy. "Pig poop is the smell of home for me. Sheep dung, too."

"What a romantic notion," she said. And she leaned toward him.

"So where are we going?" I worked myself between them, so that all three of us were walking side by side down an alley.

"Well," Thord said. "The scroll mentioned Eye of Hokum Flower, Skull of Bardur Fox, and Berry of Black Lotus Vine. That vine you brushed on that gate was a Black Lotus vine."

"Is it poisonous?" I asked.

"Only if you eat three bales. So all the ingredients are here in Gudheim. Plus there was that little riddle: *The messenger has one arm. The blade will come.* We just have to find the messenger with one arm and Banderius will come to us."

"Do you know anyone with one arm?" Megan asked.

"That's the hard part," he admitted. "Every man and woman carries a blade in this town and tends to hack away after the slightest insult. We have a horde of one-armed men and women."

"Then how will we figure out who it is?" I asked. The manure had hardened enough so that my feet didn't stick to the path.

"Oh, I may have the answer to that," he said.

"You're enjoying this, aren't you?" I hadn't realized that he had a mischievous side. He was always so serious in class.

"I am. I was rarely two steps ahead of you two."

"Only because you live here," Megan said. "If it was anywhere else, we'd be using you to wipe the floor. Intellectually speaking, that is."

"Which is why I am so enjoying this moment. I'm enjoying it so much I almost don't want to say this: here we are."

We turned the corner around a hut. A giant one-armed man stood before us.

18

THE WOLF FIGHTER

The twelve-foot-tall man's hand was stretched toward the rising sun as though in welcome.

He didn't move. That was because he was made of wicker that had been banded together to form his arms and legs and body. He was wearing trousers made from living leaves. His anguished face had been carved from the wood of a large tree.

"I give you Tor," Thord said. "He who lost his arm to the wolf that swallowed the moon. He who saved the world from being eaten."

"This is a statue of a god?" I asked.

"Yes," Thord said. "One of many. Gods, that is. And we burn it on the first day of winter because that's when he climbed down to Knifheim and, when the snow melted, he returned with wheat kernels. The priests and priestesses rebuild him every spring."

Megan reached up to touch the giant. "So he'll tell us where Banderius is?" She pulled on his hand. "He seems kind of quiet. And woody."

"My guess is someone in there will help us." Thord pointed

at the long house behind the statue. It was surrounded by so many wooden gods I assumed it was a religious building. It was timber-framed, the walls green with growing moss, and the roof was thatched. Ravens sat in a row along the crest of the house. "We'll go inside and pray. Then—and I'm crossing my fingers as I say this—our answer will come."

"Pray?" I asked. The only deity I'd ever prayed to was Belaz, the goddess of assassins.

"Yes, pray," Thord said, in a somewhat lecturing tone. "That is what people do in holy houses. It won't hurt, I promise. Follow me."

He led us through the open wooden doors and into a large central room. It was dark and the only light came from a fire in a central hearth. The smell of smoke and the stink of something dead hit me and even though I'd been trained to handle powerful smells, I had to gird myself. This was a holy house?

"There are many sacrifices here," Thord explained. "Sometimes they leave the bodies."

"Human?" Megan asked.

"Not until harvest, so we're safe. Unless there's been some catastrophe. Failed crops. Drought. Sheep sickness. Then we pick a sacrifice." He smiled as he said this last bit. Was he kidding?

A bald man in a long hooded robe nodded to us. His head had a score of tattoos that looked like they'd been written in Oldtongue. Maybe they were magical wards. He gestured to the benches around the central hearth.

"That's a gothi," Thord whispered when the man left the room. "He's a priest."

"I did read about the various religions of Ellos," I said. "And I listened carefully in class."

"You're so wide-eyed I thought you needed to know more," he said.

We sat on the wooden bench. It was whittled from a massive old tree stump and looked as if it had been there for a thousand years. We inhaled the smoke. More robed men came in and out and we waited. One thick-set bald woman in similar robes to the men strode right up to us, stared openly for several moments, then departed.

"She's a gythia," Thord whispered. "A priestess."

"I love how he talks as if we don't have a brain between us," Megan said.

I kept my laughter silent.

We said nothing. We waited with our heads bent and I watched through the top of my hood. As the morning progressed other prayerful people arrived: farmers, tinkers, old women with their knitted shawls. One man, who was as thin as a post, brought in a chicken and sacrificed it in a bowl-like indentation in the hearth, then left the body. A monk emerged a few minutes later and took the carcass away. At least the sacrifices weren't wasted.

"So that's how they get dinner," Megan said. "Clever!"

"They'd be smarter if they asked them to bring it already cooked," I whispered.

Thord shot both of us an angry glance.

An hour passed and then another and another. The smoke made my eyes water and I grew dizzy. I wondered if there was something in the smoke. Hunger grumbled in my belly.

Doubt was growing in my mind. Did we have the right place? There may be another one-armed man in some tavern waiting for us to arrive. Or even another Woden village town with all the same ingredients.

Or the letter I'd found with Banderius's name on it was fake.

"This is taking too long," I said.

Thord blessed me with a frown. "Just pray. Or at least pretend to pray. Even the simplest farmer can do it."

By Belak I'll strangle him, I thought. That was as close as I could get to a prayer.

Then a bald gythia, her face and neck a series of swirling circular tattoos, came and stood in front of Thord. One of her eyes was white with cataracts. When she looked at me I felt a sharp pain in my dragon eye.

"You are our sisters and brothers from the red robes," she said. I wasn't certain if it was a question or a statement.

"Yes. We are," Thord answered.

"You are not a stranger, Thord son of Thangbrand." She had recognized him despite his mask. "These two are."

"They are graduates of the red robes. We are searching for an old friend."

"We know," she said. "We were told to expect you by a man who once worked for us. You are not the first to come."

That must mean others had been searching for Banderius. More survivors! Perhaps we were all gathering in some secret location. A group of us could easily strike back at Corwin and the emperor.

"How many others?" I asked.

She gave me a long stare. "It is not a large number, but it is not small."

Oh, why did religious people speak in such riddles?

"The one who told you to expect us," Thord whispered. "Where is he?"

She handed something to Thord that I couldn't see. Thord looked at the item hidden in his palm, then pocketed it. "Follow the spear," she said. "It will lead you to him."

More riddles! I would have much preferred a "Banderius is in the third house on the left after the brown state house."

"There are more strangers in Gudheim," the priestess said. "Their eyes are on us now. You are in mortal danger."

I glanced around. Two square-shouldered men had come in and were sitting at a bench behind us. Hoods hid their faces, and their cloaks were dirty. They had been traveling on horseback judging by the splashes of mud. The men sat very straight, which indicated military training. They blocked our way to the door we'd entered. On the other side of the room were two more figures. One was large and the other smaller—I was pretty certain that one was a woman.

A gothi went up to talk to the smaller one, and the woman waved him away. Metal glinted under her robe.

Armor.

The waving motion made her hood move enough that the dim light revealed her face. It was a face I'd last seen on graduation night.

Scyllia. My classmate.

My enemy.

I quickly turned away.

"We have to go now," I whispered. "Scyllia is here."

"Scyllia!" Megan hissed. "Are you certain?"

"Yes. With three others. She's wearing armor and I'm sure they are, too. We have to get out of here."

"The one-eyed one speaks truth," the gythia said. I didn't know if she was referring to herself or to me. I had two eyes. "You must come with me. Now."

She turned away from us and we looked at each other. Thord shrugged and we followed her. I glanced back just as we stepped through a curtain to see that all four of the newly arrived were on their feet and heading in our direction.

The room had four doors. The priestess made a motion and two burly gothi went through the curtain. There was yelling. But I couldn't make sense of what was being said.

"All doors to the outside are being watched by Akkad soldiers," she said. "We knew one day this path to your friend would be closed."

"Then where do we go?" Megan asked.

With surprising strength the gythia pushed a stone table aside, pulled a rug away and revealed a door in the grass floor. She opened it and practically shoved us down the darkened steps. "Go this way. May Tor watch over you. And remember to follow the spear."

The door slammed above us. I heard her dragging the table into place.

Light appeared in Megan's hand. She was holding a glowing light bauble above her head. It revealed a timber-supported tunnel that stretched a long distance into darkness.

Shouting came from right above us and the dim echo of metal on metal. "Are your priests armed?" Megan asked.

"Of course," Thord said. "And the priestesses, too."

"Then maybe they'll hold them for a bit," I said. "We had better run."

And so we ran.

19

THE SPEAR

I took the lead because I could see the farthest. And we ran. And ran. The tunnel itself had a smooth floor and there were no cobwebs. Which must mean the gothi had kept this place clean. The tunnel wasn't ending. I turned back to look and saw no sign of pursuit.

Then a crash echoed down the tunnel, and shouting followed. I swear I heard Scyllia shouting orders.

"Faster!" Megan said. Though I didn't know if I could go any faster.

The tunnel suddenly branched in three directions. "Which one?" Thord asked. I could see down all three with my dragon eye, and they each looked the same. I tried to picture what direction we were running and how far we'd gone under the city.

"We've been running north," I said. "I don't know your city. Do you think one of these comes up in another holy house?"

"There is only one house of the Raven Gods," Thord said. He pointed to our left. "That direction is toward the center of town. I don't think we want to climb out in the middle of a street."

"We just have to make a decision," Megan said. "Now! In fact, I'll do it. Let's take the one on the right."

It was as good a tunnel as any, and I rushed down it, hoping there was a door at the end of this branch. All I could hear now was the sound of our breathing and, despite trying to run as quietly as possible, the echoes of our footsteps. The tunnel curved ahead.

"This better not be a dead end," I said.

We came around a sharp corner and I was pleased to skid to a stop in front of a set of stairs. At the top was a stone trapdoor. I put up my hand and listened, willing my heart to slow down. There wasn't a sound of Scyllia and her companions.

The door was heavy, but with all three of us pushing we could lift it a few inches. There was light outside. And what looked like grass. "We're outside the city walls!" Megan said.

We put our backs into it and pushed until the trapdoor was open a foot or two, the bright light blinding me. Our pursuers would see the light from a distance. But the door wouldn't go any further, so Thord held it open with his back while the two of us crawled out. Then we grabbed on and lifted.

"You can let it go," Megan said. "We've got it."

He did so, but the door slipped out of our hands and thumped down. Thord pushed on it but could only lift it the span of his hand.

"It's so heavy," I said. "How did those priests ever open it?"

"Just leave me," Thord said. He passed something to me, and I glanced down and recognized it as the thing the priestess had given him. I put it in the deepest pocket of my cloak.

"No," Megan said. "We won't leave you."

"No," I said a second later. "They'll kill you."

Then I leaned down and grabbed hold of the door as tight as I could. I stared at my hands, at the door, and with a grunt pulled up. My dragon eye seemed to flash, and my blood felt so hot it was burning in my veins. The door slowly lifted.

When I looked across, I saw that Megan wasn't helping —she was standing back and her eyes were wide. And so were Thord's eyes as he was frozen in position on the stairs. "Get out!" I shouted.

He jumped out. I let go and the trapdoor slammed shut.

"Umm..." Thord was pointing at the stone door. "How, how the Hades did you do that?"

I looked at my hands to see if they were cut. But I didn't feel pain. The blood continued to burn along every vein. "It doesn't matter," I said. "Scyllia will be here in moments. We don't want to meet her."

"She's right," Megan said. "We'll have to figure that little 'lifting' mystery out later. They'll be able to track us if they have dogs or are half good at what they do. We need to get back to our swans."

Thord led us along the hills. We raced past his parents' home. It must be odd, I realized, to know they were only a few hundred strides away. They perhaps even saw us as shadows running along their hills, but he could not speak to them.

Of course, I could never speak to my parents.

Eventually we made it back to the stone barn. The sheep were still nervously pressed against the fence. We went into the barn to find the swans sitting calmly in the corner. Brax was sleeping.

The moment we entered the swans made angry honking sounds. "They're hungry," Thord said, and he hunted around until he found two pails of wheat which he set down in front of them. They ate as Megan and Thord saddled them.

"What is it that priestess gave us?" Thord asked.

I pulled out the small object and the chain unfolded. At the end of it was a spear the length of a finger. "It's a toy spear."

"It's a compass," Megan said. "But how will that help us find Banderius?"

We watched as it turned in the air and pointed to the west.

"It doesn't even point north," Thord said. "There's something wrong with it."

I stared at it, and momentarily it seemed to glow, but when I blinked the glow had vanished.

"Let me see it." Megan stretched out her hand and I dropped it in her palm. She turned around the room. She was unkempt, but somehow it made her appear even more attractive. "No matter what direction I move, it points to the west. It's not broken."

"It just doesn't know where north is," I said. "So it's no help."

"No," Megan said. "Remember what that witch woman told us?"

"She's not a witch, she's a gythia," Thord said.

"Whatever." Megan waved her free hand. "She said to follow the spear. This spear always points in one direction, so it must be charmed. There's something Banderius has that it's attracted to. Maybe he wears a similar spear."

If it was charmed, then that explained the slight glow I'd seen. "You're right," I said.

"You're not the only smart one, Carmen," she said.

I put my hands on my hips. "I never said I was smart."

"It shows in your face. In how you'd always stick your hand up in class."

"I had the right answer," I said. "That's why I stuck my hand up."

"Let's forget about class for a moment." Thord stepped between us. "If you're right, then we just have to follow this to... to Banderius."

"There's one problem with that," I said. "And it's a big one."

"Which is?" Megan asked.

"It's pointing toward the Akkad Empire. Are we prepared to fly straight at our enemies?"

"She's right." Thord scratched at his temple, a habit of his that I'd noticed years ago. It was as if he was trying to wake his brain. "If we follow this far enough, we'll end up in the city of Deva. It's the most distant post of the Empire."

"What choice do we have?" Megan said. "We either flee now and fly in any direction, or follow the words of the witch—the gythia, I mean." She glanced at Thord and grinned. "See, I can learn things."

"Hearing the three of you argue," Brax said, his voice rumbling loud enough to startle me, "is like hearing children bicker. And I hate children. They're so hard to digest." He didn't open his eye. I rolled my eyes because I knew he was joking. Neither Megan nor Thord looked certain, though. As far as I knew Brax hadn't moved at all since we'd left many hours earlier. Then I saw the book near his foot and realized he had been awake long enough to read.

"Do you have a suggestion?" I asked.

"Yes. Be quiet. I'm trying to digest."

"You didn't eat my father's sheep, did you?" Thord asked.

"*You didn't eat my father's sheep*," Brax repeated, somehow giving his voice a high pitch. "No. I was feeling kind. Oin has fewer sheep today."

"You risked being seen?" I said.

"Hunger overcame me. You can't fly me all night and expect me not to feed. The clouds are low, so there was cover and no one spotted me. Well, except the sheep. Right before they died." He smiled at this but still hadn't opened his eye.

"Since you seem to think we're children," Megan said, "tell us what to do, Father."

This got Brax to open his eye and laugh. "Clever! I like your sharpness." Was she somehow winning Brax over? "You are either flying into a trap, or your famed Banderius is doubly clever for hiding right under the emperor's nose. Well, I guess it's a long way from his nose, since Deva is as far as you can get from Akkadium. More like his toenails. But you know what I mean."

"I say we go," Thord said. "We can't wait here. They'll soon track us down. And they, too, have figured out what his hidden message is, so perhaps they'll find Banderius."

"I agree," I said. Megan said nothing; she was already leading her swan out of the barn.

In a few moments we were in the air, winging through the clouds and heading toward the Akkad Empire.

20

FLIGHT ACROSS THE PAST

When we crossed the border, I got more than a chill. Five hundred years earlier the land below had been called Daega and was populated by artisans and warriors known for ceramics and their skill in weaving blue blankets. The Akkad Empire conquered them in a few short months. Thousands had died, and the Daegans were enslaved and those artisans ordered to build roads, temples and walls around the Akkad cities. Their ceramic bowls and plates were long broken, their exquisite blue blankets torn to shreds. But their ghosts whispered to me.

"You are inordinately pensive," Brax said. A few wing-beats later he added: "Even for you."

"Just thinking about the past," I said.

"The past is a dead land," he answered.

I pulled my cloak tighter around me. "Do you only say that because you were banished from your own lands?"

"It's dead to me. Or at least I want *them* to be dead." He said this with enough venom I shivered. "If we survive this and you fulfill your part of our bargain, you'll find out exactly how dead that land can be."

"You don't make it sound like a pleasant trip."

"It won't be. I promise." He drew in a deep breath. "Did you speak to a priestess in Gudheim?"

"Yes," I said. "How did you know?"

"You mentioned her while recounting your adventure in the barbarian city. But I'm curious, were all the priests bald?"

"Yes." Because I was behind him, I couldn't see the look on his face. "Again I have to ask: how did you know?"

"I've read about the gythia and the gothi. Very interesting tattoo artists, those Woden priests. Did you know they bury the wives of chieftains with their husbands after they die? Sadly the wives are still alive."

"They don't do that anymore," I said, though I hadn't read enough history of Woden to be sure whether I was right.

"Yes they do," he said. "They are human." He did his best shrug, that is as well as a dragon can shrug flying at full speed.

We had been following Megan for hours. The landscape below us became less mountainous and more like a prairie. Occasionally Megan would hold the spear compass out, stare at if for several moments, and then change direction. The lights of a city appeared in the distance.

"We are nearing Deva," I said.

"I see that," Brax said. "Your friends, though, with their measly human eyes, cannot see that far. We should tell them."

He sped up, but at that same moment Megan made a signal that she would turn and she circled backwards, her swan cutting easily through the air. We hadn't yet reached the city.

"It's pointing straight down," she said as she passed us. "We're here!" And, with that, she flew downwards.

We descended in a slow circle. There was nothing but blackness at first, and I worried that the ground was so dark we'd smash right into it. Then I saw massive stone walls glinting in the moonlight. An ancient fortress was below us, and the closer we got the older I realized it was. It wasn't an Akkad design, so it must have belonged to the Daegans. Which meant it was several centuries old. There were trees growing up through the smaller buildings, and the walls were mostly crumbled but the main keep itself still looked sturdy.

"You may not want the swans to see that." Brax motioned with his nose.

A dead swan, its body broken, lay among the rubble.

"Do you still want to be dropped off?" he asked.

"Yes," I said. Though the sight of a dead swan meant that an assassin had perhaps met a bad end here. "This time come right away when I make the hoot of the Whiskered Screech Owl."

"You should maybe just shout my name," he suggested. "Your owl sounds are an insult to owls."

I didn't have a smart answer to that. Plus I was watching the roof of the keep grow nearer and nearer. Since he was too heavy to alight on the old roof, I slipped off him in the air and landed softly on the main keep. Brax swept his great wings silently and took into the air. He glanced back, and I thought there might be concern on his face. Both Thord and Megan slid off their swans and landed on their own feet, then with a waved command their swans winged upward to circle the fortress.

"This place looks deserted," Thord whispered.

"I saw a dead swan," I said.

"Well that bodes ill," Megan said. "But a little death has never frightened us, right?" She drew out the spear compass which at once pointed straight down. “If this compass truly shows Banderius’s location, then he’s right under our feet.”

“Our only choice is to follow it,” Thord said.

I didn’t spot any guards. If he’d gathered together a group of assassins, you’d think he would have posted lookouts. Did he send them along to a safer place? Or was the compass pointing to some magnetic rock left in a room below? Maybe we'd find his skeleton there.

Megan led us to an open stairwell. I clutched my daggers, Thord quietly unsheathed his sword and Megan drew her small crossbow. Without a word she started down the steps, with Thord only a few feet behind. I turned to look behind and above, aware that attack could come from any direction. There were no strings strung across the steps to ring tiny bells. No traps that an assassin would have prepared for unwanted arrivals. The place had to be abandoned.

The stone stairwell circled downwards. The stairs were broken in several places and we had to stretch over them to avoid bumping the rubble. Though my ears were attuned, I heard no noise other than our footsteps. This was an abandoned fortress outside a city, but it would still make a good place to shelter. You'd think there would be poor or desperate people living here. But perhaps they thought it was haunted.

Or they'd been driven away.

If there was danger we would have to race up these stairs, as they were our only path to the roof. I tried to memorize where the broken steps were.

Halfway down the stairwell we came to a wooden door. It was relatively new, the first sign that someone had been in here recently. Megan held out the compass, which was now pointing directly at the door as if Banderius might be standing on the other side.

We nodded to each other to indicate we were ready, then Megan opened the door. It wasn’t even locked and its hinges didn't utter a squeak.

Before us was a long dining hall with an ancient wooden table that still stood on all four legs, even though a chunk of it had fallen away. There was a metal plate at one end with what looked to be the remains of a meal. A fire was burning in the hearth. One part of the wall next to the hearth had fallen in, showing starlight. How long had this place been abandoned?

A man sat in a chair staring at the flames, his back to us. He had a flask in his hand.

“Put away your weapons,” he said, without turning. “Or I will kill you where you stand.”

21

THE OATH

We stood still. I tightened the grip on my daggers.

"Perhaps I worded that too strongly," he said. "You are not in danger here. Nor are you wetlings a danger to me."

He continued gazing into the fire, not even bothering to look our way.

"Who are you?" I asked.

"You know who I am. I heard you land on the roof, so you came by swan. I am glad there are still a few swans that remain. And you were guided here. That girl is holding a compass that's aiming at my heart."

Megan did still have her right hand in front of her. The spear compass was pointing at him.

"You're Banderius." I felt stupid saying it.

"This is what our graduates have come to," he said. "Simpletons. No wonder the Red Fortress went up in flames." He took another long sip. "Please tramp over here and stand before me. I am too bored to turn my head."

I glanced at my companions. Thord and Megan both shrugged. I glanced around the room for signs of other assassins, but he seemed to be alone. We walked the twenty or so steps across the floor and stood to one side of the hearth. The fire was warm; I hadn't realized how cold my hands had become.

Banderius was not old. Nor did it look like life as a rich assassin had softened him. He was wearing obsidian armor, a thin black metal that only the richest could afford. And the rumors of his handsomeness had been true: his jaw was straight, his face well-featured and rugged at the same time. Even though he slouched in his chair, there was a lithe power to his body.

"I said you could put away your weapons."

Thord did so, and Megan and I followed his example.

Banderius took a drink from his flask. The fire crackled. "Which ones are you?" he asked. "Not that it matters."

We spoke our names. He nodded at each one but raised an eyebrow when I said mine.

"Back from the dead, are you?" he said.

"How do you know about that?"

His grin didn't make his eyes seem any warmer. "I have not survived in the madness outside these walls without knowing things. Now tell me, who else survives?"

I thought of mentioning Maestru Beatrix. No, best not to let anyone know she had survived.

"We hope there are others," Thord said. His voice sounded a little ragged. "But I found Megan as we escaped the fortress. And Carmen discovered us later."

"Then you aren't great at hiding," Banderius said. "What are they teaching you these days? Nothing practical, I assume. How is it you have swans?"

"I worked in the swanneries," Megan said. "I was able to call down two of the freed ones when I escaped the school." She spat that lie out in a heartbeat. Good for her.

"But there are three of you," Banderius said. "You only mentioned two swans."

"I found mine on my own," I said. "Swans like me."

He turned his bleary eyes in my direction. Why did he seem so angry? We had come across a great distance to find him, and he was treating us like children. Like a burden. A round stone was hanging from his neck. "That's what draws the spear on the compass," I said.

He touched the stone. "Yes. It is matched to my magnetic personality." His chuckle was ragged. "So you spoke to the gythia and the gothi?" he asked.

"Yes," Thord said. "They gave us the spear compass."

"Then you are perhaps not as stupid as you first seemed. And my missives I sent to the five realms, they worked. You obviously unraveled the riddle?"

"We did," Thord said. "Though we encountered Empire soldiers in Gudheim. Immortals chased us from the temple."

He frowned. Even with his face squished up that way he looked attractive. "I guess that way is closed now."

"The gythia said other assassins came to them," I said. "Did they find you?"

His gaze was on me again, and he seemed perturbed that I'd even asked the question. "That's not your business. You need to gain my trust before you learn a thing from me. But why would you search out Banderius, of all the assassins who remain alive?"

"Maestru Alesius told me to find you," I said.

This made him blink, and his face didn't seem so pinched by anger. "You saw him before he died?"

"Only moments before. He said you'd be able to hide us and would know what to do now."

"He was a good man." Banderius took a long swig from

his flask. The stink of wine carried on his breath as he spoke: "Such a good man. He had his high and mighty ideals. But he still thought enough of me to set you on my trail?"

"Yes," I said. "He told me to trust you."

"And did Alesius die well?" Banderius asked.

"He died fighting to the very end." My voice cracked a little.

"He would." Banderius closed his eyes for a long time. "One never outgrows one's master," he said, still not opening his eyes. Then they opened and flashed with anger. "I will get revenge for him."

The way he said it made a chill run down my spine. I would not want to anger this man.

"You can get revenge." I grabbed the hilts of my daggers. "I want revenge, too. My brother did it. He did it all. He's the one."

Banderius shook the half-empty flask at me with such vigor that some wine sloshed to the floor. "I know that, Carmen. Do you think I'm an uniformed idiot? I've watched Corwin from a distance for years. He has a very devious and twisted mind. The most devious I've encountered."

"You've met him?" Thord asked.

"Yes. I even taught him a few moves when he was younger. I thought he was malleable then, but I soon learned he was metal that would not bend. If I'd even guessed at half of what he would do, I would have put a blade through his heart."

"He killed the princeling," I said. "He killed a child. And the old emperor, too."

"You have proof of this?" Banderius said.

"I know it in my heart."

Banderius laughed. "Never ever trust your heart. But like

you, I believe he deserves death. Many times over. But now is not the time to strike. Now is the time to hide in darkness and gather power."

"So you'll help us?" Megan asked. She took a step toward him.

"Will you help me?" He leaned back and put one hand behind his head. "That's the more important question."

"Yes!" I said. I also moved closer and set my feet in a fighting stance as if to prove my words. "Yes. I will help you and any others who want to strike Corwin and the emperor down. I will. I swear it."

"Whoa!" Banderius held up his flask. "Hold up. Do you think I have an army of assassins hidden in my cloak pocket? Do you want us to fly to Akkadium and deal death left and right and then plunge a blade right through your brother's heart?"

"Yes," I whispered.

"How impetuous you youth can be. But you have misread my words. That is not the kind of help I was asking for." He winked at me. "Did you happen to bring money?"

"What?" Megan spat out. "Money?"

"Yes, gold. Rubies. Gems. Or something of value. Ancient scrolls with spells on them. Rare books. Do you have anything of worth at all?"

"We have to pay you to save us?" I asked. "What about the oath between assassins? The Red Blood Oath. It's a guild oath!"

Banderius snorted. "The fortress where I first swore that oath is gone. The people who witnessed me swear it are dead. So the oath is dead." He motioned at the crumbling hearth in front of him, at the broken table and cracked chairs. "I once lived in my own palace and had a hundred servants. Now I hide like a rat in a stone box. So how did you think this would go? When you arrived, did you dream we'd all march off to some haven with me as your… your father figure. Wrapping you up in my fatherly arms."

"You swore an oath," I said.

"Again, I ask, how will you pay?" He glugged down more wine. I didn't know if he was drunk or not. He waved his hand as though waving us away. "It doesn't matter. You could never, ever pay enough." He spoke to someone over his shoulder. "You can have them now. I've done my part."

At first nothing happened. Then several footsteps. We turned to see that eight men in chain mail were coming from behind a broken wall—they had been waiting there silently all along. They moved with precision and purpose. Each was holding a crossbow.

But the one in the lead, with no weapon at all, was the first to walk into the firelight.

It was Corwin. And he was smiling wide enough to show his teeth.

22

NOT LIKE CLEANING STABLES

"Sister, you are really, really hard to kill," Corwin said. "I thought you dead after I pushed you over that wall. I mourned for several moments. And yet you survived. That must be a tale worth telling. I'm used to the people I've killed staying dead."

I moved a hand toward my daggers but the Immortals raised their crossbows higher, making it clear I would be full of bolts before I touched the hilt. I put up my hands, palms out.

"Wise choice, Carmen," Corwin said. "And Megan and Thord it is my pleasure to see you, too, my dear classmates."

"The feeling is not mutual," Megan said. But both she and Thord were holding their hands up.

"And you, my friend," Corwin said to Banderius. "I would say you laid it on a little thick with the *I'd like to stab Corwin* part, but otherwise this was really great work."

"Easy work." Banderius shook his head. "Too easy." He turned his baleful eyes toward me and said, "I was the one who killed the emperor's child."

"You did?" I said.

He tried to hold my gaze, but looked away. "Yes. I was promised a province of my own. There is a price for everything."

"Maestru Alesius would be so ashamed of you." I continued to glare at him.

Bandcrius shrugged but still wouldn't look me in the eye. "Alesius's ideals suited him well inside the walls of the Red Fortress. But it is a different world outside."

"It certainly is," Corwin said. "The infant's death was a necessary step and helped prove Banderius's loyalty. Oh, and it wiped all of his gambling debts clean." Corwin winked at me. "I killed the old emperor, in case you're keeping track, sister. Also a necessary step."

"We were taught to have morals," I said. "To do our jobs but not seek personal glory or power."

Corwin laughed. "Morals are great fodder for old men and women, but they mean nothing in the real world. In the real world everything is a calculation. Emperor Sargon first got rid of the wizards. Now, the assassins will be gone. He will be safe from all enemies. Not that he needs too much protection."

"Will he be safe from you?" I asked.

"Oh, that's a good question!" Corwin rubbed his hands together. "He knows I would never want his crown. Because being an emperor is a thankless position. I much prefer being the emperor's right hand. He calls me his knife in the darkness. It's a charming title."

"You're sick," I spat.

"I'm a realist," he answered. "And I always win."

I had slowly backed away, sliding my feet to hide the movement. Both Thord and Megan, too, had taken a few steps backwards. It was a very natural thing to do with several crossbows pointed at us. But it brought us to the edge of the hole in the wall.

If we jumped, we'd be a pile of broken bones on the hard ground below. And it wasn't like we could send a message to our mounts. But I had to try. I cleared my throat and was about to attempt a hoot.

"If you make a shout or a whistle, you're dead," Corwin said. "I know you think you can perhaps jump through that crack in the wall, and one of you or maybe two will land on your swans. Small chance of that working, but I bet you would try it. Better than facing me."

He stepped toward us. He didn't get too close, which meant he was still wary. He knew any one of us could have vials of acid or other tricks up our sleeves.

"How is Gregum's face?" I asked.

"So that was you?" Corwin said. "You'll get to see his face soon enough. And his fists."

My dragon eye suddenly hurt. And I saw the room as a pattern of glowing lights, with each person standing there glowing, too. What was happening? The sharp pain made me stumble back a step and Megan caught me. This allowed a little more distance between us and our enemies.

I rubbed until my eye cleared.

"Yes. That's what's different," Corwin said. "You have also grown an eye. How splendid!" He pinched his chin as if deep in thought. "I'd like to know how that came about. And how you fell down a mountain and climbed out alive. It's not like you grew wings. Yes, I've decided I must have an answer to that, even if I have to pluck the eye out myself. So you're going to live for a time, Carmen." He let out a fake sad sigh. "But your companions have nothing for me, and I've learned after hours of trying that torture doesn't work on assassins. So there's only one thing to do now: Banderius, kill them."

I actually took a step forward as if I could protect Megan and Thord.

"Do I have to?" Banderius said.

Corwin looked down at where the bleary-eyed Banderius, the man we had all worshiped as the greatest assassin in Ellos, sat.

"Do you have to?" Corwin repeated. "I'm not asking you to clean the stables. Yes, you have to, and I want it done now. And do make sure there's lots of blood."

"Fine. Fine. I'll do it." Banderius raised himself shakily out of the chair, using the back of it for support. I wondered how long he had been sitting there drinking. He was taller than us and had a longer reach than even Thord. Banderius stumbled slightly when he took his first step. He stared at his foot as though surprised at its betrayal.

"We don't have all night!" Corwin said.

Banderius rolled his eyes and then looked at us. His mouth moved and I swear he whispered, "Sorry." He drew his sword.

It was a black blade covered with Oldtongue runes. I'd read about it, a famous sword that he called Lilith. He had named it after his mother.

"Don't do this," I said. "You were Maestru Alesius's favorite. You can still make good on your oaths."

He shook his head and did meet my eyes this time. His were red. "Maestru Alesius thought he could change my inner nature, but he was wrong."

Banderius brought his blade toward us and, in a heartbeat, I had my daggers out, deflecting the blow. I had hoped that the magic in my blades would make his shatter or cut right through it, but it only sparked. Lilith was clearly powerfully enchanted.

Megan darted around his other side and made a quick lunge, but he easily deflected her blow and, at the same time, kicked Thord so that he fell over. Even with the wine in his system Banderius was incredibly skilled. His black armor protected him but obviously didn't slow him down at all. My next blow was blocked, and he stopped his blade only an inch from my eye and then laughed at me. The move he had used reminded me of when Corwin had poked out my eye.

So Banderius had taught Corwin that trick.

Corwin edged closer to get a better view. I guessed he didn't want to miss a single drop of blood.

It was clear that Banderius could destroy us at any moment. He, too, was playing a game. Or he felt enough guilt he chose to give us a few more seconds of life.

I tried to work with my classmates. Thord made a move from one side, so I stabbed from the other. But Banderius was able to easily knock the dagger from my right hand with the flat of his blade and spin in such a way as to deflect Thord's blow. We backed off.

"This is taking too long," Corwin shouted. "I still haven't had my dinner."

My dragon eye started to hurt again. It filled with tears and then after several blinks came clear. We fought back and forth, near the crack in the wall.

I was able to catch both Megan's and Thord's eyes. We nodded and all three of us charged at Banderius at once.

He smiled at the challenge and dropped to one hand, then spun his legs in an arc, catching each of us in the knees so that we fell over. And from that position Banderius sliced at the back of Thord's heel. Not a deep cut, but when Thord tried to stand again, his leg collapsed and Banderius stepped on him.

I blinked away the pain from my eye. I was now seeing Banderius as a glowing figure. But with my other eye his face was clear, and it was clearly showing some anguish.

"It's better if I'm quick with this," he said. He stabbed down and though Thord twisted, the blade caught him and Thord cried out.

"Damn!" Banderius said. "That was meant to be a death blow."

"Finish him!" Corwin sounded like he'd moved closer. Both he and Banderius were near the hole in the wall.

Banderius drew back his blade. I now felt like my eye was on fire, but I lowered myself down to my haunches in order to launch myself at him.

Then abruptly I stopped.

For Banderius had burst into flames, the blaze licking around him. I threw myself to the ground. The heat was almost unbearable above me. My hair sizzled.

Banderius stood for a second or two and then fell over. Dead.

The side of the wall crumbled inwards and Brax came charging in, roaring.

"Oh dear," my brother said. "I really didn't plan for that."

23

WHAT IS FAIR?

Brax blasted out another burst of flame and half the Immortals went tumbling to the ground, screaming and shaking their limbs to try to put out the fires. The others were loosing their bows but Brax was unstoppable. Bolts stuck in his snout, his chest, and his forelegs, but he kept smashing his way through the hole and into the room.

I pushed myself up to my knees and, with a huge effort, stood up straight. The burning sensation in my eye was gone. I glanced left and right.

Corwin had fled.

I picked up my daggers then stopped. Thord lay on his back, hand clenched to his side. It was too dark to see the wound and how bad it was, but Megan packed it with some sort of healing leaves she had pulled from her cloak. "Go get him," Thord said. He lifted a hand to wave me away. "Kill him. Please."

I nodded, turned and dashed past the remaining Immortals who faced Brax. He smashed one down with his foot, snapped his massive jaws at another one. The last three kept their blades up and did their best to battle back. They were brave, I had to give them that, but they only had moments to live.

By the time I reached the door my footing grew more steady. The room brightened as Brax unleashed more flames. A wave of heat rushed over me.

I charged into a smaller room full of broken benches and smashed tables and sped as quick as my legs would carry me—my thoughts boiled with anger. Corwin's glowing footprints were easy to follow with my dragon eye. I would have marveled at the ability to see the prints, but there was no time. I went up a set of steps and into a long hallway. A black shadow swept ahead of me. Too far for a dagger throw.

"Corwin," I shouted. "Corwin!"

He didn't acknowledge me. He came to the end of the hallway, pulled up short and let out a swear. It wasn't until I'd taken a few more steps that I could see why. There was nothing but air beyond where he stood because that part of the keep had fallen in. We were far too high up for him to jump.

Corwin turned and faced me.

"Carmen!" he shouted. "It's not fair to bring a dragon to a sword fight."

I almost laughed. He'd always been so quick-witted. That was why I had once loved him.

I raised my daggers, and he drew his sword. I didn't know if I could beat him; my head was still aching, my hair smelled of smoke and even my robes were smoldering. But I had to try.

"I'm even better than I was when last we fought," he said.

"Then let's prove it." Confidence and rage rose up in me. He had ordered Banderius to kill my friends, perhaps had mortally wounded Thord. His actions had led to the destruction of the Red Assassin Keep, the deaths of my classmates and of Maestru Alesius. "You'll pay for everything you've done, Corwin. Every. Single. Thing."

"Oh, sister. I should have taught you more about how life really works." He sauntered toward me over the rubble, swinging his sword in playful arcs, then tossing it from hand to hand. "The lesson will start now." He had perhaps been holding back from showing his true skills at school. Runes were scratched along both sides of the blade in Oldtongue. It was one of the ancient swords, an enchanted blade.

My anger made me braver. I charged toward him, daggers at the ready.

Then Corwin stopped arcing his sword, and the confidence in his eyes dimmed a little. In fact he paled as I got nearer to him. He took a step back and another. Did he actually fear me?

There was a loud crash behind me and I glanced back. Brax was working his way down the hallway, shouldering stone out of his way and building up speed. He had clearly finished with the Immortals and was now trying to force his body to where we were standing.

"Ah, sis, today is not the day," Corwin said. Then he turned and ran toward the opening at the end of the hall. He whistled as he did so and jumped into the air, plummeting down to what I was certain would be his death.

I ran to the crumpled edge in time to see him flying low on a black swan. He soon arced upwards over the broken walls of the fortress and winged toward the stars in the sky.

24

THREE HANDS AND A TALON

By the time Brax worked his way to me, Corwin had vanished into the darkness. "Is there any point in chasing him now?" I asked.

"I don't have the strength," Brax said. There were bolts sticking out of his shoulders and face and he glistened with lines of blood. But none of the wounds seemed to be causing him pain. He snorted. "I was aiming for your brother with my flames, just to let you know. Not that Banderius fellow. But since you so kindly took my eye out, my aim is off. So it's your fault Corwin escaped."

"Well that doesn't make me feel any better," I said. I pointed at his shoulder. "Do any of those wounds hurt?"

"Bah," he said, pulling a bolt out with his teeth and spitting it to the floor. "Not in the slightest."

I'd have to take his word for it. There wasn't any reason for him to pretend he wasn't in pain. Besides, if he was I'd just feel more guilt. And he'd probably enjoy that. "How did you know we were in trouble?"

He smiled his dragon smile. "I've been keeping a secret from you."

“What secret?"

“I can see through your eye. Well, I can see through my eye that's in your head.”

“You can?” I rubbed my dragon eye. I remembered getting a splitting pain just a few moments before Brax arrived. “You mean everything I’ve seen, you also see?”

“No. Not quite. Once in a while I get an image. Like a picture of that ugly seven-eyed seer in Avenus. And the gythia with the horrible tattoo. And, while I was circling above, teasing the swans—I do think they’re actually starting to like me—an image flashed in my head of someone swinging a sword at you. I thought, just maybe, you could use my help.”

“We’d be dead otherwise," I said. "So thank you. Thank you." I put my hand on his shoulder, making sure not to touch any wounds.

"Don't get all smarmy about it," he said.

But my brain was already swirling with ideas. Which surprised me since I was feeling rather exhausted. "I wonder if there’s a way to control this connection between us? Maybe we could send each other messages."

He shrugged, making his wings hit the side of the hall. "What sort of messages? *Pick me up, I'm tired of walking*. That sort of message?"

"No," I said. "Just a more clear communication. I..." My thoughts were starting to slow down. My body ached from the fight. "Now is not the time. We had better go back and check on Thord.”

"If we have to," Brax said, but he turned, shouldering more of the wall out of the way, and began to rumble down the hall.

I drew in a breath when we reached the main room. The place looked like, well, it looked like a dragon had gone berserk in it. I turned away from the charred remains of the Immortals—they weren't immortal when it came to dragon fire. And Banderius hadn't fared much better. He looked far from handsome now.

Thord was in the center of the room, lit in the moonlight. Even from here I could see he was not in good shape. He had gone much paler. Megan had his head in her lap and was pressing down on the bandage she'd placed on his stomach.

"I want Banderius's sword," Thord said when I got closer. "The sword that stabbed me."

He could talk at least. I stopped by Banderius's body and grabbed the blade and scabbard, neither of which had been harmed by the flames. It was a light blade despite its size. I sheathed it, walked over, and Thord took them from me and clutched them to his chest. His hand was a little palsied.

"You need a healer," I said.

"Only one thing will heal me now." Thord's voice cracked. "Just tell me Corwin is dead."

I shook my head. "He got away."

"I don't think we'll be safe anywhere in all of Ellos as long as he is alive," Megan said. She ran her hand through Thord's hair. I bit my lip. I suddenly wanted to be the one comforting him.

"No. We won't," I said. "He has all the Empire as his resources."

"Well, I for one..." Thord was gritting his teeth, which made his words hiss a bit. "... I am angry about this hole in me. And the cut in my leg. And, I will do everything possible to hunt him down and..." He drew in a breath. "... Stop him."

"From breathing," Megan added.

"You took the words right out of my mouth," I said.

"Let's shake on it," Megan said. I had to bend quite a bit

so Thord could reach my hand. His fingers were cold. Megan put her hand on mine. To my surprise, Brax plopped his talon on top of the pile.

“I can always use a few more underlings,” he said.

We all shook, three hands and a talon.

“It’s a deal, then,” Thord said. “Now, take me to a healer. There are plenty in the villages of Woden. I just have to live long enough to get there.”

"You will," Megan said. "You've had worse than this. I have faith in you."

"I-I do, too," I said, though it sounded stupid.

It was a lot of work getting Thord onto the back of his swan and strapping him to the saddle, but soon all three of us were in the air and traveling east, away from the Akkad Empire.

I was certain we'd be flying back this way again. Corwin would hear from us the moment our wounds were healed.

PART 3: DARK WINGS

1

LUCK OF THE DRAW

I'd drawn the shortest straw so it fell to me to enter the executioner's home. We thought three assassins searching room by room would mean three times the chance of being caught. But one assassin could sneak in and sneak out without arousing any suspicion.

Or without getting killed.

That was our hope.

Besides, Thord hadn't yet healed enough to walk properly. A gythia in a Woden village had stitched his gut wound tightly, but his leg was not an easy fix: it was in a wooden splint and would take weeks for the tendons to heal. He was obstinate though and had insisted he should also draw.

And he had chosen the shortest straw.

So I'd snapped mine with my fingernail as I drew it, coughing to hide the trick. And I'd presented the teeny, tiny straw to my friends. "I win the prize," I'd said.

Megan had raised a curious eyebrow, but before either could speak I'd turned and walked straight to Brax and jumped on him. "I'll be back before you can say Maestru Belaxianariusantium." It was a saying from our school days.

He was the maestru with the longest name in the history of the Red Assassin Fortress.

I hoped I sounded braver than I felt.

Brax was now winging me toward the home of the emperor's executioner. Though I'd been on the dragon's back many times, it was still a thrill to be seated on a creature of such power and grace, feeling his wings work the air on either side of me. Sometimes, if I didn't think of the price I'd paid, I felt so lucky.

Brax let out a burp loud enough to startle a flock of geese. "Sorry," he said. "Pork tastes so good going down but never settles properly. Especially when one is forced to fly so soon after eating."

He had a gift for wrecking every moment. "We are trying to be silent," I said.

"Better out than in, as my mother always used to say."

I rolled my eyes. We flew without speaking for several minutes.

The executioner's name was Naram-Sin, and not only had he been the executioner for three separate emperors, but he also became known as the greatest Akkadian architect in the last five hundred years. He'd designed so many of the most impressive buildings in all the Akkad cities.

His home had sprung from his mind onto paper, and then tradesmen and slaves had built it on the beach near Eladium, the southernmost port of the Akkad Empire. It was an impressive building with turrets on either side and columns along each wall. The Akkadians loved their columns. There were several heated bath pools dug into solid rock outside the home. The ocean waves lapped almost to the front door. The home had been constructed in the shape of a bear's head, the largest pool being its eye. It was as if Naram-Sin knew someone would look down from the sky at his home. Maybe he'd braved a glider to examine his creation. Or perhaps he was just trying to impress the gods.

He had also designed the palace which Emperor Rexen had built. Emperor Rexen was the grandfather of the current Emperor Sargon. And Sargon had moved into that palace.

Which meant my brother would be there, too.

Which was why I was here.

For the last three nights we had been flying over this home, memorizing every detail. In all that time, not once did I see a guard patrol the grounds. Nor did I spot any guards inside the house. I found that odd. Naram-Sin might have been forgotten by Emperor Sargon, but the man was rich enough to afford his own protection. Perhaps his wealth had dwindled; after all, few lived to be as aged as him. The executioner was over a hundred years old.

So I was certain I didn't have to fear him.

"Too many stars tonight," Brax whispered. "And the moon is too bright. It would not be wise to land very close."

"I agree," I said.

"Then I suggest, instead of aiming for the roof, where any human with half an eye—sorry to mention your former predicament—could see us, we should slip into the gardens nearest the home."

"I agree with that, too. That is the best direction to approach the home. And I am certain you aren't trying to get me killed."

"Me?" He laughed quietly, but the guttural sound traveled in the air. "I swore an oath to not knowingly cause you harm. It would be ideal if you died tonight. Then our deal would be done, but I'm not saying I'm hoping for your death."

"Well, that brings me great comfort," I said.

"I wouldn't weep though," he added. He turned his head toward me as if he was glancing back, but used his left side—the side with the missing eye. I was certain he did it on purpose because he knew I felt great guilt when I saw that empty socket. And my eye—which once was his—itched as if it wanted to be back there.

Then Brax swooped silently down and landed in the massive garden. I thought we'd been discovered when I saw several men there, then remembered they were only statues—another item the Akkadians loved. The statues were of Akkadian warriors and emperors, including Augillian, the first emperor. We were next to Naram-Sin himself, who was holding a curved and deadly executioner's axe in one hand and a scroll in the other. I shivered as I looked up at it.

"He looks formidable," Brax whispered. He tucked his wings close to his body and huddled under several plum trees, hiding as much of himself as he could. "Though I bet he's not really twelve feet tall. Also, I imagine at his age he's wasting away in bed."

"I hope you're right." I made certain my daggers were loose in their scabbards.

"You'll find out. Good luck, Carmen Crow."

And with that, I marched toward the executioner's home.

2

THE BEAR HOUSE

I tightened my cloak. The dark material deflected light, and it was like wrapping invisibility around me. I pulled up my hood and padded my quiet way along the garden path. My dragon eye made everything clearer by magnifying the available light.

The circular pools had an impressive amount of steam rising from them. Either the water was heated day and night, or the executioner had discovered a rare hot water spring and built his home over it. I climbed the stone stairs, sticking to the shadows, and then chose another path that led me near the trees. I was aware of what people could see from above me if any guards happened to be at the window.

But with each step I suspected there were no guards. We could have landed right at the front door, because not a soul was out on patrol, or watching from the turrets.

I chose the side of the home where there were no windows, climbed to the second floor and drew myself over the balcony. The door had delicate gold finery and colored windowpanes, which I couldn't see through, but at least it was clear the interior was dark. I picked the lock, aware of the slight clicking of my picks. Then I slowly opened the door, which didn't squeak.

The room was an impeccably neat study. One wall was a floor-to-ceiling bookcase with row after row of books, each in tight regimental order. A slanted table, for drafting, sat in the room's center, and as I neared I saw that a half-finished drawing waited there. Perhaps, despite his age, Naram-Sin could still stand and work.

I padded across the floor, pleased that I made no sound. Every floorboard was solid. I imagined any squeaking piece of wood was banished from his perfect home. Perhaps he chopped it up with his executioner's axe.

Thord, Megan and I had discussed where his treasure room would be. We were certain he would have treasure since he'd been the emperor's executioner and architect for so many years, and that meant he'd have accumulated a great amount of gold, gifts, gems and any other riches he desired.

The Akkadians really loved their treasure.

The treasure room could either be hidden deep, deep in catacombs below his house, or located here on the top floor. Because he was an architect, I believed he'd use the top floor. Architects liked to build things high, not tunnel deep into the ground like miners, and surely the columns around the home provided enough support for the weight of his treasure. I wouldn't be surprised if he'd designed the home so that sunlight could dapple across his hoard.

It turned out I was mostly right.

I snuck into the hall and came across a central room with a stone door. It was not the entrance to a bedroom, like all the other doors made of wood. This door would keep a team of men with hammers at bay for hours. I didn't have a hammer, but if everything went right I wouldn't need one.

My lock picks fit easily into the keyhole, but there were no pins to move no matter where I poked. He had a type of lock I'd never seen before. Though I hated to use spells, especially in Akkad where magic was outlawed, I whispered, “Enderos.” And made a small gesture with my hand.

There was no click. No sign anything had changed.

What kind of lock was it? I ran through the books I'd read. We had spent hours in class taking apart and reconstructing every lock type from every corner of Ellos. But this one seemed to have no gears. No pins. And no magical wards.

Nothing at all.

So, in frustration, I turned the knob, and the door edged open an inch.

My jaw dropped. Apparently, he was brazen enough to leave the door to his treasure room unlocked. I pushed the thick stone door the rest of the way open. It moved without the slightest grinding. The executioner had built impressively well. I walked in, leaving the door open. The whole room glittered in the moonlight.

There were shiny chalices along one wall. The second wall was bare brick. And the third wall displayed ornamental weapons. I could tell that from where I was standing because the weapons were mostly made of gold and silver and crusted with gems. One good blow in a sword fight and they'd fall to pieces. There was also a table with several miniature buildings constructed of marble which I assumed were copies of his creations.

In the center was what I'd come for. A collection of his architectural drawings, each tied with a golden string.

I made my way around the table. I found it odd that the wall behind it was bare brick. You would think every bit of space would display his wealth and power. Perhaps one bare wall was a nod to the fact he'd climbed from poverty to the second most powerful position in the Empire. My dragon eye revealed the outline on the bricks of what looked like a lumpy man drawn by a child. It was some sort of art piece that Naram-Sin found attractive. Or one of his children had drawn it.

I turned and faced the table, occasionally glancing toward the open door. There was enough light to see each scroll. I went through them and discovered drawings of a house of worship for the great man-bear god Ak, plans for an armory, and the interior of the white tower that stood next to the Imperial Palace. That one gave me a shudder, since I had read they used that tower as a place to execute wizards. There was something about the walls that dulled their powers.

But I didn't need the maps for any of those buildings. What I couldn't find was his drawings of the palace itself. I seemed to have discovered every single home, tax building or wall that the executioner had designed—there was even an impressive bathroom on a mountainside. But I could not find the Imperial Palace.

The final scroll I opened made me smile. It was of the palace in Akkadium where the emperor lived.

Where my brother hid.

With these plans, my companions and I could work our way through that palace, knowing every room and every hiding place. I lifted the scroll, let out a silent yell of victory and stepped back from the table.

Something shifted behind me and made the slightest grinding. That didn't make sense because there was nothing behind me.

I turned to see that the lumpy man drawn on the wall

looked clearer. The bricks inside his outline had moved outward. How very odd!

Then his black coal eyes opened.

"Thief," a gruff voice said. His brick lips moved.

"I'm not," I said. Though I was clearly clutching the stolen item.

"Thief," he repeated, and I knew why the wall could talk. Why it could move. It was a golem. Waiting there for any intruders.

"Good golem," I said, backing away. "Nice golem."

I had read about these stone creatures made from clay or brick or sand and how they were single-minded and slow. So I edged away, confident I could quickly flee.

The books were wrong.

Because the golem lashed out with great speed and grabbed me by the arm in a bone-crushing grip.

"I break you," he said and squeezed my other arm before I could reach a dagger. "I break you in two."

3

A GRIP OF STONE

Several moments passed where I couldn't believe what was happening. Such disbelief, Maestru Alesius had taught, can kill you. Your brain stops functioning and is not willing to admit the truth of the situation.

The pain of the bones in my arms pressing closer and closer as the golem squeezed snapped me out of any hesitation. I tried to pull away, but the hands were far too strong. I'd been taught how to twist and break free of a normal human grip, and I tried this method, but this was not a grip that could be broken.

I needed more force. More strength.

It stretched out its arms, holding me far enough away that my flailing legs caught none of the items in the treasure room. After the golem had broken me, it would retreat into the walls. Maybe keeping its grip on me so my bones became a message to future thieves.

In pure desperation, I set my feet against the beast's chest, pushing as hard as I could, stretching my arms and grunting with the pain. My hands would be ripped off, but I kept up the pressure, twisting my arm at the same time.

My right hand came loose.

I was half free!

But the sudden release made me swing around closer to the beast, and he reached down and grabbed me by the head. His huge hand fit around my skull like a vice.

"Crush you," he said. "Thief. Crush thief."

He squeezed my head. Those five thick fingers were forcing five parts of my skull inwards. I banged against him with my right hand and then grabbed at his fingers, each one almost as thick as my wrist. They continued to squeeze.

I scrabbled at my belt until I stumbled across the sheath and pulled out one of the Uriken daggers. Master Alesius had said they were over three thousand years old—perhaps older than the spell that made this golem. I hoped that meant they'd cut right through him.

I stabbed at the creature and a chunk of brick came away. I slashed and jabbed again and again, knocking pebbles to the floor. Hope swelled in my thumping heart. I swung at the arm above my head and an eyeball-sized chunk flew off.

"Bad knife," the golem said. "Very. Bad. Knife."

He was squeezing so hard now I expected to hear the cracking of my skull. I stabbed again and again, but missed with the next blow and the next. My thoughts grew darker and slower.

"Crush you dead."

Darkness came, then light as I realized I was only seeing through my dragon eye. It was showing me the spell that created the golem, a tight mesh of thousands of tiny glowing stitches that held the bricks together. It was beautiful. Mesmerizing.

But still it was squeezing my skull. The darkness was coming again, and I was certain I was soon to die.

Darkness for a beat. Another beat.

Then a male voice said, “Release her.”

But it was too late. I was falling, falling, falling toward death.

4

NOT A THIEF

The fall was short.

I hit the floor and crumpled into a heap of bones and flesh. My skull was on fire, my arms feeling as if they'd both been broken. I placed my right hand on the floor and tried to push up but collapsed. I'd let go of my knife and yet couldn't open my eyes to find it.

"You're not dead," the male voice said. "It has been a long time since someone was foolish enough to try to rob me."

Speech was beyond me. Even moving my jaw sent a sharp pain along my cheek. I felt lucky that I understood what the man was saying. My head pulsed and seemed to expand, and I wondered if it had been reshaped.

Soft footsteps approached and something poked my left arm. It hurt, hurt a lot, but I couldn't move it. Then it poked my right arm. And it tapped my skull.

"Nothing is broken," he said. "You can open your eyes."

He was wrong. I could never open my eyes again. But I tried.

One did open. My human eye, and I saw a staff floating

above me. So that was what had been poking me. Testing me. The bottom of the staff was a wooden bear's paw. Its head was a bear. A hand was holding the head and beyond it was a tall, thin man with white hair and gaunt features, but blazing life in his eyes.

There was no pity there.

The executioner! Naram-Sin stared down at me, and despite his age he was not stooped. I was looking up into the eyes that had guided that axe to so many deaths. A man who could kill a prisoner in one moment and return to his study to design a palace the next. And a man who, apparently, could also wield magic.

"You're very young," he said. "But I guess the older thieves know not to visit my home. The ones who didn't have that knowledge are all dead. You will soon join them. But first: what brought you here, child?"

I tried to answer, but such was the pain that my mouth wouldn't move. The golem must have broken my jaw.

"Oh, I see." He bent down easily, showing no sign of being over a hundred years old, and picked up the plans I had been clutching. "You are an admirer of my work. Which plan could you possibly believe would be worth risking your life for?" He raised one finger. "Ah, the Vaults of Vercimax, I bet. Many would die to know the secret ways into that treasure house. You dream of jewels, do you?" He unrolled the plans and his eyes widened. "The Emperor's Palace? You truly have a death wish. Why would you want this, thief?"

This time my jaw moved, my lips made shapes, but no words would come out. Then I tried again and managed: "I—I'm not a thief." My voice was ragged, but at least it worked. I had been worried that my brainpan and the gray jelly inside it were damaged.

"You are in my home. You are clutching my architectural drawing. You are a thief."

I shook my head. It hurt, and I saw that the golem loomed right behind me with his hands open.

"I'm an assassin," I said.

He raised a white eyebrow. "An assassin. Rare birds they are these days. A dying breed, one might say."

"Not all of us are dead." I tried to make this sound angry, but my voice cracked.

"An assassin, stealing the plans to the Emperor's Palace. One, even as aged and slow-witted as me, might jump to some rather nasty conclusions."

I decided it best to say nothing. He had come to that conclusion quickly, and I now regretted telling him about my vocation. The golem had squeezed out all my good sense.

"Pick her up," Naram-Sin said, and before I could move the golem grabbed me by the shoulders and lifted me into the air. By pure reflex I had snatched up my dagger from the floor.

"Sheath your toy, child," he said, then he turned and strode out of the room, saying, "Bring her to the guest room."

I sheathed the dagger and was surprised that the executioner didn't seem to want to kill me right away. The golem followed him, carrying me with no effort. Each footstep tested the strength of the floor, made the wood creak as my own footsteps hadn't, but it had been a well-built house. We went down the hallway and into a medium-sized room with a bed, a dresser, and a view toward the ocean. The type of room built to impress a guest. There was also a padded bench. Above the bench, hanging on the wall, was his massive executioner's axe. I shuddered at the sight.

"Place her on the bench and stand next to her. If she draws her dagger again, kill her."

The golem placed me as instructed and stood right beside me. His brick face was impassive, but those strange glowing eyes watched me. They were not angry. Just single-minded. I rubbed my shoulders and my arms, bringing blood back to the muscles. The bruising and pain would take weeks to heal.

"What is your name, Assassin?" Naram-Sin asked.

"Carmen," I said.

He nodded. "Judging by your age, I'd say you are a recent graduate. Also, there is something about your left eye that I can't place. Something off." He made a gesture. "Ah, it's warded. Why?"

"It's the wrong color, that's all. Two different-colored eyes and the boys don't like that. So I bought a spell in the market."

"A vain assassin. I've met a few." I wondered if he was thinking of Banderius. Well, he wouldn't be meeting him again. "That's a powerful charm to pick up in a market. You got your money's worth."

I nodded. "She was an old, old woman. She seemed to know what she was doing."

"Now." He crossed his arms and drew himself above me. "I will assume you were not sent to kill me, otherwise you would have been haunting my chambers and eviscerated by the wards I have there. Why do you want those plans?"

"I was paid to retrieve them." I spat this out. "Paid really well."

"That is a lie," he said. He didn't even blink. "No one would pay an assassin to steal papers. Let me tell you why you tried to steal them. Emperor Sargon has declared all assassins should be executed. And you have, on your own or with help, decided to kill him, which would nullify that declaration. And the plans were your first step in completing that task. Am I correct?"

I didn't know what to say. If I agreed, then I'd be admitting that I had planned to kill the emperor. Which was a death sentence, and he was standing with his executioner's axe on the wall behind him.

"It's not correct," I said.

He raised his eyebrow again; he had an expressive face for an old man. "Oh, it's not. Then please correct my assumptions."

"I want to kill my brother."

He cocked his head to one side. "I'm listening."

"His name is Corwin. He planned the assault on the Red Assassin Keep. He betrayed the guild of assassins, and I want to kill him and by doing so eliminate the threat to assassins. It is only his skill that allows the emperor to hunt all of us down."

Naram-Sin stared at me for a long time. "It stinks like truth. A family vendetta. How very interesting. So you have no intention of attempting to take the life of my emperor?"

"If there was opportunity, I would reason with him."

This got a gruff laugh from the executioner. "No one can reason with Emperor Sargon, believe me. Now, once you are finished this task of killing your brother, you would leave the palace without touching a hair on the emperor's head?"

"Yes," I said.

"And are you employed by anyone in this task?"

"No. This is a personal job."

He rubbed his chin and then raised a finger somewhat dramatically. He turned his back on me, opened a small chest on his desk and withdrew something. He then walked directly up to me and said, "Put out your hand, palm up."

His dark, dark eyes were filled with a sense of satisfaction and delight. Like he was enjoying every moment of this.

I put out my hand.

He placed a bronze coin in my palm. It had the head of Emperor Rexen on it, so it was a very old coin.

"I want you to kill the Emperor Sargon for me," the executioner said.

5

PAYMENT FOR SERVICES

"What?" I said. I honestly believed my hearing wasn't working. My ears were ringing madly and his words echoed in my head.

"I want you to take one of those daggers you have on your belt and use it to end Emperor Sargon's life. Or use both, your choice. That is why I've paid you." He did not blink. His stare was as calm as if he were asking me to pass him a bowl of sugar.

"But, but he's your emperor!"

"His grandfather was my emperor. His father was my emperor. His brother I accepted grudgingly. Sargon, I do not. He defiles the palace I designed."

"But, why would you want him dead?" I asked.

"Are your clients required to explain why an assassination must be committed?"

"No," I said.

"Well, I will only tell you this: When I was the emperor's right hand, we were hard and we were strong. You must be that way to hold an empire together. No enemy can harbor a moment of doubt about your willingness to respond to the smallest slight. But we were logical. Sargon is not logical. He will bring this empire down."

"I-I can't just kill him," I said.

"Why not? You are an assassin. If you make it into the palace, then you are already in the beating heart of his empire—you just have to add stabbing him to your list of things to do that day."

I looked at the coin. It would only buy me a loaf of bread.

"This is not enough."

At that the executioner laughed and laughed so hard that he wiped his eyes. "It is about price? No. I will not pay you more. This is a symbol. You are in my home. You have affronted me by attempting to steal my grandest work. You are also getting your life in return for this promise."

"If I say no, you'll kill me?"

"I won't kill you," he said, though he looked at the golem. The message was clear. The golem would kill me. "But I would rather you used logic. If you kill your brother, Sargon will still continue to hunt you down. He is ruthless. He is paranoid. And he is—believe me, I do not say this lightly—the most dangerous man in the kingdom. So to strike close to his heart and not kill him means you will have all his resources hunting for you. And you and all your assassin friends will die. But it won't stop there. They will take families of assassins to the block. Merchants who sold goods to assassins, too. Anyone who gave shelter. All will die."

I placed the coin in the wallet on my belt. "It is a deal," I said.

He smiled. There was such a keen, cold intellect in his

eyes. He would have to be cold to have survived in the courts of the emperors for all these years. "Good," he said. "Now go fetch us tea."

At first I thought he was speaking to me, and I was slightly flustered and not sure how to reply, then the golem backed away and lumbered out of the room. The noise of his steps told me he was going down the stairs.

"How is it you know magic?" I asked. "When it is outlawed in the Empire."

"You outlaw that which you do not control, but that doesn't mean those in power don't use it. If you have it and no one else does you are stronger." He walked over to his desk and flipped through his papers, laying them out in neat piles. "I wasn't born wielding magic, but after looking in the eyes of so many men and women when they died, I grew curious. Where do they go? What magic keeps us here on this plane of existence until our lifelines are cut? And so I studied. I learned. With the emperor's permission. My emperor." He shook his head. His hair was clean-cut and perfectly angular. "I learned so many spells and opened so many doors, real and imagined. But I don't know where people go after death." He shrugged his shoulders. "I've learned a great amount about how to send them there. And I have gathered enough magic to protect myself." He pulled open a drawer. "Ah, here!"

He came out with a small sheet and unrolled it. "This is a copy of the palace plans that is much smaller and easier for you to carry. I shall keep my originals and use a spell to remove any smudges you have left on them—they are very dear to me." He handed the smaller version to me and said, "The monk who made this copy is dead." I decided not to ask how.

The form of the golem filled the door. He lumbered in, carrying a golden tea kettle and two cups on a tray. "Ah, the tea has arrived. Please drink with me."

The golem held the tray between us and I took one of the cups. I did sniff it for poison, and that got a chuckle out of Naram-Sin. He drank from his tea.

As I sipped, the cinnamon scent filled my nose. The taste was new—there were so many rare spices that my tongue couldn't identify. My arms felt so weak it was hard to hold the cup in my hands.

Naram-Sin held his own cup up in a friendly gesture. "Is it satisfactory?"

"It's good tea," I said. Despite how hot it was, I drank it down quickly. Fighting a golem had made me very thirsty.

The executioner set his cup down. "Well, I hope you have had enough time to clear your thoughts. I want you to remember everything I say in the next few minutes. I will begin by pointing out several interesting design features of the palace, ones that will be particularly of interest to assassins. And I will end with a description of a balcony, a description you will find quite tantalizing." He held the paper in front of me and then began to speak. It took him several minutes to tell me where various doors, including secret ones, were. A glimmering of a plan began to grow in my head. I drank the last mouthful of tea.

"You listen well," Naram-Sin said. "Who was your maestru?"

"Maestru Alesius."

"That explains it. He would be proud of you. Now, I would like you to go on your way. If you can walk, that is."

I stood. Yes, I could walk. I nodded to the executioner and walked past him down the stairs and out of the bear home.

I realized I had just accepted my first paid job as an assassin.

6

A DREAM RETURNS

"You did what?"

I had expected Megan to be the first to question my decision, but it was Thord who was staring at me with narrowed eyes. Anger pinched his features together.

"I accepted the job," I said.

"To kill the most powerful man in all of Ellos?" Thord said. When he put it that way, it sounded impossible. "Naram-Sin will betray us in a heartbeat. He was the executioner and would have no qualms about it. He could easily warn Sargon and Corwin about our plans and set a trap."

"That's true," I said. I was working hard to keep the anger out of my voice. That scenario had crossed my mind on the way back to our island hideout, and I'd even discussed it with Brax. "Though I don't see how that would get him further ahead. He already had me at his mercy and his golem could have broken my neck with a flick of its wrist. There wasn't any reason to release me unless he truly wants the emperor to die."

"Maybe he wants to get in the emperor's good books by

drawing more assassins to their deaths." Thord jabbed his index finger toward me. "Did you think of that?"

"No," I snapped. I bit my tongue to stop my next retort. It was best to remember that Thord was wounded, and part of his anger came from not being fully healed. We'd been getting food for him and even feeding the swans. He was right to press me and to test my theories. But why him? Why not Megan, who was gifted at it? They were thinking alike now.

"Carmen did the right thing," Megan said.

Or maybe they weren't thinking alike at all.

"Why do you say that?" Thord said.

"The executioner is over a hundred years old. He no longer holds influence in the court and is on the far edges of the Empire in the sunset of his life. He sees this as an opportunity to change the course of his Empire's history with no one being the wiser." She adjusted her hair which didn't need adjusting. How was it always in place, even when we were out on a windy island in the Aldric Ocean? She kept it short, which helped, and it was still dyed raven black. "And Carmen had no choice. She would be dead otherwise. Would you rather she was dead?"

"Never!"

Well, at least Thord said that with a bit of emotion.

"I'm just worried, that's all," he continued. "Our task is complicated enough as it is."

"You children should kill the emperor first," Brax said. He was lying near the fire, staring at us with his one eye. It glowed in the darkness.

"Why?" I asked.

"I am being amazingly magnanimous telling you this, but if you kill Corwin first, our agreement will be fulfilled and I'll leave you in the palace surrounded by murderous Immortals."

"You wouldn't do that," I said, not sounding confident at all. "Besides, you have a task for me to perform."

"Oh, yes, there's that, isn't there?" he said, his voice soft. "I'd almost forgotten about that." He closed his eye. "I'd scoop you up and leave your companions to die."

Megan rolled her eyes. "He likes to be dramatic," she said, loud enough so Brax could hear.

"Someday you must tell us exactly what you promised the dragon," Thord said.

"Not today," I answered. "Today we need to figure out our strategy."

"It will be complex," Megan said.

"No more complicated than memorizing Maestru Orgama's cryptic code lessons," I said. "But the best maestrus trained us." I held up the plans, not for the first time. "At least we have these." I winced when I moved my arm.

"Why are you wincing?" Thord asked.

"Well, I've not been brave enough to peek at the damage the golem did."

"Oh, stop playing the tough girl," Megan said. "Show us your arms." I rolled back my right sleeve. Even in the firelight it was visibly bruised.

"Well, that was a tight squeeze," Megan said with a smile, clearly pleased with her play on words. "Now roll back the other sleeve."

I did so, to reveal another collection of bruises and scratches along my left arm. Megan reached into her cloak and came out with a healing lotion. "Hold still," she said. "It will sting. And it'll hurt you more than it'll hurt me. Which is how I prefer it."

When she touched me, I gasped.

Not because of the pain. An image flashed in my vision —a familiar picture of her bleeding and broken at my feet and my brother laughing. It was so clear. So right there in front of me, dancing in my dragon eye.

Then it was gone.

"Sorry, did that hurt?" Megan said. "I thought you were tougher than that."

"It. It. Surprised me," I said.

I didn't know if I should tell her. I was fairly certain I wasn't seeing the future.

When I looked toward the fire, I saw that Brax was staring curiously at me. He closed his eye and lowered his head.

7

ALONG THE SEA

"You were seeing the future," Brax said.

"I was?" It was well past midnight, and we were winging our way along the coast of the Ursa Sea toward Akkadium. There was enough distance between us and my companions so our words wouldn't float back to them.

"It's a possible future. So many other things come into play that it could change. For instance, you might die before that future manifests itself."

"Thanks for pointing that out." I wanted to grab his ear and give it a twist.

"I'm just looking for the silver lining," he said. His wings ruffled in a pocket of air then were quiet again.

"Assuming I don't die, I worry about the... the vision. It's the second time I've seen Megan lying bloodied before me. I can't tell if she's dead."

"Because you've seen it twice does mean it's much more likely that it will happen."

"Well, that doesn't make me feel any better." I tightened my grip on the spike. "Why doesn't Thord appear in the vision?"

"He could be behind you," Brax said. "Or he's dead."

I drew in my breath at that statement. "Don't say that."

"You aren't going into a butterfly sanctuary. This is a viper pit. It is most likely that all three of you will die."

"I know that!"

"Don't get angry, Carmen." He turned his head to the right and gave me a glare. "I am only being a voice of reason for you ill-tempered brats. Besides, I will be out of my bargain with you. So, it's not all bad." He pointed his nose straight.

"Well, I'm glad you can see the bright side. But how do I change the future? What the eye—your eye—has twice shown me?"

"Visions are often only a quick moment painted in your mind. They rarely give you enough detail to help make a choice."

"But should I tell Megan about it?" I asked.

"Go ahead. Or don't. It won't change anything. She already knows there's a good chance she'll die."

"Why do I have to see them if they're useless?"

"You wanted my eye," he reminded me. "I warned you that you wouldn't like what you see. So, don't expect me to feel sorry for you. And as far as stopping this possible future, I find it best not to try. In the attempt to avoid one fate you can make things much worse."

"What do you mean?" I asked.

"Trust the one-eyed dragon. Things can always get worse." He turned so his empty socket was pointed at me.

I felt a flash of guilt, then I remembered something. "H-how is your eye now? Is it growing back?"

"An eye doesn't grow back overnight, Carmen. Perhaps it will take years," he said. "Please don't ask me stupid questions."

"I was curious."

"Curiosity killed the human," he said. "So don't be curious, child."

"Don't call me a child."

"I'm sorry, Master."

"I'm not your master!" I shouted this last line.

Over my shoulder I saw that Thord and Megan were staring at us. I scowled straight ahead. They were lucky: at least swans only hissed and snapped. They didn't talk. The worst thing about arguing with a dragon in midair was that I couldn't step off and get away from him.

Several minutes passed. A walled town with a small port appeared below us, glowing with the light of civilization. Those lights and fortifications would get bigger and brighter as we neared Akkadium.

Brax sniffed and said, "Something *is* itching in my socket, so maybe I won't be blind forever."

"See, sometimes things get better," I said.

"Don't use the word *see* when my vision is so limited. And don't be sunny and shiny and positive: we're flying toward the central power of the Akkad Empire and trying to kill your brother and the emperor. We're all likely to be drawn and quartered. At least I'm worth something dead. None of you are."

"Even in death you are better than us. There's your real silver lining."

He swept his wings. Once. Twice. Three times. And I wondered if he was brooding. But then he laughed loud enough that it carried through the air all the way back to Megan and Thord.

8

AN AWFUL JOKE

Of all the cities in the land of Ellos, Akkadium was the finest. Approaching it silently, on a moonless night, the size and the beauty of the capital dumbfounded me. Once it had been a jumbled mess of a city, sprung from the huts of sheepherders, camel caravan stations and docks for fishing boats. But as the Empire grew Emperor Augillian had had it razed, and then he built an ordered, awe-inspiring city on the bones of the old one.

This new city had been surrounded by a thick wall in the shape of a five-pointed star. This made it harder to attack and allowed two of those points to reach into the water and protect the port. Thousands of streetlamps burned like stars below us. Each street was in a straight line leading through the city.

I glanced at Thord and Megan. Both of them were as wide-eyed as me.

For over a thousand years this city had stood here. It was the greatest seat of power in all of Ellos's history. No wonder the Akkadians saw Gudheim as a goat town or the city-state of Avenus as a pesky flea. They were nothing compared to the glory of Akkadium.

"We don't want to get too close," Brax said. "There will be sky wards to detect large winged creatures. Swans might avoid them, but a big ol' dragon with magical blood would set them screaming."

"We'll just circle around like we planned," I said. "And look for a place where we can hide a big ol' dragon and his two closest winged friends."

"Those swans are not my friends."

We arced away from the city, but I kept staring. My dragon eye, seeing such a great distance, showed me the outline of the Imperial Palace in the center of the city. They had built it on the largest hill and it would be visible to any peasant, slave or merchant who walked those streets. No matter where they were in the city.

"It's such a big palace," I whispered. "The drawings don't do it justice." A sense of awe was creeping along my spine along with fear. We were going in there.

"Losing your will, Carmen?" Brax asked.

"No."

"Just think of it as a palace with a hundred thousand hiding spots. And a hundred thousand guards."

Well, that didn't make me feel any better.

Thord broke off to the right and motioned for us to follow. We did so. Perhaps he had seen a place to land, but since Brax and I could see much farther than him, I doubted it. I was proven wrong when he swooped his swan, rather majestically I may add, down to a set of darkened and abandoned buildings.

"Leave it to the farm boy to find this," Megan said once we had landed, and the smell hit us. The building, which looked to be a large trade station, had been abandoned because it was right beside a massive dung heap.

By massive I mean it was the size of three villages. Except instead of huts there was offal from cows, sheep, camels and whatever large animals were used by farmers and merchants. They must haul it here from the city streets.

"This smells like a good crop," Thord said, gesturing around like he'd discovered a treasure pile. "In the fall the farmers spread this on their fields and their wheat grows like mad."

"Your knowledge about dung is impressive," Megan said. "You must be such a catch at the pig slaughter dances."

"You laugh, but my knowledge has found us the perfect hiding place," he said. "And yes, I was the prince of many a dance. The secret to that was always keeping my boots clean."

"That won't be so easy here," I said. There was no actual ground to be seen. Even the wagon road was made of hardened manure. I did not want to know what this place was like in a rainstorm. "But it's no worse than the dung and carcasses in the pits near Ogra," I added. "We can survive this." And then I sucked in a rather rich scent. "At least I think we can."

The trade station suggested that they sold this dung. Maybe it did have magical properties for making crops grow. The building was older and long and square, with large doors that barely hung on the hinges. It likely hadn't been used for several years.

Megan dragged open a gate, and we went inside. It wasn't a huge space, and it was clear within a few moments, from the squawking of the swans, that they did not like bunking that close to Brax.

"I may still get a taste for swan meat," he said, and they hissed at him.

"You may lose your other eye," Megan said.

"Remember, girl, I made no promise to keep you safe."

"Oh, you often talk gruff, Brax, but I wonder if it's all a show?"

Megan was more fearless than I—after all, he'd promised to not eat me or maim me.

Brax showed his teeth in answer and then snorted out a little bit of flame from his nostrils. "I'll eat you last," he said. "I'm sure that'll give you time to decide whether it's a show."

She paled a little. But only a little.

"I know what we can name this place," I said, wanting to change the topic. And I felt rather proud of my cleverness. "The Offal House."

"I've never heard you make a joke before," Megan said.

"It wasn't a joke, it was a pun."

Thord laughed hard enough he had to hold his stitches. Megan gave me a grudging smile.

"Finally, something clever from you," Brax said.

"Oh, darn," Thord said, and something in the tone gave me a sense of alarm. He was looking down at his midsection where blood was now pooling. "The stitches have snapped."

"Not from my pun, I hope," I said.

"No," he said, staring at his now bloodied fingers. "I think flying at such speed might have done it."

Megan went over to him and I stood back. She'd had higher marks than me in our medical classes. She lifted up his shirt, revealing his muscled stomach, and a raw and red sword wound. "It's not septic, at least," she said. "But the stitches need tightening." She reached into her bag and brought out a needle. "This will hurt you more than it'll hurt me," she said.

"You like to say that," I said.

"Yes, it was my mom's favorite saying." She tested the sharpness of a pin and seemed happy with it.

"As long as one of us enjoys it," Thord said. "You might as well start now."

Megan started and Thord grit his teeth but couldn't hold in the grunts of pain. I made myself busy unpacking my knapsack.

"You must rest tomorrow," Megan said when she was finished.

"But I need to help," Thord said. "This'll be fine."

"You can't have your guts coming out in the middle of the city," Brax said. "Unless you want to be a distraction. You may have forgotten that you're wearing a brace on your leg."

"We'll discuss that in the morning," Thord said.

Then we found our places to sleep. Megan fed the swans, who had already snapped up a few mice. Brax had fed on a lone camel only a few hours before and had promised me that would keep him going for at least a day.

I cleared my throat once we had settled in. "Well now that we are done, I am wondering if we could get to the matter at hand. How do we enter the palace, kill the emperor and my brother, and live to tell the tale?"

9

A STUFFED INN

We started with the most glorious task of all: we took inventory. Audits were a necessary part of any assassin's plan. It felt as if Maestru Alesius was looking over my shoulder as we listed the dragon, two swans, four daggers, a hand bow and more, including our collection of pre-prepped poisons and potions and, finally, the palace plans. It was a rather pitiful stockpile, but it was a start. And it wasn't like we would be flying into the city tonight and invading.

Because the second most important thing was observation. Assassinations are never done without forethought. We memorized every step, every door and every lock along with possible outcomes and counterplans and, of course, the location of the nearest exits.

"I will scout around," Megan said after we'd spent a couple of hours setting out various strategies. We had begun to repeat ourselves and she was bored. She flipped the hood of her cloak up. "Plus, the smell is getting to me. I want one good deep breath of fresh air."

And before either Thord or I could answer, she was out the door.

"She has a point about the smell," Brax said. "I've been breathing through my mouth for far too long."

"The smell protects us," Thord said, then he lay down on a small pile of straw, set his head against his knapsack, and promptly fell asleep. My body ached from the travel and sleep was creeping over my thoughts, but one of us had to stay awake.

I lit a candle, placed it in the dirt and continued to read *Bartum's Revenge.* It was the tale of a group of pirates who lived on islands west of Avenus five hundred years ago. Every sentence was crisp. Every turn in the story delightful. I found the book even more interesting because I'd been near the area it described.

"Did you get to the part where the rudderman dies?" Brax whispered.

"What! No! Don't tell me things like that."

His teeth glittered in the candlelight. "I was kidding. I would never give away an important part of the story. Plus, it's the drum master who dies."

"Oh, shut up and go to sleep," I said and kept reading.

An hour later there was a cough outside and the creaking of wood followed by a chittering bird sound. Megan was back and was letting me know in case I was pointing a bow at the door. It wasn't always a good idea to surprise an assassin.

She opened the door and bumped it closed with her hips. She was clutching a body in her arms, which she promptly dropped in the straw near my feet. It didn't land with a thud; instead it fell softly.

Not a body. But a bundle of clothes. My eyes had deceived me.

"I brought clothing, bread, roast goose and dried meat and berries." She dug into the pile and came out with a cloth bag stuffed with food.

I took the bread and a goose leg from her open hand. "Where did you get it?" I asked after several bites.

"There's an inn a league away called The Salted Pig. Nasty place. I had spotted it when we were flying in. My guess that being so close to the dung hills, it wouldn't be that *poopular*." She waited as if she expected me to laugh. "Oh, your jokes are funny and mine aren't? Whatever!"

I hadn't picked up on the wordplay. "Oh, *poopular*. I get it. I get it. Good one."

"Don't fake your laughter ever again or I'll kill you." She didn't smile when she said this. "Anyway, the inn is stuffed with visitors. I mean stuffed."

"Did you speak to anyone?"

She shook her head. "I thought it best not to. I slipped in and relieved two sleeping patrons of these clothes and the kitchen of the food, but before doing that I listened. And I smiled."

"You smiled?"

She had a grin now. "Yes, because luck is on our side. The goddess Belaz is with us!"

"And what is this luck?"

"We have arrived at exactly the right time." She waved her turkey leg around like it was a baton. "It's the Feast of Friends."

"That sounds rather inviting," Brax said.

"Feast of Friends?" I said. A mild perturbation coiled around my thoughts: how was Megan remembering something from class that I hadn't? "Why does that sound familiar?"

"We studied it in Historical Happenings. Don't you

remember?" She stared long enough to watch me curtly shake my head. "It was this feast where Emperor Rexen invited all of his allies and the leaders of the Five Realms. He placed his generals at the head table. These generals had plotted against him with support from those allies. So the Immortals dispatched the generals right in front of the invited guests, leaving the bodies at their places. The emperor commanded everyone to continue to eat. And ever since that time, the Akkad emperor has held a feast to celebrate."

"I remember that now." I shuddered—it was one horror from a long list of horrific things the emperors had done. "And it's been called the Feast of Friends ever since. Though, no one else has been murdered."

"Not yet, anyway," Megan said. "This is Sargon's first time hosting, and he has invited every leader in Ellos. This is his chance to impress them with his power and to let them know there are no doubts who should be emperor."

"Let us hope he doesn't start poking holes in his guests," Brax said. "It's hard to pull off an assassination amid chaos."

"The festival is why The Salted Pig is full, along with all the inns in all the city. And that's why I'm smiling." Her teeth almost glowed. "There was a poster on the wall. The palace needs to hire extra staff." She pointed at the clothing she'd found. "Which is why I stole those clothes. I hatched a brilliant plan."

And then she told me the plan.

10

A FAMILIAR FACE

The next morning I walked alone into the city dressed in a laborer's trousers, a shirt and a brown robe. The clothes Megan had found were clean, a sign that the owner had wanted to impress her potential employer. The ward to disguise my eye was in place and a female mask hid my features, even though I knew the chance of someone in a city of so many souls recognizing me was very low. I had tied back my hair and used bear claw pins, popular in this area, to keep the bun tight. Since the coloring of my skin was darker than that of most Akkadians, I had lightened it with white paste.

Megan had left before me in a maid's dress. It had fit her as if a seamstress had sewn it around her during the night. The white bonnet somehow, and I swear this was magic, made her look innocent and kind. She would enter through the western gate.

And Thord waited at the barn for the day. Since this was only reconnaissance, there was no sense in him tearing his wound again. And his limp meant he would be memorable.

The dawn sun was over my left shoulder as I approached Akkadium's northern gate. I joined the morning craftsmen and other laborers, those not rich enough to live within the city, but who worked on the gardens or stables of their masters. The traffic gate was wide and Immortals in their golden armor stood on either side of the gate, surveying the lines of people. Their helmets were in the shape of a bear's head, and their cloaks were rumored to be from bears the Immortals had to kill themselves. Their presence made the sweat trickle down my neck. I kept my eyes cast downward, sneaking glances as I passed. Some of those men had killed fellow students and my maestrus.

I walked straighter once I was through the gates. I took a few deep breaths. The stone street led toward the market but was built in such a straight line that even from here I could see the Imperial Palace looking down upon the city. It was the beating heart of the Empire.

It was a long walk to the market, a sign of how large this city was. The street opened into a giant square featuring a thousand vendors or more; salted meats, roasting meats, and live chickens and pigs were everywhere. There were vegetables and fruits glistening on display stands. And other merchants hawked jewelry, blankets, clothing and perfumes. It all looked so rich. Half the containers were made of bronze, the other half traced with gold. This was where the wealthiest citizens lived. Ships would bring these goods from around the Empire and from the Five Realms to Akkadium.

Then I spotted a face that stopped me dead in my tracks. A man bumped into me and uttered a few choice swear words, but I ignored him.

For I was looking at myself.

On a poster. A likeness of me, admirably drawn, stared down at the gathering crowds.

And below it were the words: *500 Silver Coins for her head.*

Apparently taking me alive wasn't an option.

11

A STRONG LOOK

My face wasn't the only one on the wall. Beside me was an image of Maestru Beatrix and below her Thord and Megan. And there were four others whom I didn't recognize.

I swallowed. My mask felt slick with sweat.

Was this all that was left? Seven assassins. Of the hundreds who had graduated from the Red Assassin School. Did this mean that every other student had been murdered? I had expected as much but hoped that some had escaped.

I shuddered. Then clenched my fist.

Logic first. Emotion second.

Maestru Alesius had repeated this countless times.

Yes, my other classmates were dead. Because these would be assassins whom my brother knew personally and could recognize and describe to a royal artist. I had to accept that truth. When the time came, I would lay their deaths at his feet.

As far as my conclusion that there were only four other

assassins alive, it could be wrong. Assassins hid their faces, even from the people they worked with, so there may still be assassins who couldn't be described and were thus impossible to draw.

But the unavoidable truth was that we were being blotted from the world. And that made me feel very, very tiny.

I stepped back and stared at the images and memorized them, including the other names: *Davin, Orestes, Mai,* and *Costa*. Perhaps in the future it would be important to find them. If they lived.

Then I joined the mass of people and made my way to a line of large golden tents in the center of the market.

Despite how early it was, there was already a long lineup of workers who wanted to be employed inside the palace for the festival—all part of a general call to prepare for the Feast of Friends. Megan was in another line across from me. At least I was pretty certain it was her—I'd only seen her mask in the dim light of the offal house. She ignored me, which was the wise thing to do. No sense letting any clever observer know our connection.

The sun grew hotter and I worried about the sweat, but I had made my mask with the last of the paper putty and was confident it would hold its shape. It had been a smooth batch, which I took as a sign of good luck.

The line moved fast, which meant that most were leaving after being rejected. There were too many people blocking my line of vision, so it wasn't until I walked through the tent's door and was only five people from the front that I bit my tongue and nearly let out a yelp.

There were five Immortals, and several royal staff in their immaculate white garb, but they hadn't caused my heart to beat faster: standing at the head of the line, in glittering chain mail, was Scyllia.

And she was taking the time to stare each of the workers in the eye.

"Not this one," Scyllia snapped. "Go away." The woman nodded and stepped to her right and then exited through a side door.

I couldn't leave the line, though I desperately wanted to. That would draw attention. Each of the Immortals was standing at the ready, with hands on their swords as if eager for Scyllia to bark an order and they'd instantly behead whoever she pointed at. I patted for my daggers, then cursed my memory. We'd decided it best not to be discovered with weapons. I had only my bare hands to defend me.

"Not you, you're too ugly!" Scyllia shouted at a smallish man. "Go away."

So that was why the line was moving so quickly. She was rejecting almost everyone.

"This one," she said next. "To the library. Go through." And the third woman ahead of me walked between the Immortals to be inspected by the royal staff.

"No! Begone," Scyllia said to a hunched-over woman.

"But I need the work. I have a child," the woman said, and she reached out to grab Scyllia's hand.

Scyllia slapped her hand hard. "Begone before I have them skewer you and your children." The woman scuttled out of the tent.

It was the perfect job for her. She'd always enjoyed power.

But Scyllia was angered, and I was next in line. I breathed in through my nose, took a step forward, only glanced at her and looked down.

"Not this one. Begone!" She waved her hand.

Relief flooded through my veins. I'd taken one step away when she said, "Wait. Look at me."

I turned back and met her fierce eyes briefly, then stared at the floor.

"What's your name?" she asked.

"Gurna," I muttered. I made sure my voice was low and hoarse so she wouldn't recognize it.

Scyllia continued to glare, and I didn't dare look up. The Immortals were staring, too, and they visibly tensed. I rehearsed my reaction if I was discovered, which would be to run. Though I would have to duck and run from side to side to avoid the crossbow.

Another second passed. Another.

"You look strong," Scyllia said. "To the stables with you."

"Th-thank you," I whispered.

I kept my shoulders scrunched up as I went past her and stepped between the Immortals who watched me. I expected her to give a hand signal and for one of those blades to be stabbed through me.

But the blow didn't come.

I had made it through.

An officious-looking man with a golden amulet, a sign that he was a steward of the palace, stopped me by raising his hand. He grabbed my arm and squeezed it exactly where the golem had left a circle of bruises. But it didn't hurt as those bruises had healed quickly, another little mystery Brax had yet to explain. "Yes, you're strong enough," the man said. "I assume you've dealt with horses."

I nodded.

"Join the stable hands over there." He motioned toward a group of women and men all sitting on a wagon. I knew nothing about horses, having only dealt with them on two occasions. But they couldn't differ greatly from swans, I told myself. Except they didn't eat rodents.

As the wagon pulled away, I saw Megan join the line for the housemaids. I didn't wave but gave her the slightest nod.

The first part of our plan had worked.

12

SUCH GOOD TEETH

As we approached the palace my knees knocked together and I drew in my breath. It wasn't out of fear, for I had felt many types of fear, but it was pure awe. The walls of the palace were a smooth marble, while the perfectly rounded towers with their Akkadian curves and peaks seemed to reach right into the heavens. And the white tower, glittering like a polished elephant tusk, lorded over it all. This was a level of craftsmanship beyond any I'd seen before. The Red Fortress was a sturdy backwater structure compared to this.

Every other worker—men and women—looked to be in equal awe. So, I wasn't alone.

We didn't go in the front gate because that wouldn't do for servants. Instead, we were taken to a side gate, one I remembered from the executioner's drawings, and told to leave the wagon. The steward wiped his hands on his frock and then knocked twice, and the small gate swung open and two Immortals strode out and stood on either side of the door. A tall woman who reminded me of a crane came out between them.

"I am Horse Benalk and you will do everything I ask of you." Her voice was reedy. "The first thing I ask is for you to stand very still with your arms held in front." We did so, and she pointed at us, saying, "Search them." Two soldiers grabbed and jostled each of us roughly, trying to discover hidden weapons.

Benalk had her own inspections to do, for she walked right up to me and commanded, "Open your mouth wide." It was the kind of thing a farmer would do before buying a mule, making sure the creature's teeth were good. I nearly muttered a complaint but thought better of it and stretched my jaw to the limit. She pulled out a long metal skewer and poked my teeth. It did cross my mind to bite her, but her harsh demeanor gave me pause. "Your teeth are good and solid," she said.

And then it dawned on me. She was searching for a poison tooth or wire woven between my teeth that could be used as a garrotte. She had been warned about the different tools assassins used.

"My mother never let me eat sweets," I said.

Her measuring gaze didn't leave me. I wondered if my mask showed that it wasn't real skin. Then she said, "Stand here. Don't move. And don't speak unless asked a direct question."

I stood there as she inspected the other servants. Their teeth were noticeably worse than mine—we were fed properly at the Red Fortress. That meant I stood out.

"Follow me," she said when she was finished, and she led us through what I at first thought was a tunnel, but after several steps it became clear it was the path through the wall. That meant the palace walls were at least thirty feet thick. If any enemy somehow made it through the outer walls and defences of the city, they would find this palace to be an impossible nut to crack. And these walls would be warded by ancient magicians who had long ago died at the hands of the emperors.

We emerged into the courtyard and I glanced around. A glass conservatory stood to one side, more glass than I had ever seen with flowers in every visible space. Butterflies flew in and out the open panes. To my right were row on row of statues, so I knew where I was in the plans—the Garden of Heroes.

Judging by the direction our master was leading us, we were walking toward the stables. I should have guessed that when she'd introduced herself as Horse Benalk, the *Horse* meant she was the guardian of the stables. The stables were long buildings open at one side, surrounded by a network of wooden fences. A huge flag displaying a horse flapped above the largest barn. The scent of manure tickled my nostrils.

"You will find shovels over there," Benalk said. "Fill those wagons. I will tell you when to stop." Then she turned. "I am sure even someone with such good teeth can do this work."

"Of course," I said.

I didn't like being singled out. It meant that I had been noticed, and the last thing I wanted to do was be memorable.

I grabbed a shovel and began to fill the wagons.

13

THE WHITE TOWER

It was three hours before she gave us a break for water. My mask was still holding through the labor, and I wondered if Megan was working as hard at this point. I couldn't imagine her sweating as a maid. I realized she'd foreseen this outcome when she'd stolen the clothing and therefore took care to find a scullery dress that was the right size for her. And made sure I got the laborer's clothes.

I chuckled. Clever, clever girl. I couldn't fault her for that, though I hoped she was polishing marble toilets right now so the lords, kings and ladies could see their own reflections as they peed.

"It's a big place, isn't it?" a man said beside me. He was twice my age, though he wouldn't recognize that since my mask made me look older.

"Yes, palaces can be big." I nearly pinched myself. I hadn't meant to sound sarcastic.

But he didn't take it that way. He pointed toward the white tower. "Do you think it's true, the rumors about the bones?"

"The bones?" I searched for a memory of any stories to do with bones.

"My uncle told me that all the wizard bones ended up in the mortar in that tower. That's why it's so white. It gives me the shivers."

The enchanters had fled the Empire fifty years ago when the decree was made outlawing them. Many had believed they'd be safe in the Five Realms, but Akkad was a huge empire and had a long reach. This was where a good number of wizards were brought back to die.

"It shivers me, too," I admitted.

"There. There." He patted the top of my hand. "They're dead now. They can't do nothing to us."

I didn't like his touch, and he guessed that from my look and so took his hand away.

"I wouldn't be so certain about that," I said. "Wizards may die, but I don't think their spells die."

He nodded. "There is that," he said and then he moved further away. Either from the tower or from me.

Horse Benalk marched back up to our group, her hands on her hips. "You're only working half the speed I expected of you. Make haste! All of this"—she pointed at the piles of horse dung— "has to be gone before you leave. So get back to it. Now." She glanced at me again. Had she told some Immortal her suspicions? I clutched the shovel, my only weapon, tight. "Now," she repeated.

Once I returned to work, Benalk didn't spend any extra time watching me, and no Immortals or common soldiers came to drag me away. We filled wagon after wagon, which I guessed would end up near where Thord, Brax and the swans were hiding. We paused to let a group of horses go by. They were majestic beasts bred to race, and they outshone the ones Maestru Beatrix had shown us. Groomsmen took them inside the barn to brush and clean them while other servants tied their tails with perfect bows and attached Akkad Empire flags to their bridles. It would be a majestic display for Emperor Sargon's allies and guests.

When I glanced back up at the tower, something in my dragon eye caught the light and it painted the whole structure red. Was I seeing some spell? It went back to its familiar ivory color, but a chill crept down my back. Perhaps it was better not to know. I intended to stay as far away from it as possible.

Even though I wasn't a wizard, I'd never want my bones to lie there.

14

BACK TO OFFAL

By early evening, as the sun began to set, we finished shoveling the piles of manure into wagons. My nostrils still burned with the smell, my eyes watered and my arms ached. During two breaks for water, I'd been able to spot a rookery near one corner of the palace. That would be for messages. And the glint of armor and a protruding giant bolt in one tower indicated a ballista crossbow. So they could easily bring any dragon or swan approaching the palace down. I assumed there was at least one more ballista each in the remaining three palace towers, not to mention others planted around the walls surrounding the city.

Horse Benalk led us to the side gate and handed each worker a gold coin and a paper. I clutched both tightly.

"Your payment," Benalk said. "Arrive at this gate by six bells tomorrow, present this paper, and expect to work twice as hard as you did today."

We walked through the thick walls and onto the lawn surrounding the palace. I didn't say a word to my fellow workers, but began the long trek to the offal house. My sense of awe had vanished, perhaps from smelling horse manure for the whole day. That was a good thing—I wouldn't be approaching it with such trepidation tomorrow, the day of the Feast of Friends. I bought food in the market and left through the northern gate, winding my way to our sweet-smelling home.

"Where's Megan?" Thord said the moment I opened the door.

"I thought she would have returned by now," I answered.

"Do you think they caught her?" He was rubbing his hands together. A day trapped inside this dung house might have driven him mad.

I shook my head. "There were no warning bells. Though the palace grounds are huge, so I might not have heard any commotion. But I think if there had been an assassin caught each worker would have been inspected again or even held overnight and questioned."

"Did you even try to speak to her?" he demanded, limping a few steps closer.

"No! That wasn't possible." Maybe spending those weeks alone with her had made him more in need of her council. Or his wound was septic and the sickness was going straight to his head. I took a deep breath, calming myself, and told him what had happened, being sure to mention our wanted posters and about being face-to-face with Scyllia.

"Maybe she recognized Megan," he said. "Did you think of that?"

"Stop snapping at me, Thord. We did everything like we planned. I only know that she got past the inspection and was in a cart on the way to wherever they took the maids. There was no time to talk with her, and as you know that would only arouse suspicion."

Brax coughed. And with that cough came a puff of smoke. "Listening to your feeble intellects grapple with basic assumptions makes my stomach turn," he said. "She is spending the night there. My guess is because she and the other servants will interact with the guests, they will not be let out of the palace so they won't bring any weapons, poisons or diseases in. And, I hesitate to say this because I know how sensitive you two are, but they probably want their servers clean."

"Clean?" I asked.

"You two stink. And even Megan, who is the most concerned about her appearance, has a—how shall I put it —unattractive stench." He tapped his nose. "Trust me on that. The palace will bathe the servants so each of them smells like a rose as they serve."

"Oh," I said. "That makes sense." I sniffed, aware that I'd brought much of the smell back with me from the horse yards. I could use a hot bath, too.

"Of course it does." Brax itched at his ear with a talon. "And please don't make me spend another full day with this boring, boring boy."

Thord glared at him.

"Oh, don't give me that hurt look. You can't even discuss books. What point is there in having a brain if you don't read stories?"

"I don't have time to read novels," Thord said. "We're a little busy trying to kill the emperor and Corwin."

"One makes time for such things if one is civilized," Brax said. I was in total agreement there, but I saw that he was taking a deep breath to launch into another attack.

I put up my hand. "Food," I blurted. "Food! That'll take the edge off. I brought food."

I handed a wrapping with sausage and cheese and dried berries to Thord and then walked over to Brax and brought out a roasted chicken.

"Well, that's like feeding a handful of oats to a horse." But he poked a talon into it, shoved the chicken into his mouth, chewed twice, swallowed and begrudgingly said, "Thanks."

I joined Thord, and we ate silently for a few minutes.

"I—I am sorry I snapped," he said. "Sitting here all day. Doing nothing but staring out the crack in the door and listening to insults. It was... not exciting."

"Apology accepted," I said.

"I am glad you made it back, at least. And what Brax said makes sense."

"Everything I say makes sense." Brax snorted. "Every single thing."

"What was the palace like?" Thord asked.

"The executioner's plans don't do it justice," I said. "Those are just pieces of paper. To actually stand there inside the walls, looking up at the main keep and the white tower. It... it is almost unbelievable that they built such a palace."

"Do we wait for Megan here?" he asked.

"I don't know that we have any other choice. Perhaps when I return to the palace in the morning, I'll see her." I sat back. My bones and my flesh were weary. But it was night, and I knew this was the best time to take to the air.

"I think Brax and I should make another sweep around the city. It's time to stretch your wings, Brax."

This got a smile out of him.

15

CLOUDED SKIES

The clouds blocked the moonlight and the starlight and made it difficult to see the shadow of Brax's wings from the ground. It would have been the perfect night for flying except for a wind that had risen, filling the air with whirls and pockets where Brax would swerve or drop, which would make my heart leap in my chest as I clutched the horn.

Despite that, it felt good to be on his back again and taste the fresh air. Fresh air! We swung out into the nearby mountains. The coolness had awakened me, making me feel more alive.

"Hold on," Brax said and then he dived almost straight down, plunging hundreds of feet in a few seconds, arcing at the last minute and scooping up a mountain goat in his front talons. Its neck was already broken and I turned away as he stuffed it into his mouth. I couldn't block out the crunching and cracking of bones.

"You can open your eyes now," he said. I did so, seeing that tufts of wool were stuck to my cloak. I brushed them off, thankful I wasn't spattered with blood. "It didn't suffer and I have to eat."

I understood that. But the whole episode was a reminder of how powerful he was. The goat hadn't even had time to utter a bleat.

I put the image of the goat hanging from his mouth out of my head. We circled closer to Akkadium; the city's lights seemed brighter perhaps because no light was coming through the murky sky.

"With the cloud cover we could go right over the city," he said. "Though we won't see anything because of those same clouds."

"We must hope it is clear tomorrow night."

"Yes, and hope that the magical wards are not too high in the air."

"Yes, that too," I said. "Let's wing our way over to the port."

We circled around the city, and as we approached the port I couldn't help but be impressed by how two corners of the wall reached far into the water, leaving a large protected bay that was safe from bad weather and from attacking fleets. How many slaves had drowned to build those walls? But the port itself was jammed with hundreds of ships from around the Five Realms: Avenus triremes with their twin sails, the single-sailed and sleek Truskian ships, and even several Woden longships. The powerful were already here, with more arriving by the hour for the feast.

But what caught my eye was a line of square barges, like a floating island, beyond the wall. We edged as close as we dared, uncertain where the first air wards would be located.

"What is that line of barges?" I asked. They had been tethered and anchored in one place.

"Fireworks," Brax said.

"You're right. What a massive collection. That's enough to light the sky for hours—at least half a league of fireworks. They must be for the feast tomorrow."

"Yes," Brax said. "It will be an impressive show. We don't want to be caught in that."

As he hovered in place, I felt the excitement build, despite myself. We'd rarely had fireworks at the Red Fortress, but when we did all the students had been allowed to stand on the balcony and watch. This show would make that look amateurish.

A dark-winged shape leaving from one of the palace towers caught my dragon eye.

"Do you see that?" I asked.

"Yes," Brax said, and without a word he pushed his wings harder so we rose into the clouds. I lowered myself closer to his back, to keep from being blown off in the burst of speed. He stayed above our target and soon my dragon eye could focus properly.

It was a rider on a black swan. Obviously Corwin had stolen a collection of swans from the Red Assassin School. Could that be Corwin himself?

"It's a swan," Brax said.

"I know."

"Oh, right. I briefly forgot that you have my eye in your head."

"I'm putting it to good use," I said. "Can we get close enough to see who is on the swan? As far as I know only assassins are trained to ride the swans. I doubt an Immortal would have the skill so soon."

We followed, heading east across the water. The swan came and went from my vision as we passed through clouds. It became clear that the rider was not Corwin—he was simply too big.

Then I recognized the shape, the wide shoulders.

It was Gregum.

He glanced to the left and right as though he might have heard us. I was fairly certain he couldn't see this distance if he looked over his shoulder.

"That's one of your classmates, isn't it?" Brax said. The wind wouldn't carry his words.

"Yes, it's Gregum. He is flying east."

"Perhaps to Myra. He might carry a message."

"Or," I said, "he is hunting down another assassin."

"That seems to be his habit," Brax said. "Should we knock him from the sky?"

Turning him into a flaming chunk of Gregum that tumbled into the sea would be a glorious sight. I ran that image through my head several times. "No," I said, finally. "It may be a short trip, and killing him would warn Corwin of our presence. It's good news that he will be gone. Let's hope it will be for several days. We should turn back and take one last pass around the palace."

He spread his wings and angled them so we arced away from Gregum. The swan and rider disappeared from sight. I would have to get revenge on Gregum another day.

It was harder going back against the wind, and I realized how far we were from land. A sudden buffet of wind caught my cloak in a way that pulled my grip loose and I slid along Brax's scales, grabbing for a handhold. He had to tip himself so I stayed on.

"Do hold tight," he said. "I wouldn't want to try to find you in the sea. Plus I don't like salt water. It makes the eyes burn." He paused. "Eye, that is."

"You are getting somewhat whiny and repetitive."

"You have two eyes," he barked. "Until we both have two eyes, your ears will dine on my bitterness."

His eye couldn't grow back soon enough!

Another sudden gust hit me and unfurled my cloak. If it wasn't such a useful piece of clothing, I'd untie it and let it go. I tried to bunch it up with one hand so not so much would be open to the wind.

Something harder than wind hit me.

It smashed me down onto Brax's back, then pain erupted in both shoulders and I was yanked upwards.

Away from Brax.

But I didn't fall.

And my predicament became clear. I was caught in the talons of a black swan.

Gregum peered down at me, one hand on his reins, and he grinned like mad. Half his face was red with healing flesh from where my acid had burned him. It made him look even more frightening.

"Surprise," he said. "Your brother will be so happy to see you."

16

AN EPIC TALE

The talons were stabbing into my shoulders, threatening to pierce right through them. The swan had swept its powerful wings and climbed so high into the clouds I'd lost sight of Brax.

"Snatched right from a dragon's back!" Gregum cackled. "This is going to be so wonderful to tell Corwin about. An epic tale! Higher! Higher!"

The swan responded to his commands, pushing itself deeper into the clouds, far away from Brax. I tried to shout his name, but the wind muffled my cries. Gregum was going to fly straight above the city and dive through the magical wards and into the palace, and there would be no way for Brax to follow us.

"You won't live to tell the tale!" I shouted.

Laughter was his only reply.

"Brax!" I shouted in the vain hope he could hear me. "Brax!" Even if he was looking through my eye, all he would see was clouds.

"Squeeze her until she shuts up," Gregum said. And the swan tightened its talons, digging further into my flesh. I nearly screamed, but bit my lip because I knew Gregum would enjoy hearing my cries.

"Brax!" I gave one more shout, but the pain grew so strong I worried I'd fall unconscious.

I would have to figure my own way out.

Even though it hurt, I reached up with my left hand past one swan leg and could just grab the saddle belt. I clutched it with all my might and used my other hand to slip a dagger out of its sheath. I thrust it into the talon sticking into my left shoulder.

The swan gave a horrible hissing squawk and tried to peck at me, but I stabbed another talon and it released my left shoulder. Two quick stabs later, it had completely let go and I hung from the belt. I yanked myself up so I was out of reach of the talons and the beak. The bird was going mad with pain and anger, flapping through the sky, spiraling left and right.

"Stop that! Stop!" Gregum shouted. I didn't know whether he was yelling at me or his mount. "Stop it, you stupid bird!"

With one slice of my dagger I could cut the belt and he would fall. But so would I, and I wasn't certain whether we were above the water or land now.

I sheathed my dagger, since the plan that had popped into my skull involved climbing, and I pulled my two-handed way along the swan's underbelly, swung my legs out for momentum and then arced around and kicked Gregum in the midsection.

It was a direct hit, and he'd been looking the other way, trying to gain control of his swan. But Gregum was a lot bigger than me and had a tight grip on the reins and the saddle horn. I only knocked him halfway off the saddle.

He grabbed one of my legs and pulled but I kicked him

with the other, hitting his chain mail. He laughed at that, so my second kick was higher and struck his forehead.

The blow didn't faze him. He'd always had a tough skull and loved inflicting and receiving pain. Gregum stood in the saddle, holding tight with his knees, digging into the stirrups and pulling me up. I held as tight as I could but soon felt my cold fingers lose strength, and I let go of the belt.

He held me far enough above the swan that I couldn't reach him.

"This is where the tale ends," he said. "It's too much work to take you back alive. I'll just return with your broken body."

His scarred lips were curling into a twisted smile.

"Sorry about your face," I said. "It is an improvement!"

"I'll enjoy hearing you hit the ground," he replied. Then lifted me even higher.

Before he could throw me, the swan hissed a warning and a giant shape smashed into us in midair.

Brax had rammed the swan at full speed. It was an almost perfect blow. Gregum was tossed from the saddle. The swan's neck and wing were broken, and feathers flew all around us.

And I, having no wings, fell straight from the sky.

17

THE WAY DOWN

We came out of the cloud cover. Three hurtling gray shadows going straight down.

And we had not traveled as far as I'd thought, for we were still over the Ursa Sea. I tumbled left and right, trying to straighten out, but only managing to get myself into a horrible spin. Despite that, I searched the sky for Brax. I spotted Gregum glittering about twenty feet below me—it looked like he was trying to pull off his armor, but there wasn't time. The lifeless swan was plummeting like a rock.

Brax was nowhere to be seen.

By holding out my arms and legs and tightening my stomach muscles, I stopped the tumbling and got my feet to point straight down. I snapped my head left and right looking for Brax, hoping he'd come swooping out of those shadows. I tried to yell but the air ripped words from my mouth.

Gregum hit first, making a powerful splash. Then about thirty feet away from him the swan's body crashed into the waves.

I gulped air before striking the water.

It was like being punched on the bottom of my feet and the blow going all the way up my spine, making my bones ache.

I went down. Down. Down. The water was like ice. Further and further I went. I thought of the stories of men with webbed feet and gills who lived at the bottom of the ocean. Stories I'd read as a child. I'd be seeing those creatures soon. Further down I went until I thought my lungs would burst.

Then I slowed and could kick my legs and begin the long push to the surface. I rose higher and higher but had no idea how far the surface was, since there wasn't even a moon to look for.

They had taught us in assassin school how to sit underwater and hold our breath without letting out the smallest bubble. But I had been fighting and my shoulders ached with every movement and my legs were growing weaker. My lungs demanded more air.

But further I went. Upwards, into the never-ending grayness. The surface had to be near. It had to be.

But the need for air grew and grew so that every other thought and warning was pushed aside.

Just one breath. Maybe, I was already at the surface and I didn't know it.

One breath wouldn't hurt.

And I opened my mouth. Knowing it was wrong, but I couldn't stop my lungs from demanding it.

And I sucked in the water.

It made me cough, which forced me to suck in more. Pain shot through my head and lights flashed in my eyes.

I stopped kicking upward. My legs no longer worked.

When people drown, they don't thrash. They grow quiet.

That is what Master Alesius had told us. That the body stops working and the brain stops thinking.

I would die soon. One eye was going black.

Only my dragon eye was focusing and seeing nothing but grayness.

No. Not nothing.

Because a dark shape hurtled toward me.

18

THE SHAPE

The shape grew from being gray and featureless to a recognizable form with a glowing eye: it was Brax, cutting through the water, his wings folded against his side and bubbles of air shooting past him. He caught me up in his jaws and unfurled those wings and was able to push us higher and higher.

I could see the surface. A slightly brighter place above us.

Then everything went black.

I floated for a long time and my thoughts slowed to nothing. I had no wants. No desires. No pain. Only darkness.

It wasn't so bad. At least I didn't have to struggle.

And then a voice trickled into my ears. "Breathe," it said. "Breathe." Something was pressing on my chest and I knew I no longer floated—there was solidity under my back and legs. And yet it was soft, too.

"Breathe, child! Breathe, damn you!"

I wanted to breathe. But nothing would come in or go out.

I opened my dragon eye. Brax was looking down at me,

and I was splayed in soft sand as he pressed his paws against my chest and my stomach. I coughed, spurting water in an impressive stream. Another watery cough gargled out and another and then air, air somehow magically found its way into my lungs. I sucked in again and again until my lungs were full. Then I coughed more.

The sky was cloudy. We were on the beach not far from the walls of Akkadium and could be easily spotted by a fisherman or lookouts in their towers. It was a wonder that no warning shouts or flares had gone up yet.

Any observer would have seen there was a dragon leaning over me.

"Good!" Brax said. "You're not dead."

With the support of one of his talons, I could sit up. The lights of Akkadium danced in my vision.

"We can't linger here," Brax said. He was dripping water, his scales glistening, and without another word he scooped me up in his talons and took to the air. He was much more gentle than the swan had been.

I coughed out the rest of the water as we climbed higher. Maybe it was his intention to shake the rest of the sea out of my innards. I wanted to say something, anything, but my words had been left in the watery depths. I closed my eyes.

When I next opened them, it was as he settled me gently on the ground near the offal house and then landed beside me. I used his leg as a support and climbed to my feet. I leaned against him. "You saved me," I said.

"Yes, Carmen. It was part of our bargain. I promised to do everything I could to keep you safe."

"But you risked your life. Why not let me die?"

"I am a dragon of my word."

My wind was coming back. "Thank you," I said. And I hugged his leg.

He patted my shoulder and said, "I was only doing what I promised. Don't get emotional."

I knew it was more. Beyond our contract. He had wanted me to live, had called me child. Almost as if he were my father.

"I had no idea that dragons could swim," I said.

"It's not something I like to do."

"Did… did you see what happened to Gregum and the swan?"

"The swan was dead in the air," Brax said. "I tried to snatch you in time, but failed."

"And Gregum?"

"Unless he grew gills, he has drowned. He was wearing armor. He's at the bottom now where he belongs. The fish will nibble him down to nothing."

I nodded. I was only wearing a cloak that had threatened to drag me down, but he had been in chain mail. He was dead.

"Good," I said. He had killed so many of our friends. "That is wonderful news. Let us go inside and share it with Thord."

19

WORDS BY THE HEARTH

"By Belaz, what happened?" Thord said the moment the door opened.

I explained what I could, but was shivering too much to make proper sense.

"We must build you a fire," he said, pulling me toward the hearth.

"It might show off our position," I said.

"Not if there isn't smoke," Brax said. "I can make a fire that will warm you without wood."

He went over to the hearth and made a gargling noise like he was bringing up a horrible collection of phlegm, even working his shoulders and chest, and then he spat whatever it was into the hearth. He snorted a funnel of fire toward the liquid. It burst into flames and kept burning.

Brax could spit some liquid that would later burn. My slow, cold mind made measure of that and added it to my list of weapons.

I almost crawled over to the fire and Thord, despite his own wound, helped me. I got as close as I could to the flames and shivered. I stripped off my cloak but was too decorous to go any further. The heat would dry me soon enough.

"So Gregum is dead?" he said.

"He's at the bottom of the Ursa Sea," Brax said. "Maybe an eel is using him as a home."

"We had better hope that he was on a longer mission," Thord said. "If they expected him back later tonight, the palace will be a beehive of intrigue and accusations. I wish there was a way to warn Megan."

"There just isn't," I whispered.

Warmth worked its way through my skin, reaching for my bones. My throat and nose hurt, burned by the salt water. And my eyes were red. I was certain I looked like, well, like someone who had nearly drowned. But I didn't care. Slowly I stopped shivering. Then, not just out of vanity, I combed out my hair, finding seaweed and some other green bits. But it, too, grew dry. The flame still burned strongly.

Then the pain started—my body hadn't liked fighting Gregum and slamming into the water from such a great height. But mostly my shoulders ached, and I pulled back my tunic enough to see gouges left by the swan's talons.

"Oh, it really got you," Thord said. "Does it hurt?"

It was perhaps the stupidest question he'd ever asked. I searched for a quip, but failed. "Yes," I said. "Yes. A lot."

"It's a flesh wound," Brax added. "Get over it."

I shot him a glare and searched for biting remark, but suddenly shuddered in surprise. Thord had placed his hand on my shoulder and was already rubbing lotion over the wound. "This will soothe it," he said.

I stood stock still and even held my breath. His touch was gentle and, within moments, he had applied bandages to both shoulders. "That should do it," Thord said.

"Thanks," I said, covering my shoulders again.

"Hey, if we couldn't patch each other's wounds up what kind of team would we be?"

"That's right," I said. "What kind of team would we be?" The pain had been soothed but my shoulders tingled. I was certain it wasn't just from his touch.

"I don't know if you'll be able to go to the palace tomorrow," he said. "Those are some nasty holes."

"There isn't a choice. They'll just have to heal overnight." After my experience with the acid, I wondered if that would actually happen. When there was time to pause, I'd have to figure out what was happening to my body. "Thankfully I only have to look presentable enough to muck about in the barn."

"I'm coming with you," Thord said.

"Into the palace?" I said. "That's not possible. Will you tramp around the walls until they arrest you?"

"I am really tired of not being able to do anything."

"You'll have work to do because tomorrow night is our best time to strike," I said. "That is when the Feast of Friends begins."

"And that's when the number of guards will be at its greatest."

"Yes, but there will be fireworks to distract them," I said.

"Fireworks?" Thord asked. "How do you know about that?"

I had forgotten to mention the barges floating outside the walls of Akkadium. I described what I had seen.

"That gives me an idea," he said when I was finished. He looked at the fire, at Brax, then at me. "I think I know what I can do."

"Good," I said. "I may have a couple of ideas, too."

20

FORGETTABLE

By six bells the following morning I was at the side gate of the palace along with my fellow workers. The wounds in my shoulders had closed up, but the bruises, stiffness and pain hadn't vanished. I would just have to work through it all. We all stood silently at the door, perhaps worrying that talking would affect our prospects of work. One woman let out a cough and clutched at her stomach.

I had cleaned myself up as much as possible, but it was hard to get too clean while living in a dung hill. Maybe at this very moment Megan was stepping out of a steam bath, her hair coiffed, her underarms daintily perfumed. She was the best at mask making, so it should survive one or two dunks in a bath. I had my own mask over my face, but it already felt tight and itchy and was a little frayed around my ears. I had lightened the skin tones on my arms and neck again so I wouldn't stand out. The makeup had held the whole previous day until my delicious dip in the water.

From outside the gates, there was no sign of any tumult or extra precautions, and that suggested they didn't yet know Gregum was missing. Not that I expected them to seize and arrest every worker.

The gate opened and two Immortals came out, swords drawn.

Maybe they knew about Gregum.

But they stood on either side of the entrance as Horse Benalk strode out, her eyes red as if she'd failed to get a wink of sleep. She pointed at the woman who had been coughing. "Not you. You're sick. Begone." The woman hustled away, snuffling as she went.

Benalk again inspected each of our mouths while two soldiers searched for weapons. When she got to my mouth, she probed for what felt like five minutes. I swear she tapped every tooth at least twice. Then she stepped back and her eyes, two suspicious orbs, stared at me.

"Uh, yes," I said, hoping she'd stop her glare.

"You smell like salt," she said.

"I swam in the sea last night," I replied, then wondered if I shouldn't have said that because they might somehow know that Gregum had fallen into the ocean. Maybe the swan's feathers had washed up on the beach. He wouldn't wash up anywhere. But who would connect a stable hand with his disappearance?

"I guess that's as close to clean as you'll come," she said, then turned on her heel. "Come along, all of you. The stables await."

I followed the line of workers through the thick walls and into the palace. The grounds were already a nest of activity: slaves and workers were trimming leaves in the courtyard and sweeping the stone paths. They had set lines of tall torches along the path to light the way for the many rich visitors.

We returned to the stable, and I shoveled a fresh collection of horse poop and straw, ignoring my aching shoulders as we filled wagon after wagon. Did the emperor want the place so clean that it would appear his horses had never defecated? I took any spare moments when I wiped my brow or rubbed my arms to stare around and memorize this part of the palace grounds. I kept hoping that Megan would just wander by, but knew she was most likely working in the palace.

She wouldn't have a shovel in her hands.

Hours passed. Blisters formed. The morning turned to afternoon and stretched toward the evening, shovelful by shovelful. I went through the plan Thord, Brax and I had decided on, rehearsing each step and looking for weaknesses. Master Alesius had always said the best plans fall apart the moment you leave the planning room—I wanted to be prepared for that. I wouldn't have called it a brilliant plan, but the biggest weakness was that I couldn't pass the information along to Megan.

She'd just have to join in however she could. If she was able.

Now was the time to try the first part of our plan. And if this failed, the whole plan was for nought. I worked my way closer to the barn, waiting for when Horse Benalk was looking away.

Then fate came along and handed me a prize. For an overseer from another group of workers came running up to Benalk and said, "Mistress. The main wagon is stuck."

"They just need proper motivation," she said. "I'll provide it." She marched off in the direction the man had come from. The overseer remained to encourage us to work harder.

His guttural commands were aggravating, but he had one wonderful quality: he had a wandering eye.

First, he watched us work, but when a gaggle of servant women trundled by his leering gaze was drawn to them. Mine was, too. I looked them over quickly, but none had the same body shape as Megan.

Then, while he was still staring at the women, I took two steps backwards so I was in a shaded section of the barn that I knew was hidden from sight from several directions. It was a perfectly executed disappearance.

Except for the horse dung. Apparently, we hadn't cleaned up every last bit of it because I'd stepped right into a fresh pile. Wonderful!

I climbed into the rafters, my feet slipping on the fresh material stuck to my boots. Despite that, I made my way to the top so I'd be out of sight. I settled in and waited, sitting comfortably on a beam. Only the keenest eye would spot me.

I ran through the plan several more times. Rehearsing the jumps.

In time I heard the call that meant we were done work and was pleased it was the same man who made the call—Horse Benalk was still busy getting the wagon free. The overseer entered the barn below me and I stayed still. He gave a perfunctory look around, but didn't glance up. Then he left.

That was another good reason to not talk to my fellow workers—that way I'd be forgettable.

I wanted to be forgettable.

I stayed in that position until night fell.

21

A GREAT LEAP

It would be easier to be spotted along the ground because there were so many extra soldiers and Immortals patrolling. I had no uniform or fancy dress to wear as a disguise, so I stayed as high up as possible. I climbed out the vents at the back of the stable and onto the roof, hoping that my dark clothing hid me from view. And I moved slowly as Maestru Alesius had taught me because fast movements drew the eye. That's why a tiger creeps up on its prey before it leaps.

I spidered across to the next building, crawled along the roof and then sat still for several minutes, noting the placement of each guard on the towers above me and when they would switch. I then continued to move in the shadow. The sky was littered by a few small clouds and the moon wasn't bright, but it cast enough light to make my skin glint, so I made sure my sleeves were drawn.

I noted, too, that the lords and ladies were now streaming into the palace itself escorted by Immortals, their armor shined to a dazzling brightness that made them hard to miss from this distance. They glowed in the rows of torches and it was clear why so much light had been set around the pathways. Emperor Sargon wanted every symbol of his power to burn in the minds of his guests.

I noted one visitor was in a bright blue toga and knew her to be the female archon from Avenus, the city-state. That was their chosen color. They never sent both archons to any meetings, so both would never be captured or killed at the same time.

When I got to the edge of the building, I discovered a minor problem. My next logical step was to leap from here to a long balcony on the palace itself, but there was a rather intimidating distance between the two buildings. I estimated it to be at the edge of my jumping distance. And it meant I'd have to make the attempt at top speed.

I waited until I was certain the guards on the towers were turned away and the ground below was clear.

And then I ran quietly and swiftly along the roof. The surface was solid, and I didn't make much noise but it might be enough to attract attention. When I reached the end, I tried to jump with a good grip, but my left foot slipped on a loose tile. Apparently the executioner hadn't overseen the hammering of every single tile.

I arced through the air but I would miss the balcony, which meant I'd be breaking bones on the ground in a moment. I stretched my arms as far as I could.

And caught the very edge of the balcony.

My chest slammed into the stone, knocking the breath out of my lungs. But I was able to clutch one hand over the edge and hold myself there, despite the rediscovered pain in my shoulders. Then slowly, knowing I was in full view of anyone walking below, I pulled up. My ribs ached as I drew myself over and crumpled down onto the balcony. I sat there for a moment trying not to huff and puff.

It would have been so much easier just to fly on Brax's back. But the ballistae and the wards would have been too much of a risk.

There had been no outcry, so I hadn't been spotted. I felt my ribs, and they didn't seem broken. Though my body certainly ached from the fight last night. I was tempted to lie down here and sleep.

But that wouldn't help Megan. Or accomplish our goal.

I stood and leaned against the palace and made my quiet way along the long balcony.

It was a perfect execution, gaining the palace without being spotted. If we'd been in class Maestru Alesius would have complimented me. Everything was working out.

Until a glass door swung open in front of me.

22

A GIFTED NOSE

I hid behind a stone pot.

It was in the shape of a bear and if I squeezed myself hard enough, it hid most of my body, and the fronds from the palm plant blocked the rest of me from sight.

A man and a woman, both in blue togas, stepped out. The man was portly but steady on his feet, while the woman was tall, her spine straight.

"Ah, fresh air," she said.

"We shall need a surfeit of it after the discussions in that room," the man replied. "So much hot air. Such a bountiful selection of obsequiousness."

I was pretty certain his use of large words meant he was an ambassador from Avenus. The Avenians loved their words and gave the longest speeches.

"Everyone must bend their knee toward the young emperor." The woman had taken another step, revealing she had a bronze crown of laurel leaves in her hair—she was Thena, the archon of Avenus. I pressed my back even harder against the wall. Her protective guard would be near, perhaps just outside that door. "He's taken the assassins off the board and we have lost our only way to reach right into the throne. Together all Five Realms could face the Empire, but we bicker too much for that. With the assassins we could at least threaten a blow."

"Yes, the timing is perfect for him. I expect the drums of war to thud soon enough." The consul's breath rattled, and I wondered if he had a cold or some sickness in his lungs. "This land is too dry for me."

"The humor, too," Archon Thena said. "Scratch that—there is no humor at all. A whole empire where everyone is too frightened to laugh unless the joke is made by Sargon himself. And those Immortals are made of humorless stone."

"I'm sure they grin when they skewer someone." The man sniffed. "Otherwise, never. They appear even grimmer than when under the control of the previous."

"Their grim features perhaps suggest how the next few months will play out."

The man turned back toward the door. "Ah, I heard a summoning bell. Let's put our oafish smiles on our faces and return. One of the handlers will be along to usher us toward some new displayed glory. I for one plan to bankrupt the Empire by eating every last dainty at the table."

"We would build a heroic statue to you for that," Thena said. "A large and perfectly proportioned statue that captures every inch of your sacrifice."

They both laughed then went back into the palace. Through the crack in the door, other guests were visible being led along a long hallway. It fed into the great hall. Having memorized the executioner's drawings made it easy to keep track of where I was.

I crept along, low enough not to be seen. Then I raised my head and peered through a window directly into the great hall. Massive marble tables were set with enough food to feed all of Ellos. There were golden goblets and golden forks and golden knives and spoons—every setting had at least five of each. It was all so bright I had to squint. A garish statement about how rich and powerful the Empire was.

I reached the door and wondered if I should step past or close it and then decided to close it, thereby preventing a servant from coming along and spotting me.

But as I pushed, a hand stopped the door. I tucked myself back against the stone wall on the other side of the door. But I was far too much in the open for my liking.

The portly consul from Avenus was standing there, his arm holding the fold of the blue toga as though he were posing for a painting.

"Please don't move," he said. "I won't hurt you."

He was a diplomat who'd had every meal handed to him in the last thirty years and never done the slightest bit of labor—he certainly couldn't hurt me.

"By that," he continued, his voice smooth, "I mean I won't cry out 'there's an assassin on the balcony,' which would bring a cavalcade of grouchy Immortals here."

"I appreciate that."

"Good. Archon Thena was informed that I needed one more breath of fresh air. So we only have a short time for you to answer my questions. Since you are a member of a dying order, I want to express my sorrow."

"Um. Thank you."

He sniffed. "My guess is you are not one of the emperor's pet assassins."

"No. I'm not," I said. I set my foot against the wall. Despite his calmness and kind words, he could betray me in a moment. I would launch myself over the balcony, catch the wall, and flip down to the ground.

"Would you be willing to tell me what your aim is on this night of bragging and feasting?"

"No," I said.

"Well, that's understandable." He took a deep breath. "I'm just playing my part by breathing in so loud. We wouldn't want anyone thinking I was chatting with an assassin."

"How did you see me?" I asked. "I was well hidden."

He tapped his pudgy nose. "You may say I have a nose for things."

He'd smelled me? I should have known. My nostrils had long ago gotten used to the smell of manure and urine. It had dried, but the smell hadn't left me. There was no way to get rid of it now.

"I am curious whether you intend to kill any of the invited guests tonight?" he asked.

"No," I said.

"Ah, so it is righteous vengeance on your mind. That's my guess. There are still a few of you gloriously somber assassins alive and you are striking back." He took another deep breath and rubbed his hands together. "Good. Good. I know of an assassin who hides in Avenus—we have protected those we could. But the best are all dead."

"Will you expose me?" I was wondering if I could get around the door and bring him down before he yelled.

"No. Though it did cross my mind to exchange you for a better trade deal, but what would be the fun in that? I'm a playful sort. I like the idea of the emperor getting a nose-bleed tonight. Even if it's just payment for the boring speeches they have subjected us to. If you succeed in whatever your task is, then that helps my wonderful city. If you fail and are captured, then you will still bring shame upon him. So either way it is what they call a win-win."

"I see," I said. "Then I ask that you let me move along."

"Yes. If I had coins, I would hire you. But may I make a suggestion?"

"You may."

"There is a window just beyond the end of this balcony. I may have a nose, but I have an eye for foods, too. If you go in there, you will find a storage room—a pantry, really. You can perhaps wash yourself with pickle juice, though that is not important."

"I am aware of that room," I said, which was true. But I didn't know what was in it.

"Of course, you are. But I want to remind you it has a decorative interior window at the top, and through it I think you will get a good view of the proceedings. And I assume in your occupation you need a good view."

"Yes," I said. The window wasn't in the plans and could have been added later. It sounded like the perfect place to hide and observe the goings-on. Though I knew it could also be a way to trap me in a single room. "Thank you," I said, finally.

"I know your type are suspicious. Rightfully so. But it is not a trap. I want you to succeed. This is such a garish place. A boorish waste of an empire if you ask me." He took a deeper breath. "Ah, that is refreshing sea air," he said a little loudly and then he whispered, "Good luck, assassin. I know I need not tell you this, but the emperor is a powerful man. In ways our own informers don't even understand. I hope you have wards. May Belaz guide your blade."

When he invoked the name of my goddess, a thrill went down my spine as if I'd received a blessing.

"She will," I said.

Then he pulled the door shut, and I snuck past and over the balcony. The window was where he'd said it would be and it was easily accessible.

I'd be able to jump back out if things turned sour.

I climbed in.

23

A PEEK AT POWER

The small storage room was exactly as the ambassador described it. I landed on the floor and scraped whatever dung I could off my shoes, then threw the refuse back out the window. I then climbed to the ceiling, ignoring my aching shoulders, and peered through the circular window at the top of the room.

The ambassador had also been correct about the fact the interior window gave me an excellent view of the hall. If I'd had a crossbow, I could have put a bolt through any of the rich and pompous people gathered below.

A moment later the ambassador himself walked by and glanced up at me with a little grin and then turned, flourished his toga, and went down a set of several steps into the main floor of the hall. The archon was ahead of him. Her blue robe was stunning, and the lamps caught the bronze leaves on her head as she nodded and spoke to the people she passed. Beyond her, already seated at table after marble table, were the other heads of state or their ambassadors or princes. I could guess which countries were here by their colors—representatives from every realm.

All the servers were women in white dresses and white bonnets. I scanned each face and thought I saw one with the same features Megan had created. But I couldn't be certain from this distance, even with my dragon eye. I wished I'd stared at her mask longer. Had I forgotten what it looked like?

She went back through a set of pillars. I waited and watched, memorizing the location of each doorway. And noting the number of guards in the room and where they stood.

A glitter of metal attracted my eye. A woman in a dark cloak was walking the perimeter of the dining hall. She stopped directly across the hall and opened the door to a storage room that was the twin to this one, and then went inside for several moments and came out again.

I saw her face.

It was Scyllia. The red interior of her robe meant she had her assassin cloak on, though she was also wearing chain mail. I tightened my grip on the beams below me. She walked a few feet, stopped one servant and spoke with her, then continued on.

I watched until she reached the back of the pantry, which took her out of my line of sight. But I knew she was sweeping the room before the emperor arrived.

And it would not be long before she'd be in this closet with me.

Had the ambassador from Avenus betrayed me? I hadn't seen him leave the room, but he could have used hand signals. Or whispered to a servant.

No. If he had betrayed me Scyllia would have come to this storeroom first. The best thing to do would be to climb back outside. I listened, could hear talking on the ground. There were several guards in the garden who had paused during a patrol. I would have to risk it, just jump from the window to the opposite balcony. Or climb higher up the wall and hope they didn't see me.

Two of them were facing the window I'd have to use.

Before I could move, the door below me swung open and Scyllia walked in. She drew her dagger the moment she entered.

I reached for one of my daggers, then again remembered they were wrapped carefully in my knapsack, in the offal house under the watchful eye of Thord.

A weak assassin depends on her tools, Maestru Alesius had said several hundred times. Usually when another student was smacking me with a wooden sword. But it was why we practiced choke holds and hammer fists.

We practiced fleeing, too. But Scyllia was between me and the outdoor window now.

I could fall on her and in the surprise perhaps I would win. But she was serpent-fast, and any hand-to-hand fighting would bring the Immortals. She'd only have to hold me off for a few moments before they ran me through.

Besides, she was not my prey tonight. Though I didn't think I'd hesitate to dispatch her if the right opportunity came.

She ran her left hand along the window. Then she sniffed and I remembered that horse dung scent that had followed me from the barns.

She sniffed again and then picked up a jar that had some pickled item in it. She smelled it. Maybe that would hide the horse manure stink.

Scyllia turned to go. If she looked up, she would see me looking down—only about six feet separated us. She took a step out, but at that moment the board I was on creaked.

Scyllia stopped and glanced around the room again. She

waited for several moments. My heart was racing so quickly, I was certain she could hear it. Then she plucked a dried cherry from a bowl there, tossed it in her mouth and left the storage room, closing the door behind her.

I released my breath and let my muscles relax.

Then a gong gonged and the great hall, stuffed full of such powerful people, fell silent.

Two rows of Immortals marched down either side of the hall and stood facing the guests, grim faced and powerful. If anyone had wanted to leave they would have to walk past these men. It crossed my mind that this might be another of those meals where an emperor got rid of his enemies.

Several of the princes and women were thinking along the same lines, for I could see them clutching their knives and forks more tightly. One even pulled back a butter knife and hid it in his sleeve. It was laughable. If these Immortals could easily dispatch the assassins, then court diplomats and princes with soft words for training would be a moment's work for them.

Killing everyone wouldn't make sense. Many of these people were the emperor's closest allies.

Then the next movement at the front of the room sent chills down my spine.

A lithe man in black entered the room. I focused. It was my brother striding down the center of the great hall, displaying a sly glittering smile.

24

THE WHITE BEAR

Corwin was clad in dark armor of a kind I'd never seen before. It wasn't heavy because he strode easily through the room, wearing a slight smirk as he looked from one table to the other. He halted in front of a prince from Eshya—I recognized the colors, and, if I remembered my lessons well, he was third from the throne. My brother said something to him and the man paled visibly. Then Corwin carried on, staring at each powerful person in turn. He halted again before the archon from Avenus and pointed at her. She stared back at him without a sign of emotion on her face. That he would so brazenly threaten a head of state showed how much he thought of himself.

Or it was a display of how powerful he was. The emperor's right-hand knife.

He turned and spread his arms toward the crowd in a gesture that might be interpreted as welcoming. He was facing toward me. I could have put a bolt through his eye from here, but I could only watch, my dragon eye focusing in on his face, loathing each moment he gloated.

He made one more gesture and a gong sounded, and then my brother backed out of the room.

The doors to the interior of the palace swung wide and a large elephant covered in silver armor rumbled down the aisle, its weight threatening to break the marble floor. A white bear followed it and, like Corwin, it looked from table to table with absolute confidence. I knew these bears lived far in the north, but this one was trained well. How it held back from lunging at all the meals on dishes and the meals in robes, I didn't know.

Oh, why couldn't the Akkadians worship a sheep?

Then Emperor Sargon entered the room.

The emperor, too, was dressed in a long flowing robe as white as the cleanest, purest snow. It trailed a good twenty feet behind him. His famous bear amulet sat easily on his chest. I'd read descriptions of Sargon before he became emperor. He was thirty summers old and was described as having symmetrical features—that was our way of saying both his eyes matched and his nose wasn't too big. Some might interpret that as an indication he was handsome.

If that was their intention, they had failed in their description. Because he was eye-catchingly beautiful, his dark hair oiled and curly, and his face clean shaven and almost boyish. His shoulders were wide and clad in white bear fur. But what he had most of all was charisma—I'd seen the same in my brother, and briefly in Banderius. But the emperor was a man who, even if not dressed in the trappings of power, would draw the attention of every observer in the room. A sense of power emanated from him.

He'd only been emperor for fifty days, but he carried himself as if he had worn the crown since birth.

I couldn't look away. Such perfection. And even though I

knew I should be looking around to be sure my brother wasn't patrolling the room, I couldn't turn my head.

A spell?

And when I asked that question my dragon eye answered by showing me a gray and black vision of the room. There were red lines, like a nimbus, coming out of the emperor's form and touching the forehead of every onlooker.

It was a spell. Even though he had his own charisma, it forced us all to look.

I followed the lines and noticed that one had been deflected and was going to the roof. The Archon of Avenus had a ruby around her throat, and it looked to have created a glowing sphere that deflect the red lines. It was brave of her to bring her own magical items into the presence of the emperor.

Then Sargon waved his hand and the room filled with applause. At first I thought that, too, was some sort of spell, but I could now move my head and saw that the archon and several princes were not applauding. But his true friends were making up for them by clapping madly.

"Unlike previous emperors, I have no long speeches to give," Emperor Sargon said. His voice was deep and resonant and I heard it clearly, although he wasn't talking directly to me. Another spell? "For we will all talk one-on-one soon enough. Instead—" He snapped his fingers. "—your bounty awaits."

With that sound, the servers came out of either side of the hall bearing plates stuffed with roast fowl, fruits, vegetables, rice, breads—every sort of food imaginable. It was a perfectly timed entrance for when the servers reached the floor, each of them spun, silver trays in hand so that they seemed to dance. They spun again as one, crossing between each other. Then the individual servers each stopped before a table, bowed and lowered their trays.

There was even a smattering of applause for that display, which for the jaded nobles and lords was something. The servers just kept coming with more and more food and drink, and dancing between each other.

"Dine, my friends," the emperor said. "This is the Feast of Friends. Dine to your heart's content."

The crowd did so.

I could turn away from him now, meaning that little spell was finished. There was no sign of Corwin. Was he at the back of the room, just out of sight? Or moving around toward me?

I watched each of the servers, picking the ones the same size and shape as Megan, trying to discover her. But there were hundreds and she would disguise her normal gait. Despite the size of the crowd, the volume of conversation was low, as if they didn't dare to speak too loud in front of the emperor.

Then the door beneath me opened. I tensed my muscles, prepared to jump and when I saw who had entered, I did so, closing the door with the back of my heel.

25

PICKLES

I put my hand over the woman's mouth.

"Megan," I said. "It's me."

She looked surprised and a little confused, and I wondered if she was Megan. I was pretty certain, in that glance, that it was the same mask she'd been wearing, but what if someone just looked like her mask? Plus, they all had the same damn bonnet on!

She was reacting with fright. I'd have to knock her out before she screamed.

And then a smile split that not-quite familiar face.

"Carmen," she said. "You stink."

"What? Still!" I said. That particular problem had never been mentioned in our classes. "Listen, what happened to you?"

"They made us stay in the servants' quarters overnight—two to a bed. We had to scrub ourselves raw in the bathhouse, dress in impeccably white dresses, and then we practiced our entrance a thousand thousand times. And now I'm supposed to get the pickles."

Pickles? Why was she telling me about pickles? "Did you learn anything we can use?"

"The Immortals are within a few feet of the emperor at all times, and they also flock around Corwin. I saw both of them twice; in fact, the emperor himself instructed us on how to do our entrance. And... and there were whispers about him and about the white tower."

"What sort of whispers?" I asked.

"That's where all the captured wizards ended up. They went to that tower, but none of them came out."

"I had heard that," I said. "But does anyone know their fates? It's not like either emperor would shy away from public executions."

"Oh, the wizards are dead. I'm sure of that. But once Sargon was given the reins of the Immortals, he would visit the tower every week and come out stronger."

"Stronger?" I asked. "What does that mean?"

"That's the same question I asked when the serving girl told me. But she'd been here for years and just kept repeating, 'He's stronger. Stronger than flesh.' And she'd make the demon ward sign whenever Sargon passed."

"Magic," I said. That explained his ability to cast a charm spell on the whole crowd. Wizards had taught him. Perhaps they weren't willing teachers. "I don't know what we can do with this information."

"Just be extra careful, I guess. We don't have any wards to deflect magic."

"Thord and I have added to our original plan," I said. "Oh, and Brax."

"I'm glad he's being helpful." I didn't ask whether she meant Thord or Brax. "What is it?"

"It's too long to explain. But there will be a diversion."

"What sort of diversion?"

"You'll know. Believe me. Thord has cooked up something." I made a whispered laugh at the choice of words. "When it happens, I want you to use this window to climb out to the roof. I'll be waiting there for you."

"But how will I know exactly—"

The door opened.

I slipped behind it. "What are you doing in here, servant girl?" Corwin asked.

"Just—just looking for the pickles," Megan said, keeping her voice to a humble whisper. She lowered her head and stayed in the shadow.

"Who are you?" he asked.

"My name is Elissa," she muttered. He pushed the door so it was right against me. Any further and he'd notice that something was stopping it.

"Let me see you in the light."

She stepped into the light, but didn't look right at him.

A second or two passed. If I'd had a sword, I could have run him through from here. I pictured what would be necessary to do if he attacked her. There was a broom in the corner that could become a weapon. Laughable compared to his sword, but perhaps it would be enough to startle him.

My heart beat hard. Again. And again.

"Get your pickles, Elissa," Corwin said. "And return to serving our guests. This is an important evening."

"Yes, your lordship, I will." And she reached for the pickles.

She stepped out of the room without looking at me and closed the door behind her.

I waited for several moments, expecting Corwin to burst in with his sword drawn.

But at least thirty heartbeats passed with no sound.

So I climbed up to my lookout point, where I saw that

the meal was continuing. Corwin was already standing a few feet behind Sargon. He glared at the crowd as if daring them to strike a blow against his emperor.

I climbed across to the outside window, looked out. No one was visible on the grounds below.

So very carefully, I climbed out the window and scaled the wall, and kept going until I reached the roof of the palace.

26

A GOOD CATCH

The executioner had certainly designed a great and varied number of angled rooftops. They looked attractive on paper and were great for keeping the rain out of the building, but they were horrible to climb in the dark. I made my way up them.

I eventually came to one of the flat sections along the center of the palace. There were no guards here, but the towers on four corners of the palace looked directly down at me. Which was why I stood as still as possible and stared up at the heavens.

The sky had cleared, though there were still wisps of clouds here and there. Even with my dragon eye, the stars didn't look any closer. Nor could I spot movement up there. Did something happen to Thord?

Then came a slight glitter a great distance above me. I put out my hands as though I was catching rainfall.

Almost too late I saw the brown bag plummeting from the sky. They had dropped it from a great height and yet had hit exactly where I was. I caught the bag, even though it felt as though the weight of it would break my arms, but I didn't want it to clatter along the roof.

I lowered it down.

Brax, Thord and the two swans were flying at a great enough height that they wouldn't be spotted from the towers and shouldn't set off any wards.

At least that was our hope. It was working so far.

I scanned for the next bag, but it was not so well aimed. It smashed into the roof about twenty feet from me, breaking tiles and sliding down the angled roof and rolling over the edge.

Why had he dropped it so soon? I hadn't had time to recover from the first one. I stood still, glanced at the nearest tower. My dragon eye focused. One of the guards was now at this side of the tower, staring in my direction.

I stayed utterly still, knowing that moving would be the worst thing to do. I even held my breath and refrained from turning to look at the other towers.

The guard spat out the window then turned away.

I remained in that position for several more seconds. No alarms sounded, so I glanced at the other three towers in turn. My dragon eye revealed that the guards weren't looking my way. I knelt and dug into the bag, pulling out a black cloak, two daggers and a one-handed crossbow.

This was Megan's bag. My own cloak and daggers had fallen over the edge of the roof.

Master Alesius will be so angry at me for losing those blades, was my first thought. Then I remembered that he was dead. Well, he would be angry in the afterlife, then. For they were items of great power, I'd never find anything like them again.

"Are you looking for these?" someone whispered.

Which made me turn, Megan's dagger in my hand.

27

THE PLAN BEGINS

It was Megan. She'd wrapped a black curtain over her server clothes and climbed up behind me.

"They were hanging by a string," she said, carrying the bag. "Lucky for you, I came along."

"What are you doing here?" I asked.

"I decided not to wait for the distraction. No one will notice I'm gone—there are far too many servers. And I was certain you and Thord would muck this up without my help."

"Muck it up? Me?" I slapped my hand against my chest, feigning offence. I was pleased to see her, and she was correct on one point: there wasn't much use in her remaining down there. We exchanged bags.

She first took off her mask, then quickly pulled on her assassin cloak and dressed underneath it, putting on trousers, a shirt, dark vest and boots. I took off my mask, feeling the coolness of the wind directly on my face now. I threw on my clothes—the middle of a palace roof was perhaps the strangest place I'd ever dressed. But soon enough we had our belts tightened and weapons in place. I felt more like myself with the proper cloak and my own face. The daggers gave me strength. They had saved me several times.

"What do we do now?" she asked.

"In a moment or two our diversion will begin," I said. I couldn't hide the satisfaction of not telling her exactly what was about to happen. I wanted to see the look on her face. "What is happening in the palace?" I asked lightly.

"Fine, don't tell me about your big plan," she said. "I don't really care. And when it happens, I will continue not caring. Anyway, they were finished their first course. A musical interlude had begun, with a thousand harps playing *The Emperor Has No Pimples* or some such thing. I used that noise to sneak out."

"And Corwin and Sargon?"

"Your brother has dutifully stood behind the emperor throughout the first course, glaring at the guests until his eyeballs threatened to fall out. Though he was once called up to converse with Sargon and the king of Woden. Then he went back to his position."

"Good. Good. If they're together then they will probably both arrive at the same time."

"Arrive where?" she asked. "Oh, wait. You're still holding your surprise over my head. Once again, I'm not going to—"

The world exploded.

Well, a series of explosions ripped through the air. For over the water, in perfect view of the palace, a burning sheet of flame filled the sky. Then, one by one, the fireworks arced skyward. Thudding. Booming. And brightening the city with a thousand tiny suns.

Megan's eyes were wide, her face slightly slack. "Oh, that's all," she said.

"My idea." I didn't even try to keep the gloating out of

my voice. "Thord and Brax did the lighting. Handy to have a flying matchstick. All it took was a bit of dragon spit."

"Dragon spit?"

"Oh, I'll explain later," I said.

"Well, this will drop a plate of horse turds in the emperor's perfect dinner," Megan said. She had a way with words. "They planned the fireworks for after the third course. That's when we servers were supposed to be guiding everyone to the balconies to observe an 'amazing and wonderful display of royal power.' Sargon is going to have several heads mounted for this all starting early."

"Well, we'd better go watch them ourselves." The light of the fireworks was revealing us, though I doubted any of the guards were looking at the roof now. The whole city would stare eastward. "Now let's go! Follow me."

We had to make haste. I wasn't certain how long the fireworks would last, but I hoped that by starting one barge, the next group of fireworks and the next would fill the sky and continue attracting attention.

We jumped across a small courtyard and raced along the next roof, risking being seen from above. A white firework swan winged through the sky and circled the palace then faded away. A series of stars flew to the heavens and exploded in red and green and bright white patterns.

Even as we ran, in my mind I was following the executioner's drawings, naming every room we crossed over.

"We're heading to the balconies," Megan said. Again I'd underestimated her. "I see the plan now."

We reached the edge of the southern face of the palace and I looked down. There were several long balconies below us. And just as we had hoped, they were slowly filling with guests guided by the servers.

The emperor had decided to let his guests see the fireworks. Even though they were happening early. I could only imagine his anger that everything was not timed perfectly.

"Is that the plan?" Megan asked. "To distract them?"

"Mostly," I whispered. I pointed at the balcony below me. "That's the royal balcony."

"I know that. I memorized the same plans as you."

"Yes, well, we hope that the emperor will come out on that one, where he will be visible to everyone else. But it is smaller so he can't have as many guards." The crowd on the balcony, and another small crowd on the lawn below, gave out a cry of wonder as a lion appeared in the sky, moving its front legs as though it were swiping at something.

The fireworks were beyond impressive. I felt a pinch of guilt for the fireworks master who had designed them. They would be getting a tongue-lashing from the emperor's lackeys or the emperor himself. Or an axe to the neck.

No, that wouldn't happen. Not if tonight ended up the way we had planned.

But as hard as I stared and waited, the emperor didn't step out onto the balcony. I wondered if he had remained in the dining room in a fit of anger. Or maybe he was busy executing the fireworks master himself.

I took out a slender rope from my bag and found a gargoyle to tie it to—an ugly but sturdy demon with thick legs. Megan did the same to another gargoyle.

A firework in the shape of a white bear came charging through the skies, roaring like a god and swiping at the stars. It stood on its hind legs, stopping right above the palace. Every previous firework paled in comparison to this one.

It brought the emperor out onto his balcony. Corwin was on one side and Scyllia on the other, along with two Immortals. My brother was not watching the fireworks. He glanced around, first down then left and right, and then he turned and looked up at us.

Megan and I pulled back. I waited a few moments before I peeked over again. Corwin, along with the emperor, was watching the sky. The bear continued to roar.

"Now," I said, then dropped the rope. Megan and I went over the side at exactly the same time.

28

PUTTING AN END TO IT

Rappelling was a skill we'd practiced many times and, in all honesty, Megan was better than me. We jumped out and dropped and silently planted our feet against the wall and repeated that pattern—two shades dropping fast. No one looked up. The giant bear was getting closer and closer and lasting so long I wondered if some magic gave it strength.

Megan let go of her rope first and landed at an angle, knocking an Immortal over the balcony. I was aiming for my brother, for the second time in my life, but he must have seen a movement, for he used an Immortal to pull himself out of the way. Which meant I hit the Immortal and knocked him over the edge.

There was a sudden blinding flash in my dragon eye, which it took me a moment to realize wasn't in the real world. Was it some sort of magic ward or a message from Brax?

Megan had slipped over to the door and slammed it, jamming a dagger in and holding it there. Which left me to face Corwin, Scyllia and the emperor on my own. My brother had already drawn his sword and grinned like we'd just started a game. He was my first target. I doubted the emperor would raise a hand.

Which was when Sargon raised a hand.

"Halt!" he said. The power of the word hit me, and my dragon eye went red with pain. I froze with both daggers held out.

It was as if I was caught in amber. And in that second, Scyllia stepped past me and stabbed Megan. My friend fell before me, her shoulder bloodied. Her eyes were closed.

Just like I'd seen in the vision so long ago.

My eye flashed red again, and for a moment I saw nothing.

"You come to my place of power," the emperor said. He kept his voice loud, and I knew it wasn't just me he was speaking to: all of his enemies and allies were gathered on the balcony next to us. If there was time, they would probably make bets on how long I'd last. "You attack me in my home. For that you will die a slow and horrible death. All my enemies shall fear my wrath." The crackling of the fireworks punctuated his words. The bear roared closer as it filled the sky.

It felt as if this had all been set up. It certainly made the emperor look even more powerful.

Scyllia swung the pommel of her sword toward me, fully expecting to knock me out.

I parried the blow.

The fact that I could move surprised me. But my dragon's eye flashed, and I wondered if it were somehow deflecting the emperor's magic away from me. She swung again with the blade.

When I only had one eye, she had reveled in smacking

the blind side of my face during combat drills. Many were the bruises she had given me.

I blocked her next blow and in a swift movement, pulled a handful of dust from my cloak and threw it in her eyes. She fell writhing to the ground, scratching and rubbing at her eyes.

She wouldn't be dead. I was pretty certain. But it would be weeks before she had her vision back.

Corwin stepped up.

I parried his first thrust, catching his sword on the hilt of my ancient dagger. And I spun, plunging my second dagger toward his heart. It was a death blow.

It glanced off his armor.

What sort of armor could deflect a Uriken dagger?

Corwin laughed then moved again, making a swing that circled around and down, and I deflected it. My next stab was directly at his stomach and it bounced off.

"Ah, sister, this suit cost me a fortune," he said. "It was well worth it. Now let's put an end to this."

The move he followed up with was the same one he'd used to take out my eye. So familiar because I had relived it so many times.

And I had pictured a hundred thousand times how to parry it.

I did so, making a flicking movement with my wrist and deflecting the sword, then I stabbed his hand between the glove and the arm. He dropped his sword.

For the first time I saw puzzlement on his face. As if something impossible had just happened.

There was no sense waiting for him to get his wits back. I kicked him hard and with all my force and knocked Corwin over the balcony.

It felt good. Though it took me several moments to believe he was gone. I had beat him.

The only bad thing was the fall likely didn't kill him.

I faced the emperor.

The executioner's coin was burning a hole in my pocket. Sargon was a man of great power, but he had lived his life protected by others. He likely rarely saw his enemies face-to-face.

"Impressive," he said. "You are warded and you have an eye that glows with some unknown magic. I should have pursued you as my right arm instead of your brother. But know this, Carmen: I have been holding back." Then he shouted. "So my mighty Immortals have failed me, and you have bested my champions! And yet I feel not the slightest fear."

He would talk until my ears fell off. The best time to strike was while he was in mid-speech.

I leapt toward the emperor, daggers out, every moment of training helping me aim that fatal blow. I was an unstoppable force. Revenge made flesh.

He flicked me away.

29

THE SHOW

I smashed into the far end of the balcony as if a giant fist had tossed me there. All he had done was flick his fingers at me as if I were nothing more than a flea.

"If you are a good assassin, you will know the rumors," he said so only I could hear. "Every captured wizard died in the white tower. And that is the truth." I grabbed the balcony and dragged myself to my feet. I know the emperor allowed me to do that. He could have crushed me with another flick, but he wanted this to be a dramatic show for all the watching eyes on the other balcony. Scyllia had stopped moving; perhaps the pain had made her black out. Megan was still bleeding and completely still. "The most powerful of the sorcerers were bound there and kept alive. And every seven days, since I was handed the reins of the Immortals, I would go into that tower and I would dine on a wizard's heart. They are rather tasty. But now I have their power and their strength. And their magic."

He made a small gesture with his index finger, and my left arm snapped above my wrist. I clutched at it and bit down to hold back a scream. "See!" Sargon said. "My will is made flesh, so to speak. I could crack your neck with a word. Shatter your spine with another. But these toads who have come to my banquet deserve something bigger than the fireworks, so that when they go home they will shiver on their wooden thrones. And you have provided me with that! I am so thankful. This will hurt a little at first, then it will hurt a lot. Please scream. It will add to the entertainment."

He gestured, and I stood straight through no will of my own. He made me lift my right arm, dagger in hand.

"You dare to challenge me in my palace!" he shouted with enough ferocity that spittle flew from his lips. "In my very home. For that every single one of your bones will be crushed. Let my enemies know my wrath."

"Wh-who," I said. I tried to spit the words out.

"Who? Who what?" he asked quietly.

"Who writes your boring speeches?" I said. He looked as shocked as I was that a quip like that had come out of my mouth. But I couldn't help but grin. Maybe Brax was rubbing off on me.

He smiled a very unfriendly smile and then sent out two rays of yellow light from his hands that hit me and...

... at first I felt nothing. Just warmth. But then they my skin began to burn, my muscles to cramp and writhe and the blood in my veins felt as if it was boiling. The rays brightened so I had to squint.

I screamed. Only a little at first because I did everything I could to clamp my mouth shut, but the pain became too much despite all my years of training.

"It will feel like this will never end," he whispered. "And it won't. They came all this way for food and fireworks. Now they're getting even more." Then in a louder voice he said, "Begone, last of the assassins. Fall at my knees and die begging for your life."

He made a motion with his index finger, and I was slammed to my knees as if a hammer had hit me from above. I screamed again, though I didn't know if it was in anger or pain.

And then I struggled to rise, got one foot under me and made myself lift up from my knees.

"Never!" I said.

Sargon raised an eyebrow. Perhaps he had not expected me to resist. I was equally surprised, but I brought my left leg up and stood.

I pushed toward him step by step, one dagger raised. My other arm was limp at my side. But one dagger would be enough to pierce his heart.

I grinned at the look of shock on his face. He wasn't shouting to the crowd now. It felt as if my flesh were being peeled away layer by layer and step by step, but I pressed on.

He put a hand to his bear amulet and I was sent back, smashing into the wall of the balcony. "Enough of this!" he hissed. And this time he was moving toward me, the force coming from his hands, the sky full of fireworks.

Air was crushed from my lungs. My heart threatened to stop beating. I pushed up only to fall back. "My one disappointment," he said, "is they cannot see you well enough. But I want to let you know that I won't forget you: I'll have your eye glassed over and wear it as a jewel."

A roaring filled my ears. This was followed by a boom in the air and another boom I at first thought were more fireworks.

But it became clear they were not. That was the sound of magical wards being broken as a comet came arcing through the night air.

Brax had arrived.

30

A PERFECT MOMENT

The pain stopped. Emperor Sargon's eyes widened as the dragon descended from the heavens like a winged comet. Brax unfurled his wings to slow his flight and let out a massive blast of fire, intending to fry the emperor.

Sargon raised his hand and, as easy as that, deflected the flames so they shot harmlessly into the palace garden below. The heat made sweat trickle down my skin.

Brax swept his wings once, twice, holding his position. He let out another blast only to have it deflected again.

At that same moment two feet landed beside me, and I looked up to see Thord. He grabbed my good arm. "Can you stand?"

"Yes," I said.

"Get up, then. We are leaving." He pulled me to my wobbly feet.

"But we are not done," I said.

"The battle is lost," he replied, motioning toward the emperor, who was now sending a ray of blistering light toward Brax. "The dragon is only holding him off until we are away."

Thord stepped past me, picked up Megan and lifted her over his shoulder. He limped back to his swan and climbed on, grunting as he did so.

I hadn't moved.

Brax swiped his talons, trying to hit the emperor, but only managed to knock away a chunk of the balcony.

"This is perfect! Perfect!" the emperor said. He glanced my way and said, "Thank you!" And then he motioned at Brax as though he were an annoying moth. "Begone, foul beast!" he shouted. "Begone from my heavens!" Then the emperor pulled back his arm and threw a ball of glowing light. It blasted right through the underside of Brax's wing and out the other side.

His wing crumpled and he fell toward the ground.

"Brax!" I shouted.

"We have to go," Thord said from the back of his swan. "Take Megan's swan. Now!"

Naga had landed further down the balcony. I made a move toward her and one of those glowing balls burst between us, breaking the wall on the balcony. Naga screeched and headed skyward, following her fellow swan.

Thord was higher now and couldn't turn around—his swan already struggled under the weight of both riders. Naga followed him.

Leaving me alone. Standing there.

Sargon pulled back his arm and another glowing ball appeared there. "Goodbye, assassin," he shouted and began to throw his spell.

But at that moment Brax flew up from below, and I hopped over the broken balcony wall onto his back, grabbed on and his massive wings lifted us up higher and higher. We weaved to the left and a blast hit the tower next to us. He wove back and forth, avoiding the fireballs. The tear in his wing was widening with each movement.

But we gained height and the shouting below us faded to whispers. He aimed between the towers, avoiding the ballistae.

We crossed the outer wall. The fireworks were on our left.

Only then did I look back.

There were six swans following us with riders on their backs.

My brother was their leader.

31

DARK WINGS

"We have to split up," I shouted at Thord once we'd caught up.

He made a hand signal to show he'd heard me. The next signal seemed to suggest that he'd lose whoever followed him and circle around. Or else he wanted us to do that.

Then he, Megan and the two swans turned toward the north. We broke off westward.

I looked over my shoulder. There were three swans behind us. The other three were following Thord. His only hope would be that the Immortals were not as skilled as he was at riding a swan, even with the extra weight. And Megan's swan should also act in their defence. Swans did that for people they'd bonded with, and Naga had bonded with Megan.

The leader of the three swans that followed us was Corwin. My dragon eye showed me the grimace of anger on his face.

Brax made an undignified grunt. His right wing, displayed in the wan moonlight, was leaking blood, and the hole Sargon had torn in it widened with each flapping motion.

"I am going slower by the second," Brax said. "I had not expected such powerful magic."

"None of us did," I said.

"May I suggest we go toward the mountains." His tone was almost polite. Maybe the more blood he lost, the more polite he became. "There are more air currents there that I hope will surprise inexperienced riders."

"Yes, let's go. That makes all sorts of sense."

He turned, winging his way in that direction, continuing to grunt with each motion.

"Why did you save me?" I asked. "You could have killed Corwin and our pact would be over."

"I couldn't find him," he said, still sounding polite. "Plus, I wouldn't abandon you." And then he chuckled painfully. "I have plans for you. Corwin is only half the deal, and we were in *live to fight another day* territory."

"It was a failure," I said.

This got another weak chuckle. "We were attacking the emperor of half of Ellos. The odds were not on our side. That you got so close is amazing."

Mountains rose before us and we had to climb higher, just brushing the top of one. This small grouping of mountains was famous for its hot springs and geysers. I'm pretty sure one of the executioner's drawings was of a bathing temple somewhere in these rocks.

I shivered as the air grew colder.

"I'll let them get closer," Brax said. "And hope they don't have bows."

At that same moment, a crossbow bolt hissed over my shoulder.

"Oh, that's too bad," Brax said. "It will make surviving quite a bit tougher."

Our pursuers were near enough for me to see that the Immortals were both flying with a bow in one hand and the reins in the other. At least that would make it harder for them to aim.

"Tell me when they've loaded again," Brax said.

"Now," I said. "Now!"

"Yes! Yes! I hear you." He dived and two bolts hissed through the air over our heads.

He had tucked in his wings to increase our speed. "I am hoping my wings don't rip off when we come out of this dive," he grunted.

The others followed us, but one of the Immortals who was clutching a bow lost his grip on the reins and tumbled from the saddle when his swan followed his own dive. The man didn't make a sound as he fell to the rocks below.

"There's only Corwin and one Immortal left," I shouted.

"I guess, at this height, they aren't truly Immortal," Brax said.

He opened his wings when we were near the ground, the wind roared through them and he uttered a gargling cry of pain. Blood from the tearing wound spattered me. It widened. But his wings held together, and we missed the ground by inches and shot above it.

Then something burst below us and came rushing up. Was the ground cracking open?

No. Not the ground. We had passed into a field of geysers shooting water skyward at various times. The steam and boiling water would go as high as fifty to a hundred feet in the air, then fall back down in an icy mist. Brax swerved to avoid a direct blow from one of them.

Water turned to ice almost at once on my hair, my

clothes and hands, making my grip unsteady. I had to hold tight. I even tried to use my broken arm, but that only shot pain through my arm.

Another geyser just missed us, but it caught one of our enemies. It drenched the swan in boiling water, and the bird went screaming down to the ground, screeching its pain. His rider tumbled along the rocks.

I so hoped it had been Corwin, but a moment later my brother came into view.

He was avoiding the geysers and closing in.

We cleared the geyser field but Brax's wings barely worked properly now. He could no longer control our direction.

I glanced back to see Corwin was no longer there.

I looked left, right. "Where is he? Where is he?" I shouted.

Brax climbed up, higher and higher, because a terraced cliff wall was stretching out before us. We had to clear it.

Then, just as we were nearing the top, Corwin plummeted into us, his swan crashing into my back and smacking Brax's neck.

My grip had been broken. I was tossed through the air.

32

NOT TODAY

I landed on a cliff side, attempted to stop my rolling motion with my broken arm, and cried out in pain then slammed into rock.

But I came up standing, with one dagger drawn and my feet set in a battle stance.

Corwin had landed twenty feet away, looking like he hadn't been damaged at all. Even his hair was straight. The glare in his eyes was one of absolute determination.

Brax had vanished, perhaps crashed into the rocks below us.

Corwin drew his sword.

"That was a daring raid," he said. "Bravo, sister. But it was also embarrassing for me since I had not properly prepared. I imagine taking your head back to the emperor will make up for my failure."

"That will not happen today. Not ever." I tried to stand as tall and straight as I could, to pretend, without grimacing too badly, that my arm wasn't broken. The wind caught my cloak, and I imagined with the snow and rocks behind me it was quite the pose.

At this, he grinned. "Your arm is broken," he said. "You limp on your left so you've damaged your leg, though you may not even notice it. And you are holding a dagger, which means I have the longer reach. Advantage mine."

Pain flared in my ankle. Was it just at his suggestion? No, when I shifted weight to that side my ankle nearly collapsed.

"You betrayed your fellow students," I said. "You broke your blood oath."

"Technically, I never made that oath since no one graduated. That oath was to come at the end of graduation. And why be stuck in the past, sister? I am the future. Your loyalty to a burned-out school stuffed with dead maestrus and students is the past."

He strode ahead. His black armor caught the moonlight.

Brax, silent and sudden, raised his head over the cliff edge. He must have hit the ledge below us. He blasted Corwin with so much flame that it entirely enveloped him. He was dead. He had to be. It was an even bigger blast than had destroyed Banderius.

And I felt conflicted in my heart. Because he was my brother. And I still felt something for him, despite all the betrayals. What a fool I was.

Corwin stood in the flames, standing straight up. Why hadn't he fallen? He wasn't waving his arms or screaming or doing any of the things that one would expect a man surrounded by flames to do.

Then he moved within the flames and put up a hand that forced the fire to part. It continued to strike his armor, but he didn't melt. He stepped toward Brax.

Brax looked shocked and kept spouting out his fiery breath, to the point that the heat was reaching me and melting the snow all around.

But Corwin strode right up to him and swung his sword so that it struck Brax in the center of the head. He crumpled from the blow and fell out of sight. Perhaps even down the side of the mountain.

Corwin turned toward me and wiped a sheen of sweat from his forehead. "I planned for your dragon." He gestured at his armor. "Dragon scales from baby dragons. The most expensive suit of armor in the empire. Plus Sargon placed a ward around my face to protect against heat and flames."

The blast hadn't even affected his hair.

He now calmly walked toward me. I didn't want to back up any further since I would be trapped and have no room to move.

We crossed blades.

33

SO VERY SWEET

On a good day, I could take him. But on this day, with a damaged ankle and a broken arm, it would be a slaughter. His armor was too strong for my blade.

He jabbed playfully at me, which I parried and followed with a riposte that landed nowhere near him. He had already moved out of the way. Then he reached in and gave me a pinprick right on my shoulder. He could stand there and bat away my feeble blows.

"You won't taste victory today," he said. The most aggravating thing was that his words weren't even strained. "I will take your head, the dragon's head, and the heads of your friends back to Sargon. And he will reward me."

"Why?" I hissed. "Why do this?"

"Because it feels good. Because no one will leave me behind again, sister."

"Wrong," I spat. "The emperor will dispose of you the moment he's finished."

This got a titter of a laugh from him. "He knows that I have no desire to run an empire. Far too tedious for me. Soon there will be no assassins left. And I will stand alone."

He darted into my circle of defence and I wasn't fast enough to parry. His blade sliced my cheek.

It was a message. He could cut me at any time. He was the murderous cat and I was the mouse with one arm.

With each blow he laughed, enjoying the moment. "You will never know what it's like," he said, speaking easily as he smashed the flat of his blade against my broken arm. The pain nearly made me black out. "You wouldn't even understand the feeling of power that came over me when I was standing on the top of the Red Assassin Fortress and sent the signal to the Immortals on their winged gliders. That sense of destiny. It was I who controlled them. Who controlled the lives of every assassin in that school."

"You must be so proud of yourself." I made a quick stab toward him, aiming for his hand, but he parried it and rewarded me with another cut on the cheek.

"Ah, that matches," he said. "And I am proud. I just walked through the emperor's great dining hall with representatives of all our enemies and all our allies, and every one of them cowered before me. They all have files on my skills. My knowledge. They all know my name and they fear that one day I will crouch on their windowsill, blades in hand."

"They will kill you."

This got another tittering laugh from him. "They have no assassins," he said. "That's the beauty of it all. No assassins. All the powerful wizards are dead or they've fled Ellos. From here Emperor Sargon, with my tactics and help, will conquer the five free realms one by one. Every map will be redrawn; we will rewrite every history book and sing the praises of our great victory."

"It will be a dead land."

"No, sister. A perfect land. You don't understand power.

As long as there is a threat, that threat must be stamped out." He performed a circular cut which added momentum to his swing. I parried it, but my dagger was nearly knocked out of my hand. I knew he'd not let me stab his wrist again.

"You could have beat Scyllia," he said. "And Gregum. You are that good. Not Corwin good, of course!"

"Gregum is dead," I said, hoping this would shock him.

Corwin raised an eyebrow. "It's not like you to lie."

"We caught him over the water. He was flying to the east. We killed him."

"Well, well." His grin only broadened. "You are full of surprises. If only I had mentored you properly. I shall miss dear Gregum. Not the smartest of friends, but efficient and loyal. And this gives me one more reason to kill you. Revenge, I am told, is so sweet."

Then he began to press his attack. He was done talking.

He wanted the fight to be over.

34

PRESSING THE ADVANTAGE

He rained down blow after blow, each knocking me further back. And it dawned on me that his talking hadn't just been to air his views, but to distract and steer me to a place where there was only rock at my back and either side. Even if I wanted to jump over the edge of the cliff to rob him of the fatal blow, I'd have to get past him.

He kept pounding, staying just far enough back that neither dagger nor powders would reach him. I was barely deflecting the blows, sweating like mad now as it cooled on my forehead and ran into my eyes.

He saw that. Winked at me and sliced above my right eyebrow. Now blood was blinding me and I had to stagger further back, using my broken arm to wipe it away.

I reached in and found a burning pepper powder and tossed it, filling the air between us. But he didn't even blink, and I found it was my eyes that burned even more.

"I put that in my eyes every morning and night. It helps me sleep."

I blocked his next blow at the last moment. It had been aimed at my neck.

. . .

"The sand in the hourglass dwindles for you," he said. "Sweet sister, enjoy these last few breaths."

He might have added a few more taunts, but I was too busy dodging each blow. As I did so I listed my weapons. The poisons and dusts waited in each cloak pocket, but he was immune to anything I could toss at him.

I was not immune to his blade. This time he nicked my stomach and I screamed.

"Ah, that's what we were looking for. A little reaction from my sister who always faces the world with such coolness. Not so cool now as your life dribbles away."

My eyes continued to water, but the dragon eye stayed clear and focused. And through it I saw Corwin as a series of red lines, moving toward me. I could see his beating heart. Even the magic ward was visible. He was completely protected.

He hammered me with a downward blow that I had to block, using both hands. The shock made the broken bones grate in my arm and I fell to my knees, but his blade was turned away.

It was also perhaps the last time I would use that arm. It hung limp at my side.

"Impressive," he said. "I thought that was your death blow. At least you are going out with a fight. There will be a chapter in my book about you. My sister was heroic, but she tragically chose the wrong side."

"No. You—you chose the wrong side." It wasn't the snappiest reply, but I just had to keep him talking. "No one would read a book about you."

"Oh, that hurts, Sis," he said.

What was my advantage? With a broken arm and now tired beyond endurance, I could think of nothing. I had two daggers, one arm, a cloak and one good ankle.

And the answer came to me.

I shifted to one side and threw my dagger. He made a quick twisting motion, and the blade hissed past him.

"Oh, a desperate move, Sis. As if a thrown dagger would ever catch me. Now you have only one weapon."

I drew my second dagger.

The thing he didn't know was that my blades would cut rock.

My dagger had hit the wall to his left and stuck there.

I made a feint to his right and he spun away from it, but that gave me room to jump and place a solid foot on the dagger protruding from the wall.

I used that leverage, that extra height, to throw myself overtop of him.

A look of confusion and surprise crossed his face as I flipped, and when I was directly above him I cut the tie on my cloak.

It was weighted on the bottom. It fell over Corwin's head, blinding him. I landed, grabbed the cloak and twisted so that it was wrapped tight around him and threw him to the ground. I kicked his hand so that his sword went clattering along the rocks.

Then, as he struggled, I smashed him again and again with the hilt of my dagger.

He reached up, grabbed my broken arm and pulled, and the pain came close to knocking me out. But I kept hammering at him.

In time he stopped moving.

I didn't. I continued swinging. Just to be sure.

I'm not certain when I stopped. I looked down to see that he was breathing but otherwise motionless. I had won.

But when I pulled away the cloak, he was staring at me.

35

TURN YOUR BACK

I drew back my arm to hit him again, then realized he had been knocked out. He'd trained his whole life to sleep with his eyes open. His eyes weren't tracking movement. They stared straight into the stars.

His face was bruised. Blood was leaking down his hairline.

I didn't know why I hadn't used the sharp end of my dagger. I guess I still had some hope for him.

Or a conscience.

I went to his swan, who hissed at me, but I met its eye in the way Maestru Arvid had taught me, showing it who was master. I retrieved a circle of rope from his saddlebag. It was a struggle to tie him with one hand, but I made sure each knot was tight. I kept expecting him to awaken, but my blows had been hard.

Then I retrieved my dagger from the wall and stumbled over to the edge. Brax was on a line of rocks below me, not moving.

"Brax?" I said. "Brax?"

He didn't reply. His wing looked like it was missing a chunk and perhaps was broken in several places.

"Brax!"

His good wing flapped raggedly and he turned his head. There was a gash in his skull. But he was alive! "Do you have to be so loud?" His voice was a whisper.

"I'm so glad you can speak. Can you move?"

"I really hate your brother," he said. And he moved his other wing.

"I'll come down there," I said.

"And what? Carry me on your back? Just let me take a few good breaths." He struggled but was able to pull himself to all fours. "I assume he is dead now."

I shook my head.

"You didn't kill him?" Brax nearly spat these words out.

"No."

"You are a mad child," he said. "A soft mad child."

I shrugged. "It was my decision." I saw that the cliff angled up. "You can climb up to where I am if you are able."

"I can see that. I'm not completely blind," he said. "I just hope I don't leave any pieces behind." But he started dragging his damaged body up a slanted series of rocks.

A motion caught my eye. Three swans were moving through the distant sky, only visible because they blocked the stars. Three meant the Immortals had defeated Thord and Megan. I rushed to Corwin's swan and took out the crossbow, struggling to load it with one hand, cranking back the string and setting a bolt in place. I wasn't certain I could take on the remaining Immortals now. And Brax was not in the best of conditions either.

I raised the crossbow and aimed.

Thord was in my vision. With Megan riding the second swan. A swan with an empty saddle followed them.

I lowered the crossbow and waited.

By the time they landed Brax had worked his way to me. I was surprised that Corwin's swan hadn't fled, but he must have imprinted it. It backed away from Brax.

Thord slid off and then turned to help Megan, who was clutching her side. She couldn't hold herself up so she leaned on him. Her black clothing hid the severity of her wound.

They struggled over to where Corwin was lying and looked down.

"Why is he still alive?" Megan's voice was raspy.

"Exactly what I asked her," Brax said. "I don't mean to be critical but you're not a very good assassin, Carmen. You failed at your only job."

"I couldn't kill him," I admitted. "I couldn't. He's my brother."

"Do you want me to do it?" Brax asked. Blood still flowed from where Corwin's sword had cut him. "Just say the word."

"No."

"We can't leave him alive," Thord said. "And it's not like he would have given any of us mercy."

"No. He wouldn't have," I said. But I thought of all our years together—our childhood playing with toys, running around at the feet of the maestrus. "He wasn't always so horrible."

"Well he is now," Megan said. "And if we release him then he crawls back to the emperor. Honestly, just turn your back, Carmen. I'll be quick about it. Unless my hand slips."

"No," I said. "There is one thing we—"

"Oh, isn't this splendid!" Corwin interrupted. "It's a reunion of family and friends. How glorious."

36

A TEAR OF SORROW

I looked to be certain his hands were tied tightly. They were, but even having his eyes glare into mine made my stomach sink.

"I suppose you're drawing lots to decide which of you will get the pleasure of stabbing me," he said.

"We were just discussing that," I answered.

"Ah, so there is a quarrel. And you, sweet sister, couldn't finish me off. How inept." He sneered toward Megan and Thord. "I can tell by the look in their eyes they agree with me." Then he glanced at Brax. "And he agrees, too. And... Hey, your dragon only has one eye. Did you know that?"

"Of course," I said.

"And you... you have a gray eye. It looks oddly like his. I wonder..." He smiled. "Oh, sister. A magical dragon eye. How clever of you. A shame you didn't have the guts to join me. We could have ruled all of Ellos with Sargon as our puppet."

"I have better things to do," I said.

"There is nothing better to do." His smile never faded. "So what's the decision? I could offer you gold. Or freedom.

Or you could strip me and let me walk chastised back to the emperor. He might execute me himself, he's a little chop-chop-choppy that way. Or is this where you want me to beg for my life? Ha. Never. But I won't beg to you idiots. So do your worst."

"Thord," I said. "Can you take the pommel of your sword and—"

"Thord," Corwin said. "You're getting Thord to do your dirty work?"

"—and press down on his jaw?" I finished.

Thord drew his sword. He limped over, leaned down and set the pommel on Corwin's jaw.

"Press hard. And keep his mouth open." He did exactly that, putting his weight into it. Corwin tried to jerk away from the pressure, but Thord held tight. Any harder and he might dislocate the jaw.

I lifted my cloak from the ground, reached into one of the pockets and found the item I wanted.

"Powsion?" Corwin said, his words garbled. "Yah caneven stab me? Poesin?"

"No, brother, I will make you forget."

"Fohrget?" His words were slurred. "Fohrget." Then it came clear. "No! No! No!"

I dumped the contents of the vial into his mouth. "Now close his mouth."

Thord grinned as he grabbed Corwin's jaw and head and squeezed so Corwin couldn't spit the stuff back out.

"You're right, Corwin," I said. "I'm too weak to kill you. Too soft. But you know what the corporthium pill does: you will shortly fall into a coma, and the alchemy will work on your brain so you forget everything." His eyes widened, then narrowed in anger. "You will forget your skills. Where you came from. What it was like to see those Immortals fly down to the Red Fortress. It will erase your first kill from your memories. And your second. And third. All the things you love about life will one by one be taken from you. And finally you will forget your own name and be nobody. Nothing. You won't even be my brother anymore."

There was a tear coming from his left eye. I knew it wasn't from the pain. It was a tear of sorrow.

"Goodbye, Corwin," I said.

Then he blinked and blinked again. By the third blink he closed his eyes.

He had already forgotten how to sleep with his eyes open. The next time he opened them, he would no longer be Corwin.

"I still think we should have just killed him," Brax said. "It seems like a waste of good powder."

"So what do we do with him now?" Megan asked.

"I have an idea about that, too," I said.

A plan had just landed fully formed in my mind.

37

TO THE SKIES

We took several minutes to strip him of his armor, wrap him in a blanket, and strap him to the back of his swan. I emptied the saddlebag of everything that would give him a hint of where he was from and left him with only a bit of hard bread and dried meat.

"He is not dead," Brax said. "But the oath we swore in that cave so long ago involved his death. Do you consider our debt settled?"

"Yes. You have fulfilled your part of the bargain. You are free."

He smiled, showing his teeth. "Good. Then before we discuss the second part of that bargain, I have one more thing to do."

He turned back toward where Corwin was strapped to the swan. It squawked and hissed but before it could move, Brax blinded Corwin in one eye with a quick flick of his talon. "It's only fair," he said. "Your brother left you this way and you're too pure to take revenge."

I swallowed. "But, but—he'll bleed to death."

Brax spat in Corwin's eye. I thought it would burn, but

the liquid bubbled up. "It will heal, if that's what you are about to ask. Dragon's bile will heal it—I may have forgotten to tell you about that particular property. Besides, it's a good look for him."

I could see it wasn't even bleeding any longer.

"There," he said. "We dragons do worry about what is fair and what is not. And that seemed eminently fair." He glanced at Thord and Megan. "And I am certain your companions agree."

Both of them were pale, but they nodded.

Brax rubbed his talons together. "Good. We're agreed. Now about the rest of your plan."

I explained it to the three of them and they agreed that it made sense. Then we spent the next few hours eating the rough bread and dried meat we found in the saddle of the extra swan. Thord stitched up Megan, who didn't cry out loud once. Then Brax spat on the wound.

"Why didn't you use that on me when I was wounded?" Thord asked.

"I don't like you," Brax said, simply. Neither of them laughed.

We drank from the waterskin. Brax allowed Megan to sew his wing closed so that the tear was no longer bleeding. He flapped it and grimaced, but said, "Good as new." He stood taller, making it clear that his strength was returning. "And now for the second part of our deal, Carmen Crow. Do you remember what you swore?"

"Yes. I will become your servant for the space of one year and I will kill someone for you."

"Yes, that's it. You are officially my servant now, Carmen."

"I am," I answered.

"What is this?" Thord said. "You can't do that."

"I swore an oath," I said. "A Red Assassin never breaks her oath."

Brax nodded at that. "Your friends don't have to worry. I will be a good and kind master."

We packed our goods, filling the bags of each swan. We had at least taken all the assassins away from the emperor except Scyllia, but she was nowhere near as dangerous as Corwin. Sargon may still plot and plan, but without the cleverness of my brother to guide him, he would find it hard to unearth the hidden assassins.

I still had a contract to kill the emperor, but it wouldn't be fulfilled tonight.

We took to the sky. Thord led my brother's swan by its reins.

We flew to the west for many hours, until we were near the edge of the mountains. We landed on a plateau that looked out over the ocean. I slid off Brax and took one last look at Corwin, and then nodded. Without a word, Thord let loose the reins of the swan and smacked it on the side.

It flew in a direct line away from us. Further and further west.

"It will keep traveling until it tires," Thord said. "Many hours from now. Your brother will be hundreds of leagues away. Perhaps they will land on an island and he'll spend the rest of his life there."

I knew that in time he would wake up and not know who he was or even how he'd been blinded.

"He's no longer my brother," I said. "He will become someone new."

"Goodbye to a rotten sibling," Brax said. "He was a waste of bones and flesh. Speaking of flesh, the time has come for you to say goodbye to your friends."

I turned to them. Megan was still pale, holding her side.

Thord met my gaze. "I will fulfill my oath to Brax," I said. "And I will return to find you both."

"You had better treat her properly," Thord said.

"Oh, the puppy barks at the dragon," Brax said. "Yes, I will be the greatest master she has ever had. I will feed her thrice a day. I want her to do her work."

"Look for us in Avenus when you return," Megan said. "We'll leave word with Maestru Beatrix."

"I will," I promised. "I will."

"Now, come Carmen Crow Slave, enough of this," Brax said. "Get on my back for your work has only just begun." I climbed on and with a few powerful swoops of his wings he was in the sky. He began flying north.

I waved one last time at Megan and Thord, then stared toward the distance.

On my right the sun was rising. Perhaps that was a good omen.

PREVIEW OF DRAGON ASSASSIN 2

1. ABOVE BITTERWATERS

We would die before I fulfilled my promise to Brax.

When we were halfway across the Bitterwaters, his wings began to freeze. Chunks of ice formed along the bony edges, getting thicker each moment. Most of the ice would break off if he folded his wings in or flapped them harder, but it was obvious he was tiring.

There wasn't anything I could do from my perch on his back, other than huddle in my cloak and hold tight with my slowly freezing hands. Every once in a while I'd reach out and brush off the snow nearest me.

I'd long since lost the feeling in my toes. I had bought thick mittens, a scarf, and three sweaters at a northern Akkadian village (all of which I was wearing). They had been the last clothing from a merchant who'd sold the rest of his stock to Akkadian soldiers marching east. Since it was the end of his wares he'd charged me double.

It was a good thing I had that extra layer of warmth, or my fingers and the rest of me would have long turned into icicles. I could only wait helplessly, expecting us to plunge into the waters at any moment.

The Bitterwaters, a sea legendary for causing the deaths of thousands of sailors, was a wasteland of water and ice that stretched forever in all directions. The ice hadn't formed in large enough chunks to land on. I'd lost count of how many hours we'd been in the air. The sun was shining somewhere far behind us, but not directly here. If the rumors were true, the sun never shone on Bitterwaters.

Brax made no complaint, but he was not one of those rare dragons with fur—he had scales and nothing else to keep his blood and organs warm. Flying made that blood move, but the wind and cold took its toll. Ice had frozen over his empty eye socket and he didn't bother to brush it away.

The joy of being in the air had long since been frosted out of me.

So had the fear of where we were going. Few mortals had traveled across the Bitterwaters to the Land of Beasts and lived to tell the tale. There weren't even maps. Only stories of boats returning with burnt sails and oars broken and most of their crews dead.

The Land of Beasts, or "that horrible place beyond Bitterwaters," was mostly believed to be part of the shared imaginations of crazed sailors. A dreamed-up place. Except it became quite real when the occasional dragon made its way across the water and burnt down a village or two.

It became even more real when one of those dragons decided to go back.

And this mystical, dangerous land that Brax himself called Drachia was where he was carrying me.

To kill someone he wouldn't name.

It was almost hard for me to believe it had been less than two days since I'd flown my separate way from my friends, Megan and Thord. And seen my brother fly on the back of a giant swan, unconscious and blind in one eye, toward the west. That had all happened a hundred years ago. In a land that no longer seemed real.

Only the cold was real now.

A *crack* indicated that another section of ice was falling off Brax's wings.

"Can you fly with that much ice stuck to you?" I asked.

"I have no choice."

"Was it this bad when you crossed the first time?" The scarf over my face muffled my voice.

"It's colder now. And I didn't have a passenger weighing me down, so it's taking twice as long. Have you ever considered losing weight? You could start with your head."

I bit back my reply, not that it was all that clever. He was not in the mood for talking and I wanted him to direct every bit of energy toward staying aloft.

I did the only thing I could—reached out and brushed away snow and ice as far as my arms would reach on either side. At least I was helping in some small amount, and it kept me warmer. Though I nearly slipped off more than once with the effort.

Again, there would be no hope of rescue from the Bitterwaters. I'd fall into that bone-chilling cold and freeze into a block of human ice and then sink to the bottom.

After at least another hour—or five minutes, because time had perhaps been frozen itself—I spoke again.

"Does the sun ever shine here?" I asked.

"No, child, it does not. They say this is where the tears of the moon fall. Thus the ice."

"Who are *they*?"

"People from Woden—simpletons like your friend Thord. But that isn't the moon's tears below us. It's death."

"That Woden tale is a way of explaining things with a story."

"I know that, Carmen!" he snapped. "I'm angry with everyone and everything right now. It's the only emotion that keeps me going. Now be quiet for a long time because I need to concentrate."

There was another large crack as a ragged chunk of ice broke from the tip of his right wing. But there were ever-growing sections of ice in the center that forced his wings to droop. If I had a pole I could have reached them.

Slowly, my eyes closed. I could not slip into slumber. My hands would unclasp and I would fall.

But my eyes didn't care about that. They were getting tired. And sore. I kept them closed for several moments.

Or longer. I wasn't sure because I felt like I was in a dream, and in that dream I was getting warmer and warmer. Someone had lit a fire in a hearth and I was under several layers of blankets.

No. My mind was tricking me. But when I tried to open my eyes, I failed. The frost had iced my eyelashes together. I wiped at them with a rime-covered mitten but still couldn't see. There was another cracking sound. And another.

Then silence.

I stopped rubbing at my eyes and listened. There were no more sounds of the ice cracking, though the wind had picked up enough to make the hood of my cloak flap.

Wait! That wasn't wind. We were going faster and my position had shifted so I was leaning forward.

Which meant we were falling straight down.

And I was blind.

ABOUT THE AUTHOR

Arthur Slade was raised in the Cypress Hills of southwest Saskatchewan and began writing at an early age. He is the author of over twenty books, including *Dust* (which won the Governor General's award), *Flickers*, and *Amber Fang*. He currently lives in the mythical city of Saskatoon, Canada where he writes on a treadmill desk while listening to heavy metal.

It's true.

Connect with Arthur Slade online:

www.arthurslade.com

art@arthurslade.com

Printed by Amazon Italia Logistica S.r.l.
Torrazza Piemonte (TO), Italy

13016435R00228